WOMEN, WIVES, MOTHERS

Women, Wives, Mothers:

VALUES AND OPTIONS

JESSIE BERNARD

Research Scholar, Honoris Causa
The Pennsylvania State University

ALDINE PUBLISHING COMPANY
Chicago

ABOUT THE AUTHOR

JESSIE BERNARD is Research Scholar, Honoris Causa, Pennsylvania State University. She was educated at the University of Minnesota and Washington University, and has had a distinguished professional career that includes a term as president of the Society for the Study of Social Problems. Dr. Bernard has contributed numerous articles to professional journals and has written extensively about women. Her many books include *The Future of Marriage, Social Problems at Midcentury,* and *Women and the Public Interest* (Aldine, 1971).

First published 1975 by
Aldine Publishing Company
529 South Wabash Avenue
Chicago, Illinois 60605

ISBN 0-202-30280-6 clothbound edition
ISBN 0-202-30281-4 paperbound edition

Library of Congress Catalog Number 74-18210
Printed in the United States of America

CONTENTS

ACKNOWLEDGMENTS

"RESEARCH ON SEX DIFFERENCES: An Overview of the State of the Art" was presented at the December, 1972, meetings of the American Association for the Advancement of Science at the invitation of Dr. Dale Harris, Pennsylvania State University. This paper is an MSS Modular Publication, Module 26, 1973.

"A Developmental Paradox" includes material from Jessie Bernard, *The Future of Motherhood* (New York: Dial, 1974); it was part of a course given at George Washington University, fall, 1972.

"Sex-Role Transcendence and Sex-Role Transcenders" was presented at a conference on "Freeing Sex Roles for New Careers," at the University of Maryland, June 24, 1974. This conference was sponsored by the American Council on Education, the National Institute of Education, and the American Personnel and Guidance Association. It was also presented at the Center for the Study of Sexual Identity, September 15, 1974. The research on "role transcenders" was based on data gathered by the American Council on Education and was done jointly with Engin Holmstrom of that organization. Appreciation is hereby expressed to the American Council on Education for the use of its data and to Ms. Holmstrom for her cooperation.

"Adolescence and Socialization for Motherhood" was prepared for a conference on adolescence sponsored by NICHD, Fall, 1973, at the invitation of Dr. Sigmund E. Dragastin. The papers prepared for this conference are published by the Hemisphere Publishing Company.

"Ages and Stages of Motherhood" includes material from Jessie Bernard, *The Future of Motherhood* (New York: Dial, 1974); it was part of a course given at George Washington University, Fall, 1972.

"Middle Motherhood" includes material from Jessie Bernard, *The Future of Motherhood* (New York: Dial, 1974). The section on "Continuing Options" was presented at the Menninger Foundation Symposium on the Middle Years, New York, March 1, 1973.

"Late Motherhood" includes material from Jessie Bernard, *The Future of Motherhood* (New York: Dial, 1974). The section on "Whatever Happened to Mother?" was prepared for part of a series at Stanford University, February, 1974.

"Age and Attitudes on Feminist Issues" was designed to fill a specific spot in the September, 1974, issue of the *Annals of the American Academy of Political and Social Science*. The editor, Dr. Frederick Eisele, sketched the general nature of the contents needed for that spot. In the present context, however, it seemed more logical to separate age and class as related to feminist issues.

"Class and Feminist Issues" is expanded from the preceding paper.

"The Impact of Sexism and Racism on Employment Status and Earnings" was presented at the Spring, 1972, meetings of the Southern Sociological Society at the invitation of Dr. Jacqueline Jackson. This paper is an MSS Modular Publication, Module 25, 1973.

"The Bitter Fruits of Extreme Sex Specialization" was prepared for a series at Stanford University, February, 1974, at the invitation of Dr. William R. Scott.

"Policy-Relevant Research on Motherhood: The State of the Art" was prepared for the February, 1974, meetings of the American Association for the Advancement of Science at the invitation of Dr. Jean Lipman-Blumen.

"New Societal Forms" was prepared for a conference on "The American Woman, Who Will She Be?" organized by Dean Mary Louise McBee at the University of Georgia, August, 1973. It appears in *The American Woman: Who Will She Be?*, edited by Mary Louise McBee and Kathryn A. Blake (Beverly Hills: Glencoe Press), 1974, pp. 81-93.

Appreciation is hereby expressed: to Dial Press; to The Heritage Press; to MSS Modular Publication; to the Annals of the American Academy of Political and Social Science; and to Glencoe Press for permission to reproduce materials from their publications.

WOMEN, WIVES, MOTHERS

INTRODUCTION

WHEN VIRGINIA WOOLF went to the British Museum in 1928 to do research for a talk she was preparing to give on women at the women's colleges of Oxford, she became exasperated with the inadequacy of what she found. She went conscientiously through dozens of learned books by men which told her more than she cared to know about the authors but netted little about women. I was far better off when I did the research for the papers in this book. For now there is a goodly band of researchers who are working hard to create and accumulate the knowledge needed to bring us up to date and then to help us keep up with what is now going on in the world around us. A brick here, a brick there, and little by little holes are filled in. By industriously chipping away at our ignorance we are beginning to know a great deal more than we did even a decade ago. Not, to be sure, nearly enough. For even as we work, the need grows apace and we have to run fast to keep up. We are just beginning to know what we need to know. We are still handicapped by inadequate conceptualizations, models, paradigms, research techniques for finding the right questions to ask and ways to answer them. But we are learning.

You Are There

A popular television program in the 1960s reenacted historical events, such as the trial of Socrates or the assassination of Julius Caesar, as they would have appeared if reported by Walter Cronkite in the modern manner. The most important historical events do not, of course, happen dramatically. Some may take vast periods of time. We are therefore in an unusual position today, for one of the most important series of historical events—the restructuring of sex roles to adapt them to modern life—is unfolding before our very eyes. We are here. We are actually watching it. We have ringside seats from which to observe it.

The changes now in process are comparable with those that came with the transition from gathering to the domestication of plants, from scavenging carcasses left by other animals to hunting and trapping, from nomadic to fixed communities, from agricultural to industrial economies. Most of those changes took centuries, even millennia; the last, part of which we are now living through, less than 200 years. I view the current restructuring of sex roles as no less epochal than the restructuring of the class system which was one of the first consequences of the industrial revolution. When I read eighteenth century British tracts,[1] for example, that taught poor people to recognize their betters, to know their station in life and be content with it, to use their brains to make the most of what they had and not to try to get more, to accept the fact that societies were rigidly classified and the duties of all laid down,[2] I find it easy to substitute "women" for "the poor" and see in the changes in the sex-role structure now beginning to take place an analogue to the changes in the class structure then beginning to take place. No one reporter can, obviously, cover this whole story. It takes a wide array of researchers on many fronts to keep abreast of this fast-breaking "news." The papers assembled in this book constitute only a minuscule part of the story. But every little bit helps.

Most of these papers were requested and the topics assigned to fit into a given context. It is surprising therefore that they are as coherent as they are. Although they were not written to conform to an outline, there is an intrinsic logic in them, as I discovered when I began to collate them. As I have noted elsewhere, a book is an autobiography of the author while it is being written. These papers reflect my own preoccupations of the last year

1. One of the most successful of such tract writers was Hannah More, a contemporary of Mary Wollstonecraft's, who condemned "the infamous doctrine of the Rights of Women" (Jones, 1968:195).

2. Miss More established schools for the poor where they were taught to be content with their lowly station, long hours, low wages. They were taught that "rigid social distinction was God's own benevolent plan and that it was therefore wrong for the poor to try to raise themselves to higher economic or social levels by means of workers' unions or by efforts to change laws which bore harshly upon them. Ambition to leave a lowly station was reprehensible, discontent was sinful, and rioting was atrocious. Her writings reflect the general—but not universal—uneasiness at the possibility of laborers getting out of hand. Her plan for avoiding this was to make the poor physically comfortable by showing them how to utilize what they had, and submissive by showing them that joy in heaven was the recompense for deprivation on earth" (Hopkins, 1947:7, 203) Miss More was writing in the second half of the eighteenth century and the first years of the nineteenth.

or two. Little attempt has been made to impose more coherence on them than was inherent in the original papers themselves.

Alvin Gouldner once paid me the compliment of saying I never repeated myself. That is a record hard to maintain. There may be repetition in these papers when I felt that excising material would distort the context; but there is, I believe, only as much as was inevitable.

A reviewer of one of my books once gave it bad marks because so many of the references in it were to papers presented at professional meetings. It had not occurred to him that that is where much of the thinking on the cutting edge of knowledge is presented. I do not claim that the papers here assembled necessarily represent such a cutting edge, but I do hope they are near enough to the frontiers of current thinking to help us see what is happening in our society today as it goes through the throes of revamping its sex-role structure. We need all the help we can get from whatever source to keep up with the process.

References

Hopkins, Mary Alden. 1947. *Hannah More and her circle.* London: Longmans, Green.
Jones, Mary Gladys. 1968. *Hannah More.* Westport, Conn: Greenwood Press.

PART I

SEX DIFFERENCES

THE SINGLE PAPER IN Part I deals not so much with substantive sex differences as with research on sex differences as an institution. This research has not apparently been notably successful in its manifest functions, which have varied over time, but it has been remarkably successful in its latent function of legitimizing the status quo by demonstrating the inferiority of women on most of the variables that are highly valued in our society. In the selection of variables for study, in the value placed on them, and in the interpretation given to results, it has shown a male bias. The most valued variables have been those having to do with maleness. Women have accepted the assessment of their own inferiority until recently, when many have been converted to the male evaluation of power. They now see power not so much as a sex phenomenon as an institutional one, and they are trying to learn how to achieve and use it. This conversion is, in my opinion, regretable, if inevitable. There are some men who argue that in the future the values we view as female values will be more and more needed, and that it is therefore a mistake to underprize them now.

ONE

Research on Sex Differences:
An Overview of the State of the Art

Men and women, Senator Ervin is quoted as saying, are as different from one another as horse chestnuts and chestnut horses. At the risk of alienating some of my consoeurs, I am willing to go along with this, at least part of the way.[1] Men and women are different. A highly sophisticated corpus of research documents biological, psychological, social, and cultural differences between them. This paper does not propose to resurvey the differences reported nor to reinterpret them. It seeks rather to view research on sex differences as itself a sociological phenomenon, an institution, in the context of the sociology of knowledge, examining such questions as: (1) the objectives, latent as well as manifest, to which research on sex differences has addressed itself; (2) the questions asked, that is, the kinds of sex differences the research has concerned itself with; and (3) the methodological and ideological stance the research has taken.[2]

The Objectives of Research on Sex Differences

The article on sex differences in the International Encyclopedia of the

1. I have dealt with sex differences in greater detail in Bernard, 1971, and 1972b.
2. Many scholars and students as individuals, as well as the scientific community as such, have taken a stand against research that has the effect, if not the purpose, of demonstrating innate racial inferiority among blacks. This is not because they wish to hobble the advancement of science, but because in the absence of conditions which make adequate research possible, such research can be used against blacks when taken as the basis of policy.

Social Sciences notes that "the study of sex differences has been undertaken in order to answer important practical questions and in order to contribute to our knowledge of the ways in which many sorts of individual differences in personality come into existence" (Tyler, 1968:213). The specific objectives have shifted from time to time. At the beginning of the present century, for example, "the feminist movement generated interest in the question of whether the intelligence of women was or was not equal to that of men. What most investigators hoped to find was scientific evidence for the equality of the sexes" (Tyler, 1968:207). In the 1920s and 1930s research on sex differences was extended to encompass other, especially emotional, aspects of personality, including those derived from Freudian concepts and insights. Clinical, counseling, and therapy uses were major concerns: "the social objectives were to prevent neurosis and improve relationships between the sexes through understanding the differing emotional needs and ways of expression in men and women" (Tyler, 1968:208). In the 1950s there was another shift, this time to the study of sex roles and the way the child learned them. The objective of the research of this period was not just to understand sex differences for their own sake, but to utilize information about this highly visible aspect of personality development as a source of clues about the developmental processes through which many other aspects of personality may have come into existence" (Tyler, 1968:208).

Today research on sex differences must—in addition to continuing its counseling concerns—address itself to "feminists who wish to assert new alternative roles for women" (*Science*), 1972:1127). We have, in effect, come full circle. If the early feminist movement raised questions about the intelligence of women, the modern feminist movement raises questions not only about intelligence but also about roles; and "it may be creating myths about social roles just as erroneous and confusing as those which it seeks to discredit" (*Science*, 1972:1128). The present objective is, therefore, to face this new challenge. The "crucial task is to extricate scientific fact from wishful fancy concerning the behavioral attributes of structural sex differences and [to show] how both are, covertly and more grossly, reinforced and bent to social ends" (*Science*, 1972:1128). Exploitative social ends, some of the same feminists add.

The record of achievement of these ostensible objectives in the past cannot be said to be spectacular. The first was reached not by research but, in effect, by fiat. Intelligence tests were designed in such a way as to equate the intelligence of the two sexes. Nor was the second objective, the understanding of differing emotional needs of men and women in order to prevent neurosis and improve the relationships between the sexes, achieved. The clinical and counseling use of masculinity-femininity tests proved a disappointment, so that "the hope has been largely abandoned that M F scales might play a useful part in counseling situations to help individuals find work and living situations that would fit in with their basic temperamental qualities" (Tyler, 1968:212), let alone prevent neurosis.[3] And now the feminists' challenge of the role structure of our society is calling into question the utility of much of the recent role-oriented research on sex differences.[4]

Whatever the stated objectives of research on sex differences may have been, its latent function has been, in effect, to rationalize and hence to legitimate the status quo, including of course its role structure, especially the inferior position of women. The inferiority of women was self-evident from the research. "One persistent question has stimulated research interest throughout all these periods: why have women's achievements failed to match those of men? Why are there so few outstanding female artists, scientists, or statesmen?"

It is becoming increasingly clear why research on individual differences in intelligence or intellectual ability alone will never be adequate to answer this "persistent question." Research on the sociology of science has sensitized us to the importance of the sociological conditions necessary for scientific achievement. Thomas S. Kuhn has shown us the part played by the community of scientists; we now see the necessity of a shared ambience, of communication, of an audience that can reward achievement (Kuhn, 1962). Very few women have ever had the opportunity to enter this world and fewer still have been admitted fully (Woolf, 1929). For most of human history most women have spent most of their adult lives gestating, nursing, and caring for small children; these functions have preempted their entire lives. They were ignored for all high-level purposes, shut out from the world that supplies the conditions for productivity. Most ladies of the gentry in England could not even read until well into the eighteenth century. Women are only now beginning to enter the world that makes productivity possible, and even yet there are many barriers—as a voluminous research literature makes abundantly clear.[5]

3. The clinical use of the Freudian conception of sex differences, which identified power with the penis, took the form of trying to reconcile women to an acceptance of their inferiority. In effect it reaffirmed the old advice: be good, little maid, and pretty, and let who will be witty.

4. When research on sex differences turned to roles as well as to sex differences per se the political implications became increasingly clear, especially to women in the reemerging women's movement. Sex was assigned to roles: that is, roles as well as human beings had gender. Some strange inconsistencies were left unaccounted for in matching sex differences with sex roles. Women, we are always being reminded, have not produced any top-drawer artists. And yet on masculinity-femininity tests, artists tend to show up on the feminine side. Again, more girls than boys excel in the verbal skills, still in most of the studies of the amount of talking actually done in two-sex task-oriented groups, men talk more than women. If sex-related skills were matched with roles, there would be many more female surgeons and dentists using the fine-muscle superiority reported among girls. Except for the gestating and lactating function—a powerful enough exception, admittedly—there are no societal functions that cannot be performed by at least some individuals of both sexes. Nor, within each function (with the above exceptions), are there roles that cannot, similarly, be performed by at least some individuals of both sexes.

5. See, for example, reference to the "stag effect" in Bernard, 1973:157, 303. See also Rossi and Calderwood, 1973.

However equivocal the performance of the manifest function of the research on sex difference may have been, the performance of its latent function has been remarkably successful. The research explained why women "have been relatively unsuccessful within the present culture" (Theobold, 1967b:14). This success derived in part from the fact that women themselves have accepted their own inferiority: they have accepted the low value placed on them. They have a frighteningly poor opinion of themselves.[6]

Research Questions and Answers: The Superiority of Men

Lawrence Kubie, (1953) once analyzed the reasons why individual scientists chose the problems they did. Some selected problems that would keep them engaged for a lifetime; others sought the equivalent of a fast buck, that is, a project that would bring early returns in the form of publications. But when we add up all the research done by all the researchers, whatever the individual motives of individual scientists who conduct it may be, interesting trends show up.

Although sex differences, for example, are of many kinds, which among the potentially thousands of such differences have actually most preoccupied researchers?[7] How does it happen that so much is made of the fact that the blood of males has more androgen than that of females, but nothing is made of the fact that it also has more uric acid? And how does it happen that the net effect of the vast corpus of research leads to the conclusion that men are superior to women on all the variables that are valued highly in our society, namely: muscular or kinetic strength, competitiveness, power, need for achievement, and autonomy? In brief, the components of the archetypical macho[8] variable, offensive aggressiveness? These are the variables that interest men. These are the variables they judge one another by. These are the variables that are rewarded in our society.

6. See McClelland, 1965:173, and Bennett and Cohen, 1959. An article signed with a wo-man's name is rated lower by college women than the same article signed with a man's name (Goldberg, 1968). A lecture delivered by a man carries more authority with students of both sexes than the same lecture delivered by a woman (Bernard, 1973: 255–257). Still, it must be noted, on transcripts of discussions by groups consisting of two men and two women, neither male nor female judges could correctly identify the sex of the discussants more than slightly above a chance basis, and that slight margin resulted not so much from the contents of the contribution itself as from the sex-related words used and the more tentative feminine style (Bernard, 1973:167). The inferior pay accepted by women doing the same work as men is further evidence of the low opinion held by women of themselves (Bird, 1972).

7. The man who shouts *Vive la difference!* has one kind of difference in mind. How about the greater susceptibility of males to hemophilia, baldness, and color blindness?

8. Since the term *masculinity* has been shown so clearly to refer to cultural phenomena, a new term seems called for for the "he-man" phenomena originally referred to. The term *macho* is useful for this purpose, both as noun and as adjective. *Machismo* refers to the cult of macho.

These are the variables we need to know about in order to operate successfully in our society. These are the prestige variables. Furthermore, in all kinds of variables, regardless of their importance for success in our society, those in which males excel are almost automatically, if only implicitly, assigned higher value.[9] Except in IQ, maleness is assigned superiority.

Ruth Benedict noted a long time ago that cultures could be described in terms of certain characterizing patterns. Our culture, which was created by men and has been operated according to paradigms that have neglected, if not ignored, women, can be described as characterized by machismo, the cult of macho. The Adam Smith paradigm, for example, which guided policy well into the twentieth century, paid little attention to women or their world; Adam Smith wrote a separate book on the theory of the moral sentiments. The economy was run by an economic man, a man motivated wholly by rational judgements of gains and losses. Political Science has had almost nothing to say about women except—when women asked for suffrage— to deny that they had the qualifications to exercise it or to enjoy civil rights. Until recently the neglect of women in policy decisions could be justified on the grounds that women did not inhabit the male world. Polemicists and didactic writers never tired of telling us that women had their own sphere, one that operated on quite different principles from those of the male world (Bernard, 1971:24–28). It is understandable, therefore, that men have been superior in the world they made for themselves along male values. And it is equally understandable that "the failure of women to emerge as equal partners with men [in a world they never made] is due to the fact that they have not adopted the characteristics which can be clearly seen as crucial for success in the present socio-economic system" (Theobold, 1967b:13-14).

Research evidence so far leaves little doubt that more males than females test high on offensive aggressiveness, this typical macho variable, this Ur variable on which, it may well be argued, much of the superiority of males in so much of the research rests. The male body is better equipped for it in size, speed, and musculature, and better fueled for it by androgens.[10] It is the one sex difference most jealously insisted upon by men.[11]

9. At one time, for example, a great deal was made of the smaller ratio of brain tissue to body weight among women; but when it was later found that beyond a certain minimum size, brain weight was not related to ability, brain complexity, not size, being the important variable, at least that sex difference was rarely heard of again. In the nineteenth century, when it was believed that there was greater dispersion of attributes among women and greater central tendency among men, it was argued as a sign of male superiority; men were more stable than women. But when the reverse was found to be the case, women hugging the average more than men, this sex difference also lost its appeal. The case of the name given to different styles of perception between the sexes on the rod-and-frame test is also relevant. The invidious term *field-dependence* was given to the characteristically female style rather than, for example, *restricted perception* to the male style.

10. That, I can hear Freud muttering under his breath, is exactly what I meant.

11. A young woman once said: "I have learned that when I talk to a man, if right at the outset

The indifferent, neutral, and antimacho variables belong to women. More females than males, for example, show nurturance and the most loathsome of all antimacho variables, namely dependency as defined by the psychologists.[12] They also show the perhaps not altogether unrelated variable, mental illness (Bernard, 1972: Chapters 2–3; Gove, 1972). Women are magnanimously recognized as the more viable sex. But so what? There is little value in a longevity that keeps powerless older people alive.

The conceptualization of aggressiveness and dependency as polar opposites, one characteristically male and one female, illustrates how the paradigms of sex differences with which we start influence what we see and how we see it. It is harder to see dependency in men, aggressiveness in women. But the two qualities are not necessarily opposites. More males than females may be aggressive, but the fact that marriage is so much more important for the well-being of men than of women (Bernard, 1972a: Chapters 2, 3), suggests that more of them have great dependency needs. (Or else, of course, that more women than men supply the dependency needs of spouses, so that the dependency of men is not left exposed.) It might also be argued that only the form, not the incidence, of aggressiveness and dependency is different in the two sexes. Female aggressiveness tends to be defensive,[13] often in the protection of the young, as in the case of the lioness. Among human beings, it tends to be verbal. The frequent characterization of dependency as passive, finally, may be erroneous. There can be active dependency as there can be passive aggressiveness. Indeed, one of the indexes of dependency as reported in the research literature is the female infant's *seeking* of skin contact, hardly a passive quality. Walter Mischel, it may be added, rightly questions the utility of the term *dependency* in describing behavior (Mischel, 1966:68).

I grant that men are bigger, stronger, more powerful than women, he will concede anything else. Of course women are smarter, more clever, better copers, and the like. All he insists on is superior power. Concede that and you can claim everything else." Even Harvard professors concede usefulness (to men) in the womanly virtues of docility, willingness to be programmed, and skill in the "expressive role." One even asks, dear me, dear me, "Why is this functional role, which has been traditionally a feminine responsibility, so undervalued in our time?" (McClelland, 1965). Diana Baumrind asks: "Would McClelland *himself* relinquish the instrumental assertive role and its rewards in exchange for the opportunity to manage 'the interpersonal and emotional relationships which hold the society together'?" (1972:184).

The young woman quoted above might be exaggerating, but the use even today of such ploys as "you great big strong man" and "poor little weak me" suggests that there is a kernel of truth in her observation. One is reminded of Desmond Morris's description of the ritualistic obeisance shown by monkeys to the dominant male. "A non-sexual female monkey can present her rump to a male as a sign that she is simply not aggressive. It acts as an appeasement gesture and functions as an indication of her subordinate status. . . . If a weak male is threatened by a strong one, the underling can protect himself by behaving as a pseudo-female. He signals his subordination by adopting the female sexual posture" (1969:101).

12. Sociologists see human interdependence in a quite different perspective.

13. In some of the communes of the counterculture, the females, who were almost pathologically dependent, could express aggressiveness only in behalf of their children (Speck, 1972:106).

The research on sex differences has, in brief, been a predominantly male enterprise, reflecting male perspectives and values. This is true even when it is engaged in by women, for women pursue science as defined by men. Since they use the male-oriented conceptions, definitions, and paradigms, the fact that research is done by a woman does not mean that it necessarily reflects the interests of women or that it embodies a female point of view. Researchers, as Kuhn indicates, work under the surveillance of the community whose paradigms they share. They select problems and execute their research under the watchful eyes of their scientific colleagues. Since most of these have been men, the researcher—male or female—has a male audience in mind when he or she designs a project and reports results. If the project does not pass muster before the male audience it drops into limbo and is never seen or heard of again. The "censoring" function performed by a community of scientists has been well documented by Kuhn (1962).

Only very recently are women beginning to supply answers to the questions the male researchers never asked. They are analyzing scores of behavior patterns that men never noticed in themselves before: that they do not listen to women colleagues, that they interrupt women more than they do men, that they use language that ignores women. They challenge a whole corpus of research on female sexuality. They see quite a different array of sex differences.

Backlash

Since sex differences have been used against women, feminists have understandably reacted strongly against the research that, by demonstrating their inferiority, has justified their low status[14] and shown that they get just what they deserve.[15] This backlash has encompassed several strategies, including denial of differences, agnosticism with respect to differences, rebuttal, and scientific challenge.

14. Especially useful has been recourse to menstruation as the undeniable proof of their incapacity. Women are absolutely unfit for the responsibility of power or even consideration for it. Their glands are against them, poor dears. Edgar Berman, in the so-called Battle of the Raging Hormones, is the classic example of this line of argument. In a Democratic Party task force, he argued that the leadership capacity of women was limited by their hormones. He was, ironically, bested by a woman, Patsy Mink, representative from Hawaii, and forced to resign from the committee. It seems futile to reply to this argument, but women continue to do so. First, they point out, not all women suffer the disqualifying premenstrual jitters attributed to all women. Second, their bodies are glandularly most nearly like men's in this period. Third, positions of power and responsibility are usually held in our society by persons of either sex who are 50 or older. And finally, if one's glands are to determine one's qualifications, the susceptibility of men to pretty breasts and legs, as Cynthia Epstein has noted, disqualifies most men for judgements concerning the hiring and firing of women.

15. "It is . . . argued in much of the literature that the failure of women to emerge as equal partners with men is due to the fact that they have not adopted the characteristics which can be

The strategy of denial underplays sex differences.[16] The argument states that with the exception of actual gestation and lactation of infants, there are no relevant differences between the sexes so far as role assignment is concerned. Sex differences do not predetermine sex roles; anatomy is not, as Freud insisted, destiny. Certainly there are no differences that justify discrimination against women in role assignments. The burden of this critique has been that our common species heredity is far more pervasive than the specialized reproductive component of heredity (Bernard, 1972b: 44–45).[17] These critics are consistent; they reject the greater moral virtues attributed to women as well as their greater infirmities. My personal objection to the denial strategy is the concession it implies to male values. It implies that to prove themselves worthy, women must prove themselves no different from men. We're just like you, see? I do not accept the idea that recognizing the existence of sex differences means ipso facto recognizing male superiority, though I recognize that this is how it has been interpreted in the past.

A second feminist response to the research on sex differences that are relevant for role assignment or for policy, but they have not yet been proved (Weisstein, 1970). Skepticism is always an honorable scientific stance, and it is just as well to have a strong streak of skepticism in any scientific field. Henri Poincaire once noted that even all mathematicians are not equally convinced by given proofs. My own feeling is that we have to begin with the admission that we can never really know what the sexes would be like if there were no cultural conditioning, if we did not begin with pink and blue

---

clearly seen as crucial for success in the present socioeconomic system, and that women should therefore concentrate in developing these values and 'strengths'" (Theobold, 1967b:14–15). In brief, if women would only shape up, they, too, could succeed; it was their own fault if they did not.

16. An interesting reversal of this denial of sex differences is the current tactic of emphasizing rather than soft-pedaling them on the theory that the denial strategy has had dysfunctional consequences for women. Many aspects of femaleness have been swept under the carpet. It was poor taste to talk about them. Hardly anyone in polite society or scientific company spoke of rape, abortion, menstrual cycles. There was, therefore, always something forbidden about women, something that had to be kept under cover. The motives behind this kind of conspiracy of silence may have been benign, not to embarrass women by reminding them that they were not men. But the latent function was to put women in an exploitable position. Problems peculiarly theirs were not given the attention they deserved. Militant feminists now follow the strategy of "politicizing" such peculiarly female issues as rape and abortion. They even attack the use of the menstrual cycle as an excuse for discrimination against women.

17. It should be noted that denial of sex differences refers only to the relevance of differences for role allocation. A careful canvass of all the sex differences apparent in infancy, and hence least culture-based, specified: smaller size, lesser muscle mass, lower metabolism and energy level, less vigorous overt activity, lower pain threshold, greater sensitivity, less interest in novel or highly variable stimuli, interest in people, and greater clinging to mother. Certainly not a very impressive inventory with which to explain the variety of sex roles within each sex or between sexes. David B. Lynn notes that in the past, cultures could reinforce these potentials and thus foster domesticity in women. "Today, however," he concludes, "a new adaptation may be demanded for the species to thrive" (1972:243–245).

blankets in the nursery, dolls and trucks in the preschool, ballet and baseball in the preteens, cheer leaders and football players in high school, and so on. Since children cannot survive outside a cultural matrix, by the time we can examine them we have already begun to shape them. The skepticism is thus likely to focus less on the existence of differences themselves than on their precise nature and their inevitability.

A third critique accepts the existence of sex differences but challenges their intrinsic or unchangeable nature as determinants of roles. One of the favorite forms of this critique is to canvass the inventory of cultures throughout the world for examples of role patterns which reverse our own. A classic example of this approach was Margaret Mead's (1933) study of the Arapesh, the Mundugumor, and the Tchambuli.[18] Among the Arapesh, she reported, everyone, male and female, showed the nurturing qualities we identify as feminine in our society. Among the Mundugumor everyone, male and female, showed the ruthlessness and aggression we identify as masculine in our society. Among the Tchambuli the men showed qualities we identify as feminine and the women, qualities we identify as masculine. There have been other reports on cultures in which our conceptions of masculine and feminine qualities are reversed.[19] Another form of this critique challenges the intrinsic or unchangeable nature of sex differences by showing that they vary not only from place to place but also from time to time in the same culture. In the nineteenth century, for example, diabetes was more common in males, and ulcers more common in females. Today there is a reverse incidence. Both are psychosomatic illnesses. More women than men used to suffer from hysterical illnesses; now the hysterias are rarely found in either sex. Courtly men of the late eighteenth century were more like women in their love of adornment and vanity than they were like men a century later. O tempora, O mores!

18. No book, it may be noted, was ever more welcome than this one. *Sex and Temperament in Three Primitive Societies* set the mold for thinking about sex and roles for a whole generation; it appeared on the reading lists of a wide variety of college courses. My own critique (Bernard, 1945) received little attention.

19. For example, Hall, 1963:10. More recently a report on women in Ghana showed women as having more of the initiative and entrepreneurship we think of as male and the men as having more of the passivity we think of as female. One successful woman "noted that under Ghana's former British colonial regime, Ghanaian men with education had been encouraged to work in clerical and office jobs. Many men, she added, had the education to make them successful in business 'but they prefer the security and prestige of white-collar jobs. They are not as courageous as the women,' she said. 'Maybe we have nothing to lose, so we don't mind. We go out and do things, but the men would rather sit in an office and earn $50 a month, knowing very well that it's not enough and yet they won't branch out'" (Jones, 1972). Anthropological reports on women in Africa show that such enterprise is an old story, illustrated by the custom of the Mammy Wagon also.

In a news conference, Denmark's new queen and king told reporters they enjoyed their work. The queen found her work "very rich" and the king was "happy with the job I have, helping my wife" (Pedersen, 1972).

One final example of the use of reversals. It was originally believed that man came before woman; he was the first, she the second, sex. Then prenatal research showed that without spritzing with genetically provided androgens, the fetus remained female, and even when the

David V. Tiedman and his associates noted some time ago that women did not object so much to statements that their psyches *were* different; what they minded was insistence that their psyches *had* to be different (Tiedeman, O'Hara, and Matthews, 1958:37). Because the implications of this issue are so profound and so ramifying, it has seemed to be of enormous importance to determine whether sex differences were ineradicable or subject to modification. At this point we are back once more to the old nature-nurture controversy, though on a somewhat more sophisticated level than in the past, for we know considerably more about both nature and nurture.[20] Because the male-oriented research tradition has tended to prove the inferiority of women, it has seemed important to feminists to prove that the differences were not the result of genetics.

Currently the most acceptable view is that the role-relevant traits are the result of socialization, and thus the developmental approach to the interpretation of sex differences is widely discussed. We can "examine our best evidence concerning sex differences, their contribution to social roles, and the patterning of roles through social and learning processes" (*Science*, 1972:1127). Human development has, in fact, become a major preoccupation among researchers in recent years; in the case of sex differences, the part played by early socialization has almost preempted the field.

The Challenge to the Socialization Paradigm

Few aspects of socialization are more thoroughly scanned today than the processes of instilling gender identity in children and preparing them for their gender roles. An enormous research literature has documented the sexist bias in games, toys, readers, media programs, and the like. Increasingly we recognize how early and how profoundly, if uninten-

---

genetic material is female, spritzing with androgens will masculinize it. Now some of the radical feminists could crow. The essence of the argument is that human heredity, which has not changed very much since it was laid down some ten thousand years ago or so, has to explain a bewildering variety of sex roles as defined by scores of cultures in many different times and climes. Only two constants can be relied on as explanatory factors: (1) gestation and lactation have always been components of the female role, and (2) the greater size, speed, musculature, and, presumably, more androgen among males have given them a power advantage. Otherwise roles have not been matched on a one-to-one basis with sex traits. It was the Indian squaw who walked, carrying the burden, for example; and it is the man who sits on the beach overseeing the Japanese women who catch the fish.

20. It is worth pointing out that so far as eradicability is concerned, the genetic versus acquired formulation is inadequate. It is sometimes easier to modify a genetic than an acquired trait. A genetic trait can sometimes be changed by fetal hormones, by surgery, by medication, or mitigated by prosthetic devices. The enormous advances now in process in so-called genetic engineering, in sex change, and the like enhance the cogency of this point. An acquired trait, on the other hand, may be invulnerable to change, as in the case of some addictions. Disappointed psychiatrists could probably add scores of examples of acquired behaviors not amenable to change.

tionally, unwittingly, and unconsciously, by our differing responses to the pink-clad and the blue-clad infants we participate in producing passive, dependent, submissive, noncreative females, fit primarily for subservient and inferior roles in our society. We are left in no doubt that the socialization of boys and girls is different and produces appropriately shaped adults who can fit easily into the roles defined for them in our society. And there, precisely, is the rub, according to feminists' critiques.

For even this seemingly favorable orientation—emphasizing as it does the acquired rather than the inherited origins of role-related sex differences—is now challenged by some feminists as a copout, as a placebo. Carol Hanisch (1971), for example, views it as a diversionary tactic, distracting attention from the real basis for the roles of women,— power. Not traits socialized—the new word is "programmed"—into girls determine their adult roles, but the superior power of men. She finds that males can cheerfully accept the socialization interpretation of the sex differences which determine the roles of women because they gain greatly in substituting a socialization paradigm for a power or institutional paradigm. She therefore sees the emphasis on socialization as, in effect, a respectable way to exonerate both men and women from responsibility for the discriminatory effects of such sex differences: sorry, girls, too bad you haven't got what it takes; you're afraid of success and all that. I know it isn't your fault; I know it's the way you were socialized as a child; you'd be just as superior as I am if you had played with trucks instead of with dolls. But what can I do about it, after all?[21] The blame for the discrimination is placed on the shoulders of women themselves.

The alternative proposed by this critique is not a return to a theory of innate differences but a shift to a power or institutional or structural explanation. Proponents of this viewpoint note, for example, that when women have institutional support their sex makes little if any difference in role assignment. Class and caste support powerful women in the Third World; women hold high office, even exert power, and it is acceptable.[22] In our society the institutional structure does not support women in power positions. Thus maleness-cum-institutional-support has enormous advantage over femaleness-sans-institutional-support, whatever the nature of sex differences may be.

The feminist critique of the socialization paradigm does not deny that children are socialized for different roles, but it argues that even if socialization no longer emphasized the differences between the pink-clad

21. The socialization paradigm can be used by victims also. It is a cliché that members of minority groups can find a secondary gain in their handicaps. Failure is not due to their own inadequacies but to their race, their ethnicity, their religion.

22. In many cases, to be sure, they are primarily agents of their families, contributing to the power coffers of fathers or husbands. In the United States, caste has served a similar function. A white woman could operate a plantation, holding power over black men, because the institutional structure wiped out sex differentials in macho.

and the blue-clad infants, the infants would still grow up in a world that retained an institutional set of biases. If by some miracle we could change the socialization of girls without other institutional changes so that they were not oriented so exclusively toward motherhood or occupations such as teaching, typing, laboratory assistant and were, instead to the same extent as boys, prepared to be doctors rather than nurses, would their adult experience be different from what it is today? Would they be as likely as men to gain acceptance in medical schools? The feminist critics say no; so long as the institutional structure of our society favors men, they ask, can women, no matter how well prepared psychologically and intellectually, expect to be dealt with on the basis of their merits rather than on the basis of their sex? Emphasis on socialization merely offers an easy out; it does not open doors. Not more and more research on sex differences per se nor on the development of such differences, whatever the process, is called for by these critics, but an attack on the institutional structure that embalms these differences in the form of discrimination against women. The name of the game is power.

Critique of the Ideological Bias in Research

Another form the backlash takes is an attack on the assumptions, presuppositions, and especially the political implications of research on sex differences itself. Here the critics touch an issue which, though a long-time concern, has become especially sensitive in recent years, namely the influence of ideology on science.

In 1949, Nicholas Pastore published a book on the nature-nurture controversy in which he explored "some of the dynamic factors that have influenced the leading scholars in formulating their inquiries and their interpretations" (Pastore, 1949). He concluded, as Goodwin Watson tells us, that "there is interaction of a circular kind between the political and psychological dogmas. Interaction . . . implies some effect of social assumptions upon scientific findings and correspondingly some departure from the ideal of objectivity" (1949:viii). Even then, almost a quarter of a century ago, Goodwin Watson saw the relevance of the issue for sex roles. And he called "for a new advance in scientific methodology in the biological and perhaps also in the physical sciences" (1949:viii), to help overcome ideological biases.

Pastore had found among the twenty-four men he studied that, with the exception of Terman and John Watson, those who were liberal in their political ideologies tended to favor the "nurture" interpretation, and those who were conservative, the "nature" one. The policy implications of the conservative "nature" view is that the individual should accept the establishment or system or institution or social order and adjust to it; the liberal "nurture" view is the reverse.[23]

Twenty years later young radicals in all the behavioral and social sciences were making the same points as those made by Goodwin Watson. They were calling both for "new advances in scientific methodology" for their disciplines in "formulating their inquiries" and for greater sensitivity in their interpretations. Sociologists were being rebuked for the class and racist bias in the formulation of research projects; their work, it was alleged, was, in effect, a kind of espionage, a gathering of data which could be used by those in power to exploit others, especially the poor and the blacks. A whole generation, in brief, triggered first by opposition to the war, was beginning to question the sacredness of the social order. They were using the venerable Thoreau tradition against the war; they used the anarchist tradition against the bureaucratic system. Until then it had not seemed untoward that schools and other socializing agencies should prepare young people for positions in the social order—ministers for the church, teachers for the schools, workers for industry, everyone for sex roles. Now many were challenging the right of any institution to "program" them in any way, to shape them for the "slots" of a system they rejected. They wanted to do their own thing, not anyone else's, certainly not the system's. They did not want to be molded to fit bureaucracies, nor shaped for fixed sex roles in a world they never made and did not approve of in any case. Unlike the researchers they did not take the status quo for granted. The disaffection of the young men was caught by the young women. The grievances seemed to be especially relevant in their case.

A review of the research literature on women found that it did indeed harbor an ideological bias which, implicitly or explicitly, accepted the status quo and took for granted that women adjust to it regardless of whether or not its roles were congenial to them (Astin, Suneiwick, and Dweck, 1971).[24] The authors of the review went beyond the findings to examine both the interpretations and their implications for the future. In addition to defects of methodology,[25] including instruments, they found

23. There are, admittedly, illogicalities and inconsistencies in this formula. "Adjustment" in the case of women could take the form of acquiring the male characteristics called for in our society, as some commentators advised (Theobold, 1967a) or of learning to grin and bear the ignominious roles assigned them. The first alternative implies a "nurture" ideology, the second, a "nature" one. In practice, the counseling-clinical objectives of the twenties and thirties had been in the direction of the grin-and-bear-it type. I find my own stance illogical. I am what is now called an old-fashioned liberal, yet I find myself siding with the "nature" side of the controversy in the sense of accepting sex differences but wanting those associated with women more highly valued, a goal calling for the exercise of power. Suppose we could, indeed, by changing our socializing patterns, produce more females who excelled in male-type accomplishments. Why should we? What's so great about macho?

24. See also the August and November, 1971, issues of *The Journal of Marriage and the Family*, edited by Pauline Bart.

25. Rae Carlson (1971; 1972) found that much research on the psychology of women was

ideological considerations weighing heavily. They distinguished two schools of thought on the basis of hypotheses and interpretations: the moderate-equivalent and the progressive-equal. The first accepts the status quo, as the conservatives did in the Pastore study, and shows how women must adjust to it.[26] The second does not accept it and its thrust is increasingly in the direction of calling for institutional change to overcome the built-in discrimination against women, in the tradition of the liberals in the Pastore study.

In the backlash against the latent function of research on sex differences, as in the case of the research tradition itself against which it is protesting, there is a latent function being performed. Many of the women themselves belie the old research results. They are active, not passive; they are autonomous, not dependent. They are, in fact, not at all the kind of people we used to think women were, not at all the kind of women the old research said they ought to be. They are calling for new conceptualizations not only by their verbal critiques but also by just being the kind of female persons they are. They are themselves data belying the old stereotypes. They will become *scientific* data when someone studies them, as, no doubt, someone soon will. For they are performing an important function. David B. Lynn has noted that "if the Women's Liberation movement did not exist, society would have to invent one to help awaken the nation to the necessity of undertaking the new adaptations demanded of it" (Lynn, 1972:245).[27] Similarly it could be said that if this scientific backlash did not exist, the several disciplines would have to invent one to help awaken them to the necessity of reexamining their old assumptions.

Sex Stereotyping

It is ironic to note that a branch of psychology called Individual Psychology, and hence ostensibly concerned with individual differences has become, in effect, a branch that underplays individual differences and overplays group or population differences. It has become an instrument for

inadequate because it used the "agentic" approach preferred by males, but unsuitable for studying women.

26. Some of the researchers of this school believe that "nothing should be done because women's current status is a natural state. They believe that women should not take their inferiority to heart, that they should accept their status and endeavor, by embracing their womanhood ever closer to their psyches, to help the world appreciate their natural qualities. They usually point to the virtues of modern men and women and suggest that the relationship between the two should be a complementary one, in business, in school, and at home. They call on men and women to live as superior and inferior beings for their own and society's good. From an objective perspective, this approach to the issue gives rise to the claim that research conducted under the moderate-equivalent school is biased against women" (Astin, Suneiwick, and Dweck, 1971:16–17). Among the researchers cited as especially biased in ideology is Mervin Freedman. The study by the Brovermans, Clarkson, Rosenkranz, and Vogel is referred to as demonstrating the bias of the moderate-equivalent school (Ibid: 18).

27. I made the same point in *Women and the Public Interest* (1971:277–278).

violating the concept of individual differences, a concept that calls for dealing with the individual in terms of his or her own special qualities. Research on sex differences has inadvertently contributed to this unanticipated consequence.

In both psychology and sociology a fundamental tenet is that intragroup differences are often greater than intergroup differences. Still, in reporting research finding we tend to concentrate on the 10-point difference between, let us say, the average black child and the average white child, overlooking the 50-point spread between the highest and the lowest child among blacks and whites. And so, analogously, do we look at the distribution of sex differences.

A considerable body of research has documented some of the intrasex differences among women under such rubrics as career-oriented versus home-oriented, or pioneers versus housewives, and so on.[28] Recent work on fetal hormones suggests that some of these differences may be due to androgenization. And, I may add here parenthetically, I do not shrink in horror from the idea that achieving women may be more androgenized than nonachieving women. Some achieving women are as demure in habit as the old stereotype of the feminine woman. Despite all the evidence of great intrasex differences, however, we still speak—and think—as though "women" were a homogeneous population.

Our speech habits contribute to such stereotyping. They can have subtle consequences for our perceptions and thinking. One is to negate the basic axiom about intra- and intergroup differences just referred to. In the article on sex differences in the *International Encyclopedia of the Social Sciences*, for example, we read that "females appear to excel in verbal ability," "females are less able than males to disregard the visual field in which a perceptual pattern . . . is embedded," men "are more oriented than women toward abstract ideas, practical success, and power," and so on (Tyler, 1968:208–210). Such formulations, I am convinced, encourage categorical, that is, stereotyped, thinking. The author's reminder that "individual differences far outweigh sex differences" does not undo the mischief.

The sloppiness of our reporting has consequences. Because the researchers tell us that boys have more mechanical aptitude than girls, we shut *all* girls out of shop courses. An analogous situation would be one in which *all* men would be denied driver's licenses or shut out of jobs requiring color discrimination because more men than women are color-blind. Or no men would be put in hiring positions because more men than women are susceptible to visual sex stimuli.

I would recommend as a simple first step in changing our speech habits that instead of saying, for example, that males are more aggressive than

28. My own work has always emphasized intrasex differences, especially *The Sex Game* (1972b: 43–69) and *Women and the Public Interest* (1971: 7–13).

females, we say that more males than females are aggressive. We do not shut out the female who is more aggressive than the average male nor, conversely, her opposite number, the male who is less aggressive than the average female.

Another speech habit that has consequencs is the term opposite sex. Perhaps our bilateral symmetry predisposes us to think in terms of polarities: "on the one hand . . . on the other hand," "on one side . . . on the other side." But the sexes are not necessarily opposite except in coitus. Thinking in terms of opposites leads to non sequiturs. If men are A, women must be Z. If women cease to be C, men will become C. And so on.[29] I suggest that we speak of the *other* rather than of the *opposite* sex. If the sexes were, indeed, opposites they would never be able to share any roles. If a role fit one sex it could not fit the other.

Stereotyping, however easy and congenial to lazy types, runs counter to the long-time macrosociological trend of substituting individual achievement for ascription in the allocation of roles and the accompanying statuses. Such individuation is not an easy goal to reach;[30] making decisions on the basis of sex is much easier than seeing the individual woman. Stereotyping saves the time and attention required to judge the individual. What feminists ask is that such stereotyping be eliminated and that women be permitted to achieve according to their individual abilities. Research on sex differences could help rather than, as now, hinder this end.

If individual differences were acceped, if the education and the counseling of young people emphasized individual differences and if jobs were allocated on the basis of individual qualifications, it is likely that the sexes would distribute themselves along the lines of the respective sex distributions of these qualifications. If, under the conditions just specified, it still remained true that only a small proportion of girls liked physics and were good at it, they would show up among the professional physicists in that same proportion, however small. They would not be discouraged from entering the profession because "most girls" were not interested in a career

29. For an excellent statement of the use of polarities in psychological conceptualization see Carlson (1972: 22–25). She makes the point that the polarities are within both sexes rather than between them. The most opposite "dimensions" can occur within the same individual. And, according to the Jungian system, they should. In the words of Erich Neumann, "the peril of present-day mankind springs in large part from the one-sidedly patriarchal development of the male intellectual consciousness, which is no longer kept in balance by the matriarchal world of the psyche. In this sense the exposition of the archetypical-psychical world of the Feminine . . . is also a contribution to a future therapy of culture. Western mankind must arrive at a synthesis that includes the feminine world which is also one-sided in its isolation. Only then will the individual human beings be able to develop the psychic wholeness that is urgently needed if Western man is to face the dangers that threaten his existence from within and without" (1963:xlii).

30. David B. Lynn has suggested some of the difficulties involved in dealing with even schoolchildren on the basis of individual ability rather than sex. Two individuals with the same ability may have different cognitive styles and there are many elements involved in cognitive style itself. Even so he concludes that research on grouping by some interaction of cognitive style and ability rather than sex is possible and in order (1972:256).

in physics or talented for it. There would be as many women physicists—or anything else—as there were women in the population who were interested and talented in it. That would help; it would be a step in the right direction toward matching talents and roles. But only a first step. For unless we changed our evaluation of sex differences, whatever occupations showed large concentrations of women would be low in prestige and in rewards.

Changing the way people think about women—as the critical activity discussed so far has aimed to do—is important in its own right. It contributes to the advancement of science. It does not, however, immediately improve the value placed on sex differences, nor does it solve the urgent need to overcome the low opinion women have of themselves. If we did not change our evaluation of sex differences, female roles and occupations would remain lower in status than male roles and occupations —unless women achieved power. On the basis of current standards, respect and recognition are accorded to an individual not because he or she contributes indispensable, even invaluable, services—as women admittedly do[31]—but because he or she has the power to compel them. Converting women to an acceptance of power has been one of the most significant successes of machismo. In addition, therefore, to activating theoretical and intellectual changes, women are now seeking power.

This would be the logical place to end. The major points have been made, namely that: (1) research on sex differences achieved few if any of its ostensible objectives; (2) such research has had the effect of rationalizing the inferior status of women by explaining it in terms of their demonstrable inferiority (an inferiority they have themselves accepted); (3) it has been guilty of a male bias in the selection of variables, in the methods used, and in the interpretation of its results, all reflecting the values of a male world in which the cult of macho prevails; and (4) it has had the effect of preserving sex stereotyping. A strong backlash has alerted us to these defects. Only recently have women been converted to the use of power as well as of the pen as a way of counteracting these forces, to activism as well as to science. But I cannot leave it at that—I beg leave to add a few more words. They do not have to do with scientific research on sex differences but with the possible effects of such differences, whatever they are, in the future.

Women and Power

I think I have no hang-ups about sex differences. I am quite willing to concede male superiority in offensive aggressiveness. Despite tales of

---

31. There is no hesitation to grant that women perform the integrative function that holds "the society together," to admit that "a society would quickly collapse into anarchy" without such integrating services. There is even willingness to concede that "the world is suffering from an overdose of masculine assertiveness." And readiness to admit that integrating contributions "natural to women" are undervalued (McClelland, 1965: 172-192). But *pay* for holding society together and for preventing its collapse? Perish the thought.

matriarchs and Amazons and even stories of real-life heroines like Deborah and Joan of Arc, it is hard for me to believe that if women had had power there would have been enough of them to build empires or ravish the earth as mercilessly as men have done. I am even willing to grant positive value to the culture men have created. One of its components, modern technology, has improved the living conditions of most of us; our health is better, we live longer, we are richer.

But I am not willing to grant that this male accomplishment has been an unmitigated joy to the world or without enormous human cost. I do not believe that the harsh driving macho cult has been an unqualified success. It is not very wholesome for most of us; but it is worse for women than for men. To paraphrase an old anti-war slogan, it is not emotionally healthy for women or other living things. The mental health of women, for example, is not good; the typical emotional state of women is depression. I have called the mental health of housewives Public Health Problem Number One (Bernard, 1972a: Chapter 3).[32] I do not view the failure of women to excel in such a society as much of a disgrace.

My concern, then, is no longer with proof of the existence of sex differences, whatever they may be, so much as with the values placed on them and the uses made of them—including power.

For a long time the idea of power was anathema to women. Power was associated with maleness. Women looked hopefully to a time when human beings could transcend power. Their hopes have faded. Increasingly they accept the necessity for securing power and learning how to use it. No one, they have sadly learned, surrenders power; it has to be wrested.[33] The issues have been encapsulated as follows:

> certain women's groups, such as Women's Strike for Power . . . have argued that feminine values are crucial to the controlling and development of the world even today. They claim that women have the capacity to do certain presently crucial tasks better than men. Believing that force is counterproductive on the national and international scene, they state that women must now take the initiative because men have been taught to try to achieve "power" in all situations.

This view is countered on two levels. First, it is argued that the only way

32. The costs to women of macho are equally great in Mexican-American culture. Here, we are told, women are masochistic, feel inferior, and tend toward depression; they are even more disturbed than their counterparts in Anglo culture (Torrey, 1972:126). A study of two Mexican communities confirmed the relationship between the status of women and psychiatric symptomatology: Women whose status approached that of men reported fewer symptoms (Langner, 1965:360–392).

33. Not necessarily, of course, by force. When blacks were resorting to violence they were reminded that in this arena they were bound to lose. The same is true in the case of women. No matter how skilled in self-defense they become, no matter how clever in the use of arms, violence is not their best bet. They may yet prove the old saying that the pen is mightier than the sword.

to bring about change is to force through a new idea or a new technique—that cooperation cannot be effective in changing the behavior of people. Second, it is argued that it is, therefore, naive to look for alternative techniques which would eliminate force. At the next level of analysis, these two arguments appear effectively identical; it is claimed that competition is necessary and will prevail over cooperation (Theobold, 1967:14).

The moral, obviously, was that "women should therefore concentrate in developing these values and 'strengths' that were crucial for success in the present economic system" (Theobold, 1967a:13). Women who had once hoped to make themselves felt without resort to the use of power have now concluded that they too must learn how to achieve and use it.[34] This conversion may, in fact, constitute the most significant—and deplorable—evidence for the practical superiority of the macho values. I wish women had not had to concede on this matter.

What about the Future?

Even among those who grant that "women have been relatively unsuccessful within the present culture" and who do not deny that "women could change and be more successful," there are misgivings about this capitulation by women. They argue

> that the areas *presently* valued will not be important in the future and that it is therefore absurd to abandon female values at this point . . . .
> The major areas of work in coming periods will be education, the human care of human beings, and the creation of the good community, and . . . these will demand empathy, intuition, and cooperation which appear to be predominantly female characteristics. (Theobold, 1967:14)

A similar thought was expressed almost half a century ago:

> It is not necessary to assume that behavior forms that are highly efficient in one period of national development will be equally efficient throughout successive periods of national life. It is quite likely that an individual most markedly endowed for successful behavior in one period of national history may be least markedly endowed for successful behavior in some other period. (Murchison, 1929:4)[35]

34. The organization of Women's Lobby, Inc. was announced in November, 1972. It will lobby for a variety of women's issues *Washington Post*, November 21, 1972). Even the conventional American Association of University Women now views the acquisition of power as having greater priority for women than service "as a means of molding a more humanistic world of 1990" (Bloom, 1972).

35. The subtitle of Murchison's book, *The Psychology of Political Domination*, has always struck me as remarkable prescient.

The same thought has been expressed by others. Sociologists note, for example, that in one age the warrior is the hero; in another age, the priest is the wielder of power.

Any number can play the futurist game. At least three views are relevant to a discussion of sex differences and the future. One describes a world not too different from the present except that women have more power. The other two view quite different structures, one pro and one con with respect to the key factor of technology.

In the past it was one of the arguments in favor of equality that if women were in positions of power they would vastly improve our society. Women were more nurturant, more person-oriented, more concerned with human welfare, less belligerent and militaristic. If they were given more power, therefore, a better human society could be expected.

This argument is no longer acceptable. In the first place, it implies moral superiority in women, a sex difference that is not demonstrable and one, in any event, that they are not willing to accept. It assumes, further, that women have to promise to be good before they are granted what is truly their due, rather than having it as a matter of justice. Further, no one can be better than the system. If women are in positions of power they have to act according to the logic of the system; anyone who occupies a strategic position has to act according to the rules of the game, regardless of sex.[36]

Still, on the basis of what we think we know about women, Gloria Steinem—under protest—did make a projection of this nature. She noted that women did not want simply to imitate men and do what men have been doing; what they did want to do was "change the economic system to one more based on merit." They would guarantee free access to jobs. They would not eliminate violence, for they were "not more moral than men . . . only uncorrupted by power so far." Given power, they might turn out to be as aggressive as men. "But for the next 50 years or so," she concluded, "women in politics will be very valuable by tempering the idea of manhood into something less aggressive and better suited to this crowded, post-atomic planet" (1972:184–188).

Of the other two views of the future, one is pro and one is anti-technology and, strange as it may seem, the future of both orientations—including the counterculture—lie in the direction of reduced machismo. Stranger still, the impact of the protechnology and hence expectably more macho-oriented viewpoint is more favorable to women than the anti-technology one.

Those of the counterculture who revolt against technology—not all of them do, of course—make a persuasive case against machismo. They

36. The Women's Lobby referred to above followed the same pattern as other lobbies; it planned to lobby in behalf of the interests of women, including child care, pension plans, Social Security and tax reform, abortion reform, welfare reform, minimum wages for domestic workers, health care for women, the Equal Rights Amendment, the Women's Educational Act, and credit reform.

proclaim a new humanism (Speck, 1972:183–185). But the damping of machismo does not automatically produce this new humanism, nor improve the position of women, as the research reports now beginning to come in show. In rejecting macho the men often reject its virtues as well as its vices; they show little of even a minimum amount of achievement drive required to keep a household or operate a commune. The new humanism sometimes shows up therefore as no more benign for women than our present culture, and in many instances it is far less so.[37]

Protechnology futurists do not see a continuation of the present world in which women have to take over male characteristics in order to succeed, but rather a new kind of society, one created by technology rather than by revolution, in which the values characterizing women up to now will be called for rather than imposed. In the industrial age the traits associated with maleness were called for; in the postindustrial or cybernetic age, the traits associated with femaleness as we know it today will be in demand. The basis of society in the cybernetic age will be an information net, the effective functioning of which calls for "an honest, cooperative society . . . [and] greater acceptance of what might be defined as female characteristics" (Theobold, 1967:15).

I would not like to put all my eggs in a cybernetic basket. Technology may have its ineluctable consequences, but, as in the case of Marx's inevitable triumph of the proletariat, a little help from women cannot be out of order. I do see a future different from the present and a future which may, indeed, be more congenial to women than our macho culture of today. Who knows? It might even be more congenial to men. For not all men cherish the cult of macho. Remember individual differences?

37. Women are relegated once more either to the status of household drudges or to that of pet or mere adjunct. In some cases they retain the traditional weaknesses—dependencies, passivity—to an almost pathological extent (Speck, 1972: Chapter 6). Among the communes I know, Twin Oaks does improve the position of women. The pioneer leader is a woman and both sexes choose their roles.

References

Astin, Helen; Suneiwick, Nancy; and Dweck, Susan. 1971. *Women, A bibliography on their education and careers*. Washington, D.C.: Human Service Press.

Bennett, Edward M., and Cohen, Larry R. 1959. Men and women: Personality patterns and contrasts. *Genetic Psychology Monographs 159:101–155*.

Bernard, Jessie. 1945. Observation and generalization in cultural anthropology. *American Journal of Sociology* 50 (July):284–291.

———. 1971. *Women and the public interest, An essay on policy and protest*. Chicago: Aldine.

———. 1972a. *The future of marriage*. New York: World; New York: Bantam, 1973.

―――― . 1972b. *The sex game, Communication between the sexes.* New York: Atheneum.

―――― . 1973. *Academic women.* New York: Meridian.

Bird, Caroline. 1972. From each according to her ability. *The School Review* 80 (February):184.

Bloom, Karen L. 1972. AAUW members and the future: A Survey, November, 1972. Unpublished report.

Carlson, Rae. 1971. Sex differences in ego functioning: Exploratory studies of agency and communion. *Journal of Consulting and Clinical Psychology* 137:267-277.

―――― . 1972. Understanding women: Implications for personality theory and research. *Journal of Social Issues* 28:17-32.

Goldberg, Philip. 1968. Are women prejudiced against women? *trans-action* 15:28-30.

Gove, Walter R. 1972. The relationship between sex roles, marital status, and mental illness. *Social Forces* 51 (September): 34-44.

Hall, Edward T. 1963. *The silent language.* New York: Premier.

Hanisch, Carol. 1971. Male psychology: A myth to keep women in their place. *Woman's World.* 19 (July-Aug.):2.

Jones, Brendan. 1972. African women show enterprise in business. *New York Times,* February 7, 1972.

Kubie, Lawrence. 1953. Problems of the scientific career. *American Scientist* 41 (October): 605-606.

Kuhn, Thomas S. 1962. *The structure of scientific revolutions.* Chicago: University of Chicago Press.

Langner, T.S. 1965. Psychophysical symptoms and the status of women in two Mexican communities, in Murphy, J.M., and Leighton, A.M., ed., *Approaches to cross-cultural psychiatry.* Ithaca: Cornell University Press.

Lynn, David B. 1972. Determinants of intellectual growth in women. *The School Review* (February):24-245.

McClelland, David. 1965. Wanted: A new self-image for women, in Lifton, Robert J., ed., *The woman in America.* Boston: Beacon.

Mead, Margaret. 1933. *Sex and temperament in three primitive societies.* New York: Morrow.

Morris, Desmond. 1969. *The human zoo.* New York: Delta.

Mischel, Walter. 1966. A social-learning view of sex differences in behavior, in Maccoby, Eleanor, ed., *The development of sex differences.* Stanford: Stanford University Press.

Murchison, Carl. 1929. *Social psychology of political domination.* Worcester: Clark University Press.

Neumann, Erich. 1963. *The great mother; An analysis of the archetype.* Princeton: Princeton University Press-Bollingen.

Pastore, Nicholas. 1949. *The nature-nurture controversy.* New York: King's Crown.

Pedersen, A.E., 1972. A queen's rich new existence. *Washington Post.* November 7, 1972.

Rossi, Alice, and Calderwood, Ann, eds. 1973. *Academic women on the move.* New York: Russell Sage.

Science. 1972. Sex role learning in childhood and adolescence. September 22, 1972.

Speck, Ross V. 1972 *The new families, youth culture, and the politics of drugs.* New York: Basic Books.

Steinem, Gloria. 1972. What it would be like if women win, 1970, in Martin, Wendy, ed., *The American sisterhood.* New York: Harper & Row.

Theobold, Robert, et al. 1967. *Dialogue on women.* Indianapolis: Bobbs-Merrill.

Tiedeman, David V.; O'Hara, Robert P.; and Matthews, Esther. 1958. *Position choices and careers.* Cambridge: Harvard Graduate School of Education.

Torrey, H. Fuller. 1972. *The mind game, with doctors and psychiatrists.* New York: Emerson Hall.

Tyler, Leona E. 1968. Sex differences, in *International encyclopedia of the social sciences,* vol. 7. New York: Macmillan, Free Press.

Watson, Goodwin, 1949. Foreword to Pastore, 1949.

Weisstein, Naomi. 1970. "Kinder, Kuche, Kirche" as scientific law: Psychology constructs the female. Paper read at meetings of American Studies Association, October, 1968, and reproduced in Morgan, Robin, ed. 1970. *Sisterhood is powerful.* New York: Vintage.

Woolf, Virginia, 1929. *A Room of one's own.* New York: Harcourt Brace.

PART II

YOUNG WOMEN

EVEN IN THE AMBIENCE of zero-population growth ideology, most girls are going to want to have babies, at least for the foreseeable future.[1] In the past practically all have wanted to. With this central and built-in goal in mind from infancy on, it has been almost impossible for girls and young women to invest themselves seriously in the pursuit of any other goal. A biological deadline stared them in the face. Or at least they felt it did. Part II deals with these young women.

The first paper describes a paradox well known at least since Mary Wollstonecraft pointed it out at the end of the eighteenth century, the paradox of preparing women for the most demanding of all roles, that of mother, by fostering weakness in them rather than strength. Perhaps this paper should have been written in the past tense, for the situation it describes is on its way out. Still, for a considerable period of time the effects of the paradox it refers to will shadow marriage and motherhood.

The second paper pursues the topic of the special nature of adolescence today and the implications for both women and the social order of the attrition of virginity as a first line of defense against irresponsible motherhood. It introduces the concepts of "tipping points" and "turning points" to help get a perspective on the direction of current trends.

A large part of my own writings over a long professional lifetime has been devoted to intrasex differences, especially among women. It is one of the most serious casualties of our research biases that our concern with

1. A random national sample of youth in 1972 reported that 89 percent expected to have children (Roundup of current research, *Society* 11 (March–April, 1974), p. 10.

31

intersex differences has all but overshadowed our interest in intrasex differences. We ought to know a great deal more about these intrasex differences, and we will when we stop thinking that the only controls to impose on our studies of women are male samples, in which women almost uniformly come through as inferior men.

An intrasex difference we do know something about is one that has to do with a variable subsumed under the rubrics "pioneer" versus "home-maker," "career-oriented" versus home-oriented, and the like. Practically all studies show the presence of this difference. The third paper in Part II highlights it among young women just entering college. I found the "Pioneer" an especially intriguing type of young woman. Pioneers show a minimum fear of success. They are involved. They participate. They want everything. Dionysian as contrasted with the more moderate Apollonian traditionalists, they seem to have high "social metabolism." Unlike the traditionalists who are high on the people-related values but low on the others as compared to pioneers, the pioneers are high on the characteristically male values having to do with power, influence, and success, but also on the people-related values. They seem to be true "androgynes," more male than men on the male values, more female than other women on the female values.

The young women discussed in Part II will have a great deal to do with the future. I have confidence in them.

TWO

A Developmental Paradox

To be a good mother, a woman must have sense, and that independence of mind which few women possess who are taught to depend entirely on their husbands. Meek wives are, in general, foolish mothers. Unless the understanding of women be enlarged, and her character rendered more firm, by being allowed to govern her own conduct, she will never have sufficient sense or command of temper to govern her children properly. —Mary Wollstonecraft, *Vindication of the Rights of Women.*

Female Identity via Males

Today, as in 1792 when Mary Wollstonecraft wrote the above passage, the model for the role of mother calls for strength and courage, among other virtues. Still, strange as it may seem, although we have expected practically all girls to become mothers, we have not emphasized these qualities in them. Quite the reverse, we have rewarded them for being "feminine" which has, upon examination, turned out to mean dependent, helpless, and weak. The reason for our emphasis has been paradoxical but not perverse, for in order to become a mother in our society a girl has first had to get a man. And that, in turn, has meant learning how to be attractive to men.

33

When Erik Erikson turned his attention to the development of women he saw their achievement of identity in terms of their relations to men. He told us that "much of a young woman's identity is already defined in her kind of attractiveness and in the selective nature of her search for the man (or men) by whom she wishes to be sought" (1968:283). As a matter of fact, no matter what a girl's goals may have been—marriage, job, career, or whatever—her path has been determined by her success in pleasing men. Pleasing men has, therefore, been the major preoccupation of the first several decades of her life.

There is nothing inherently dysfunctional in this situation, except that at least in our society until today, attractiveness and pleasing men and "femininity" have gone together. "The competition for men was stiff, so that these young women felt keenly the importance of looking feminine and attractive" (Coup, Greene, and Gardner, 1973:131). The "attractive" part is fairly simple to achieve: "they have both the wherewithal and the motivation to follow fashion trends and to experiment with various forms of 'self-improvements,' visually speaking" (Ibid.). But the "feminine" part is something more deep-seated. A large component, indeed the characterizing component, of feminine attractiveness has consisted of dependency. Dependency is therefore the touchstone in understanding the development of girls and women—at least until now.

Dependency the Touchstone

Erikson, in fact, saw all female development in terms of dependency. He told us that the identity of women is achieved when they commit themselves to the future father of their children. "The stage of life crucial for the emergence of an integrated female identity is the step from youth to maturity, the stage when the young woman, whatever her work career, relinquishes the care received from the parental family in order to commit herself to the love of a stranger and to the care to be given to his and her offspring" (Erikson, 1968:265). Thereafter she will identify herself primarily if not exclusively as Mrs. John Smith. Mary Jones will have disappeared. She may reemerge as Mary Jones Smith, but all this tells us is that she used to be dependent on Mr. Jones and now she is dependent on Mr. Smith. Her identification may have changed but in either case she remains dependent.

It is interesting to note in passing that Erikson does insert a brief interlude of delay of adult functioning. During this "psychological moratorium" the young woman is permitted to become "masculine" and invade the "outer space of the male world." She may throw off the restraints of her "inner space" and explore the wide world as young men may. But this free time is, in fact, not completely unfettered. For it is at this time that she picks the man she wants to bear children for. But it is interesting also to note how differently women see their own development. Sheila Tobias, for example, sees women enjoying no such free-wheeling moratorium but rather sees them deprived of it. And some women see these years not as a moratorium but as an almost frantic time devoted not to intellectual exploration but to seeking commitments from men. And among counselors, this period of youth in women is viewed as a moratorium not in their preparation for motherhood but in their worker roles, a time when women become so obsessed with marriage and motherhood that they find it almost impossible to look beyond.

In any event, the role script according to which we have thought we were rearing girls and boys went something like this. Little girls are going to grow up to be wives and mothers. They should be sweet, gentle, submissive, even subservient, and look up to males. In return men should protect and take care of them. With such a combination of traits families would be harmonious and free from conflict.

The illogicality of this script—training girls in dependency for a role demanding strength—seems to have escaped us. As an ideal it may never have fit any but the upper-middle-class Victorian family, if even that, but somehow or other it has persisted. Only recently has it come to be challenged.

The Nature of Dependency

Not all researchers conceive of dependency in the same way. Some see it as a structural, others as a subjective, fact. Sociologists see human inter-dependence as the basic fact of life. It is the kind of dependency John Donne reminded us of in the seventeeth century and Ernest Hemingway in the twentieth when they told us that no man was an island unto himself and that therefore we were not to ask for whom the bell tolled. It tolled for all of us whenever it tolled for any one of us. Economists see interdependence as a basic fact in the market, where the division of labor makes everyone dependent on others for goods and services to exchange for his own. But the psychologists who have used the term have had something else in mind.

It is not always clear what psychologists refer to by the term *dependency*, and some think the term should be abandoned. But whatever it is, dependency manifests itself in the need for protection, help, love, approval. Laboratory researchers examine such behavior in nursery-school children, including clinging to the mother, asking for help, seeking physical contact, creating disturbances when separated from the mother, staying near the teacher, and approval-seeking from adults and peers (Maccoby, 1966:326–327). Kenneth Keniston, speaking of dependency in connection with young women, has in mind "need to be nurtured, . . . desire to be protected, admired and cared for, . . . petted, pampered" (Keniston, 1971). And Milton Sapirstein, writing about dependency in marriage, has in mind the security that permits one to be helpless on occasion, knowing that one will be protected (1948:170). To distinguish the structural sociological and the economic conceptions from this psychological or subjective conception, the term used here for the first is "dependence," and for the second, "dependency."

The development of girls to date may be delineated in terms of first "achieving" dependency and then—in the case of at least some of them—of overcoming it. In the earliest years, dependency is parent-sponsored, later it is peer-sponsored, and finally it is self-sustained.

The Same Scratch

On the basis of the criteria used by researchers, boys and girls start life from about the same scratch where dependency is concerned. Differences between them are minimal, even nonexistent in the earliest years.[1] Infants and small children *are* dependent, little boys as well as little girls. Both must depend on mothers and teachers. In the case of boys, however, dependency must be outgrown; that is one of their first developmental tasks. But the "psychological work" in the first stages of female development is not to overcome dependency but to retain, even exaggerate, it. Thus, although "no strong sex differences in dependency are observed at early ages–at older ages (high school and college) girls are consistently higher on dependency measures" (Mischel, 1966:74).

The Achievement of Dependency

As in the case of boys, the normal thing would be for girls to slough off infantile and childish dependencies, to surge forward to more and more autonomy. But they are not permitted this course. Dependency must be

1. In this respect dependency is quite different from—offensive—aggressiveness, with which it is often contrasted. The research evidence is quite convincing that more human males than females at all ages from nursery school through college tend to be aggressive. In all but 9 out of 57 studies reported, more males than females showed this trait. In the four studies in which more of the girls than of the boys were aggressive, it took the form of verbal aggression in one, of covert aggression in another, and of pro- rather than of anti-social aggression in a third. And when little girls did show aggression, they showed more feelings of guilt about it (Maccoby, 1966:326). On the basis of other data, it is the form rather than the frequency of aggressiveness that differentiates the sexes, being more defensive in the case of females, offensive in the case of males. Defensiveness appears especially with respect to protection of the young.

bred into them, not only not discouraged but actively encouraged. The process by which it is built into them has been charted by the psychologists. Thus, although in infancy and in the early years of childhood a variety of dependent behaviors may be sanctioned for both sexes, later on "dependency in boys becomes increasingly unacceptable" whereas in girls it is condoned and positively rewarded (Mischel, 1966:77). "The greater incidence of dependent behavior for girls . . . seems directly explicable in social-learning terms. . . . For girls the dependent behavior may lead to an acceptable and even prized outcome. . . . Dependency seems to be . . . even desired. . . . In our culture girls receive more reward for dependency than boys" (Ibid.:74–78). Dependency is thus reinforced in girls and punished out of boys.

An analysis of 134 books used in elementary schools documents the process by which girls are processed for dependency and pseudo-dependency. "Little girls endlessly play with dolls, cry over dolls, give tea parties, look on helplessly or passively or admiringly while boys take action. . . . When one girl merely reports a forest fire—what anyone breathing might be expected to do under similar circumstances—the author is so overcome that he pours praise on her as if she had put out the blaze single-handedly at the risk of her life. Girls often depend on boys when they are quite capable of handling the situation themselves. One finds she can only skate when she has Mark to lean on; another can only reach a jar if a boy brings a stepladder. . . . Girls, small and large, are helped out of one difficulty after another by their brothers, older or younger (New Jersey NOW; 1972:17).

The process may not be easy but it is eminently successful. As a result of this relentless conditioning, the desired result is achieved. The kinds of behavior that have been uniformly reinforced over a long period of time now show up in sex differences. By the age of 8 all the studies show more females than males who are dependent (Maccoby, 1966:95). Mission accomplished.

At puberty new constraints on young women are added. For now her virginity has to be protected. Margaret Mead has called our attention to the discontinuity involved in the development of women resulting from the responsibility we place on them—or at least used to—for enforcing the mores with respect to premarital virginity and the sexual responsiveness called for after marriage. The impact of this preoccupation with virginity and the consequences for female character have been enormous. We inculcate distrust; males want one thing, her body. She must be wary. At least in this fundamental area of moral judgement we do not permit, let alone encourage, development beyond conventional conformity. Everything she does has to be monitored. Independence and autonomy are too dangerous to be permitted.

The Rewards of Dependency

The process of thus "gentling" females has been compared to the erstwhile binding and crippling of Chinese women's feet. The rewards for women must be fairly considerable for the process to succeed. They are. In high school the boys will like them; they may even become popular. They can feel protected and cherished. They can enjoy their helplessness. And the more dependent they appear to be, the more adorable they will seem to the boys. The girl who must turn to a boy to help her with the punch bowl will enchant him; she will make him feel big and strong and masculine.

Girls who do not want to conform to this pattern have to struggle "against many of their own feelings . . . their deeper need to be nurtured, their dependency, their desires to be protected, admired and cared for. Consciously or unconsciously, they . . . have to deny themselves full enjoyment of many of the real gratifications available to other girls in high school—the gratifications of being petted, pampered, admired, and taken care of" (Keniston, 1971). Other rewards take the form of "a dispensation from the terms of adulthood" and an "unworked-for feeling of importance" (McLaughlin, 1972:624).

The rewards for dependency may be so considerable and the punishment for its absence so severe that the girl may never wish to forego it. It becomes self-sustaining, or it may become so thoroughly entrenched in her character that even if she wished to overcome it, she could not. She is fixed forever in a mold of dependency.

> If we examine the rather meager literature on the development of women in late adolescence and early adulthood, there is considerable evidence that women today find it more difficult to move toward individuation than do men. Research on student activists, on the development of autonomy in women, and on the development of high levels of moral reasoning all concur in finding highly developed women more psychologically conflicted and fewer in number than highly developed men. The difference between the sexes is of course relative, for all men and women find the path toward individuation difficult and only a few come close to achieving it. But . . . it seems that for most women to move toward individuation in American society requires them to come into many direct conflicts with their social environment. For men, in contrast, social expectations generally assist rather than obstruct this movement, at least up to a point. (Keniston, 1971)

Some Costs of Dependency

As long as it can be made to last, it is, indeed, delightful to have the boys falling all over themselves to serve you. It is delicious to be pampered, petted, made much of—ask any of the middle-aged "girls" who affirm how much they like to be girls. They want nothing done that might deprive them of their soft nest and the protection of men.

There are costs, however. By indulging, even using, their dependency and their helplessness, girls may well attract boys. But at the same time they are buying future trouble, in marriage, in motherhood, and beyond. According to Sapirstein, for example, dependency leads to the seeking of an omnipotent parental figure, denial of their own capacities, submissiveness, hostility, incapacity to express guilt adequately, hypochondriasis, neurotic depression, and, once more, anxiety (Saperstein, 1948:84).

Equally serious is the fact that dependency, a "dispensation from the terms of adulthood," becomes counterproductive when the girl becomes a woman. The helplessness that is so cute in the girl becomes ridiculous in the woman. The inability of the bride to balance a checkbook may be adorable, her tears appealing. But at some point her dependency becomes an incubus rather than a charm, a bore, not to say a nuisance—not to say a real drag on a relationship. For there is a hidden joker in the way we socialize boys and girls.

Marital Costs of Female Dependency

A major discontinuity in a woman's development occurs at marriage. The dependency that was so well rewarded before marriage is rewarded no longer. She must now cater to the dependencies of the stranger to whom she has committed herself. For men as well as women have dependency needs, however well they may be papered over. Wives are called upon to satisfy the dependencies of husbands as well as the other way around and, in fact, sometimes instead of the other way around. Dependency is not solely a female prerogative. There are times when everyone, male as well as female, wants to be petted, pampered, taken care of, allowed to be helpless. These needs are part of the common human condition. And it is one of the "primary functions of an effective marriage" to fulfill them for both partners.[2]

> The intimacy of the marital relationship should create a haven of emotional security where both partners can relax completely, and if necessary, be helpless on occasion without feeling threatened or losing self-esteem. . . . Neither partner should be required to play full-time superman, and neither partner should be helpless to the extent of denying the other's dependent needs. . . . They should both be capable of being effective adults most of the time; have a marginal leeway for feeling inadequate some of the time; be able temporarily to play a protective parental role (Sapirstein, 1948:170).

2. Men may also pay excessively for their dependencies (Sapirstein, 1948:159–160). Too generously indulged in they are destructive in both sexes.

While ostensibly women are more dependent than men, actually the reverse may be the case. The greater importance of marriage for men (Bernard, 1972: Chapter 2) than for women suggests that it may be.

But are we really talking about the same phenomena when we speak of dependency in the case of men and women? A number of observers have noted that any act performed by a man looks different from the same act performed by a woman (Bernard, 1966:255–257). And so when men show dependency it is one thing; when women do, another. The wife who takes her husband in her arms after a rough day at the office is "mothering" him and this is in no sense denigrating to him. In fact, satisfying the dependency needs of others, especially of males, is one of the major functions assigned to women in most societies (Bernard, 1971: Chapter 5). The interpretation and styles of catering to dependency vary; when men do it, they are condescending; when women do it, they are appeasing.

The wife, reared to expect her dependency to be rewarded, finds herself in a position where she must supply the dependency needs of her husband but, often enough, finds her own needs unmet. If she asks her husband to cuddle her after a rough day with the children, she is made to feel that she is making unwarranted demands on him. What, after all, has she been *doing* all day long that should entitle her to such indulgence? Blood and Wolfe, for example, speaking of what they called the "mental hygiene" aspect of marriage, found that only 8 percent of their sample of city wives and only 3 percent of their sample of farm wives had husbands who performed this mental hygiene function of marriage for them. "Clearly," they concluded, "most housewives cope with bad days on their own. . . . The husband's own problems, preoccupations, or known incapacity to help . . . discourage the wife from turning to him. . . . Their [the wives'] most characteristic device is to go to bed early, to sit down and relax, or just to forget about their troubles. Reading and TV are common distractions at home, going for a walk the favorite way of getting out of the house" (Blood and Wolfe, 1960:185–186). Whatever may be the ideal for marriage, the run-of-the-mine marriage does not seem to provide well for the dependencies of wives. They have been kept childlike and then sent to do an adult's job. No wonder they find this period of their lives "relatively trying." The "relationships with husband can be more or less demanding or tender than they can feel comfortable with" (Coup, Greene, and Gardner, 1973:132)—probably more demanding and less tender.

Economic Costs: Dependence and Psychological Dependency

There are, no doubt, some women who are in the satisfying position of having their dependency needs fulfilled to their complete satisfaction. But some women may continue to exploit their adorable helplessness all their life. They come appealingly to ask a man to please help them with this little mechanical chore that he finds easy; they can be amusing and even adorable in the process. The helpless woman who flags down a passing motorist can be charmingly flattering to his ego when she cannot get her car started and he unerringly finds out what she has done wrong. These and a thousand little ways in which female helplessness may manifest itself can have a delightful flavor for both the woman and her gallant rescuer. She feels grateful and he feels superior. Some women remain "cute" forever.

But many women would like to achieve autonomy. It is not possible for them. For quite above and beyond the kind of dependency that everyone of any age or sex experiences, their situation is complicated by economic dependence. Women who have been reared for a position which, according to the old script, would be provided for, do not take preparation for economic independence seriously. It will be a subordinate option. All her thinking about herself will rest on the assumption that she will be "provided for."[3]

In a time when most of the productive work a woman did was going to be done in the home, easily combined with motherhood, there was no conflict between economic dependence and psychological dependency.[4] Although that situation applies for fewer and fewer women, it still shapes the mentality of enough women to make them vastly underplay their own skills and talents. Only in times when a large part of a woman's productive work is done in the outside world does psychological dependency become a crippling handicap. It disqualifies her for top positions (Bernard, 1971:94), and may even prevent economic independence at all, thus foreclosing a wide variety of options.

Role Costs: Motherhood

There are, finally, costs of dependency in what Erikson called the core of female identity, a "biological, psychological, and ethical commitment to take care of human infancy" (Erikson, 1968:266). Motherhood brings its

3. In the 134 school readers referred to above there were only three working mothers.

4. There is really no inevitable or intrinsic incompatibility between economic dependence and psychological dependency. Many have been struck, for example, by marriages in which the attraction the wives felt for their husbands was hard for outsiders to understand. One competent woman who was supporting her husband—quite inferior to her so far as the usual criteria could be applied—remained with him because, though he did not support her, he satisfied her dependency needs. He petted her, babied her, cherished her, made her *feel* protected, cared for. And this is a desideratum many women are willing to pay a good deal for and which they are reluctant to give up. It is fear that change may deprive them of it which leads many women to reject "liberation." The dependency of the prostitute on her pimp, whom she supports, is another example of the lack of any intrinsic relationship between economic dependence and psychological dependency.

own demands. Mothers have to be strong. Nurturance, not succorance, is required. The mother is assigned enormous responsibilities that demand qualities quite the opposite to those considered so attractive when she was a girl. She must reorganize her whole personality. Her husband, if he is humane and sympathetic, may offer some help, but he is not likely to relieve her of the reponsibilities. The role of mother as institutionalized in our society cannot be adequately performed by dependent, passive women. As a result, it exacts enormous emotional costs.

References

Bernard, Jessie. 1974. *Academic women.* New York: Meridian.
———— . 1971. *Women and the public interest, An essay on policy and protest.* Chicago: Aldine.
———— . 1972. *The future of marriage.* New York: World. Bantam, 1973.
Blood, Robert O., and Wolfe, Donald M. 1960. *Husbands and wives: The dynamics of married living.* New York: Free Press.
Coup, Roger F.; Greene, Shirley; and Gardner, Burleigh B. 1973. *A study of working-class women in a changing world.* Chicago: Social Research.
Erikson, Eric. 1968. *Identity, youth and crisis.* New York: Norton.
Keniston, 1971. Themes and conflicts in "liberated" young women. Karen Horney memorial lecture, March, 1971.
Maccoby, Eleanor E., ed. 1966. *The development of sex differences.* Stanford: Stanford University Press.
McLaughlin, Patricia. 1972. Comment on *Women on women. American Scholar* (Autumn):624.
Mischel, Walter. 1966. A social-learning view of sex differences in behavior, in Maccoby, 1966.
New Jersey NOW Task Force. 1972.*Dick and Jane as victims.*Princeton: Published by the authors.
Sapirsteiñ, Milton R. 1948. *Emotional security.* New York: Crown.

THREE

Sex-Role Transcendence and
Sex-Role Transcenders

1. Androgyny and Sex-Role Transcendence

A stable or slowly changing, non crisis-prone society can afford to socialize and train children for a future not too different from its present. And, assuming that a stable society has had a chance to achieve a suitable division of labor and functional specialization not too intolerable for its members—itself an index of stability—there is a kind of logic in preparing for the future by replicating the present. Roles will remain much the same.

But in a dynamic, crisis-prone society like our own in which, as Jean Lipman-Blumen (1973) has shown, roles become de-differentiated and reconfigured such justification no longer exists for, as Robert Hefner and Virginia Davis Nordin (1974) point out, "it is all but impossible to educate individuals for future life roles in a rapidly changing technological society" in which role de-differentiation and reconfiguration are endemic. Young people have to be prepared "to choose adaptive strategies rather than . . . forced into rigidly assigned appropriate behaviors" (Ibid.). Millions of women—as well as men—today are paying the price for an early socialization that, by limiting their options, makes it impossible for them to adapt to the role reconfigurations, now in process.

There is as a result, widespread dissatisfaction, even malaise, especially about the way sex-role socialization takes place today. But there is not as yet a general consensus on what changes we should aim at. Just what do we want in the way of sex-role socialization? Do we simply want a new

43

polarity? Do we want a sex-role reversal that would be equally polarized, as some hostile critics charge? Do we want to turn little girls into little boys, or little boys into little girls? Do we want unisex, monosex, or what?

Questions of this nature are calling for a reexamination of the concept of androgyny and eliciting new concepts, such as "sex-role transcendence." This paper addresses itself to a consideration of these concepts.

TWO CONCEPTUALIZATIONS OF ANDROGYNY

Androgyny may be viewed from two perspectives, according to the nature of the unit—dyad or individual—involved. The dyadic conceptualization appeared in Plato's *Symposium,* in which he recounts how an original being was severed into halves, one male, one female. Incomplete, each has ever since had to go about seeking the other half in order to complete the dyad once more.[1] It is the dyad that is androgynous, not the parts. The other conceptualization sees not the dyad but the individual as the androgynous entity. The androgynous individual is not a truncated semicomplete being, part of another whole but a whole being in herself or himself. The difference in conceptualization is important.

If we accept the view of the *Symposium* we validate a concept of the sexes as polar opposites.[2] If one is rational, the other is intuitive; if one is aggressive, the other is passive. Each is incomplete, dependent on the other for fulfillment as part of a whole. Neither can function without the other. Each is truncated without the other. The moral is clear-cut; we are all incomplete because we have only one set of virtues; in order to be complete we must join with the other sex that has the complementary traits.

The dyadic conception of androgyny is a good approximation to the actual sex-role specialization that prevailed in preindustrial societies. In such societies there is a division of labor that corresponds to the Platonic concept; our own frontier West is an example. On a farm, neither sex can operate independently. The homesteader needed a wife as a partner, and mother of his children. There was "women's work" in the garden, in the barnyard, in the household that she could do even when pregnant, nursing, or tending the children. Her work was as essential as her husband's. There was genuine interdependence. A great many of the differences we instilled into the sexes reflected that difference in work roles. The enterprise for which they were prepared was androgynous.

The division of labor that came with industrialization and urbanization in the early years of capitalism called for a harsh, competitive, almost dog-

1. Carolyn Heilbrun notes that there were three original circular beings, one all-male, one all-female, and one both male and female, which were severed. Thus "each person seeking his [or her] original half might be in search with equal likelihood for someone of the same or of the other sex" (1973:iii). She reminds us that some of the restored units would be homosexual and some lesbian.

2. See "Research on Sex Differences: The State of the Art," in this book.

eat-dog mentality in men. Drives for power and dominance were important for survival. It called also for a supportive personality in women. "Masculine" came to mean, as Carolyn Heilbrun reminds us, "forceful, competent, competitive, controlling, vigorous, unsentimental, and occasionally violent"; "feminine" came to mean "tender, genteel, intuitive rather than passive, unaggressive, readily given to submission" (Heilbrun, 1973:xiv).[3] Two quite different mentalities were created in individuals of the two sexes; the houshold, however, was androgynous.

The emerging world today renders the old polarized distribution of traits by sex anachronistic, even destructive: "by developing in men the ideal 'masculine' characteristics of competitiveness, aggressiveness, and defensiveness, and by placing in power those men who most embody these traits, we have, I believe, gravely endangered our own survival. . . . So long as we continue to believe the 'feminine' qualities of gentleness, lovingness, and the counting of cost in human rather than national or property terms are out of place among rulers, we can look forward to continued self-brutalization and perhaps even to self-destruction" (Ibid.). These are a woman's words; here are a man's: "Western mankind [sic] must arrive at a synthesis that includes the feminine world—which is also one-sided in its isolation. Only then will the individual human being be able to develop the psychic wholeness from within and without" (Neumann, 1963:xliii). In brief, changes in our total society no longer call for the sex specialization of the past. It calls for whole individuals.

Still the long shadow of the past hangs over us. An inappropriate—and exaggerated—sex-role specialization still prevails. In another place I have documented the dysfunctional consequences that ensue when we carry sex-role specialization, based on a dyadic conceptualization of androgyny, to the extremes we do in our society today.[4] It is good for neither fathers nor mothers, for neither children nor parents, for neither marriage nor parenthood.

Yet we cling to it and shape boys and girls to conform to it. We still socialize differing psychological traits in the two sexes to correspond to the differing roles assigned to them. Rather than the division of labor and specialization of function resulting from sex differences, many sex differences result from the division of labor and the specialization of

3. It may be noted that the concept of the mutual complementariness of the sexes has been extended beyond the dyad to whole societies and cultures. Here, ideally, the "male principle" and the "female principle" should also be in balance. But what has happened has been a take-over by the "male principle," much to the detriment of the total society. Thus Erich Neumann, a Jungian scholar, tells us that "the peril of present-day mankind springs in large part from the one-sidedly patriarchal development of the male intellectual consciousness, which is no longer kept in balance by the matriarchal world of the psyche. In this sense the exposition of the archetypal-psychical world of the Feminine . . . is . . . a contribution to a future therapy of culture" (1963:xlii). And Carolyn Heilbrun agrees that "what is important now is that . . . before it is too late, we deliver the world from the almost exclusive control of the masculine impulse"(1973:XIV).

4. See "The Bitter Fruits of Extreme Sex-Role Specialization" in this book.

function we socialize individuals for. As a result we get truncated individuals.

But a modern society calls for whole individuals, for individuals in which the virtues of both sexes are cultivated, the weaknesses of both muted. The goal comes to be seen not as specializing the virtues and the weaknesses in one sex or the other, but as aiming for well-rounded, complete individuals capable of flexibility and adaptability to change. Heilbrun speaks of "a condition under which the characteristics of the sexes, and the human impulses expressed by men and women are not rigidly assigned" (Heilbrun, 1973:x). She calls this condition androgyny. It "seeks to liberate the individual from the confines of the appropriate" (Ibid). It is a movement "away from sexual polarization and the prison of gender" (Ibid.:ix). It presages a world "in which individual roles and the modes of personal behavior can be freely chosen" (Ibid.:x).[5]

THE CONCEPT OF SEX-ROLE TRANSCENDENCE

Hefner and Nordin at the University of Michigan are engaged in research on what they call *sex-role transcendence*. They use this term rather than *androgyny* because, as commonly thought of, the dyadic conceptualization rather than the individual conceptualization of androgyny tends to prevail. "The popular use [of the term 'androgyny'] puts too much emphasis on polarity *combined* instead of polarity *transcended*" (Hefner and Nordin, 1974:49). They define sex-role transcendence as:individual behavioral and emotional choice that is based on the full range of possible human characteristics. This choice is appropriate and adaptive for the particular individual in the specific situation and is not determined by adherence to sex-role stereotyped conceptions of appropriateness. (Ibid.). It is the third of three stages they posit in sex-role development: (1) a stage in which there is an undifferentiated conception of sex roles; (2) a stage in which there is an overdifferentiated, polarized conception of sex roles; and (3) a stage—as yet in the future—in which there is a flexible, dynamic approach to human roles that transcends sex-role constraints. The model "is patterned after the stage-models of developmental psychology," such as Erik Erikson's of personality and Lawrence Kohlberg's of moral development (Ibid.:41).

Stage 1. Gender-Identity Development. The child's conception of sex-role differentiation cannot occur until the child has learned that there are two sexes and acquired an identification with one of them. Although both *gender* and *identity* are controversial terms (Stoller, 1968:x), they are useful in the present context, the first referring to "behavior, feelings, thoughts,

---

5. Heilbrun distinguishes androgyny from homosexuality and bisexuality. It should be distinguished from the dictionary definition of hermaphroditism.

and fantasies that are related to the sexes and yet do not have primarily biological connotations" (Ibid.:ix), and the second, to a sense of self.

> Those aspects of sexuality that are called *gender* are primarily culturally determined; that is, learned postnatally. This learning process starts at birth, though only with gradually increasing ego development are its effects made manifest in the infant. This cultural process springs from one's society, but a sense of this is funneled through the mother, so that what actually impinges upon her infant is her own idiosyncratic version of society's attitudes. (Ibid.:xiii). Gender *identity* starts with the knowledge and awareness, whether conscious or unconscious, that one belongs to one sex and not the other, though as one develops, gender identity becomes much more complicated, so that, for example, one may sense himself as not only a male but a masculine man or an effeminate man or even a man who fantasies being a woman. (Ibid.:10)

Stage I of the Hefner-Nordin model corresponds to the first stage of gender-identity development;[6] the child's conception of sex-role differentiation cannot occur until gender identity has been achieved. The child has to identify herself with the female sex before she can begin to distinguish which roles are appropriate for her. It doesn't take very long.

Parents, of course, know the sex of the child from the instant of birth and they lose not a moment in conveying this information to the infant. They fondle boys and girls differently in infancy and are at great pains to deal with them in culturally gender-suitable ways. There is probably no aspect of child rearing that is more insisted upon than the inculcating of the culturally-approved gender identity. And most infants are pliable enough to accept it.

> The process proceeds subtly and without stirring much conscious awareness . . . so long as there is acquiescence to the parents' wishes. However, if the child deviates from the norm in his behavior, the parents' anxiety may be stirred. This, converted into anger, embarrassment, tense coercion, or the like, signals the child that to proceed further with that particular bit of behavior will threaten him with loss of parental esteem. Thus, this gyroscope, the parents' attitudes toward their child's gender identity, guides the child's development. (Stoller, 1968:231–232)

Having, then, been dealt with as a girl, the child develops appropriate feminine feelings, thoughts, and behaviors so that by the time she is two-and-a-half years old—some students say 18 months (Ibid.:232–233) —she is fixed in her responses, and even if the world treats her as a male, her identity

6. Hefner and Nordin summarize five models of sex-role development (psychoanalytic, cognitive-developmental, social-learning, biogenetic, and sociological), as well as empirical studies (1974:7–14).

remains that of a female. Beyond the age of three it is almost impossible to change gender identity. With gender identity firmly fixed, sex-role differentiation can proceed.

Stage II. Coalescence of Gender Identity and Sex-Role Differentiation. Freud made the child's discovery of the penis or lack of it, somewhere between the ages of three and five, the critical point in gender development. Whether or not this is so, some time during this period qualitative human differences come to be telescoped into dichotomies so that children learn to see the world, including sex roles, in polarized terms. By the time children enter school, they already "stereotype occupations by sex. By fifth grade, when asked to describe a typical day in their adult lives, even those girls who dream widely about occupational choice describe themselves running a household, whereas boys talk about their occupational roles" (Schlossberg, 1974). Since mothers are the only females most girl-children know well, once they have recognized that both they and their mothers are of the same sex, the first, and probably most powerful, sex-role model they take over is that of mother.

In this stage of sex-role learning the child not only accepts conventional sex roles but even, according to the Hefner-Nordin model, overdoes the acceptance as a means of obtaining security. Individuals now "view the fit to the stereotypes as necessary and as a major step in gaining entrance into adult society. Strict adherence to the feminine or masculine role is highly regarded and required throughout their whole life span of all members of our present Stage II society" (Hefner and Nordin, 1974). Indeed, our society has tended to see this as the terminal stage in sex-role development.

Stage III. Sex-Role Transcendence. So far we do not know much about Stage III, except that it is not a return to Stage I. Nor do we know much about how it is reached by individuals. Hefner and Nordin do not believe it is a gradual movement, as from Stage I to Stage II.[7] Rather, they suggest that it is "the resolution of a crisis which produces both a lack of fit with Stage II conceptions and the awareness of Stage III that leaves behind the defensive need to cling to the pole to which one has been assigned" (Hefner and Nordin, 1974:47). Although a long period of preparation may lie behind this transition, it is a "quantum leap" when it happens. In the women's movement, the short hand term "click" has been used to describe the sudden insight that produces such a quantum leap (O'Reilly, 1972).

7. Actually, we do not know much about the transition from Stage I to Stage II. There may be, as Hefner and Nordin suggest, several substages in Stage II. Although gender identity may be fixed very early, learning what gender means takes longer. Only gradually do gender identity and sex roles coalesce. In our society, one step in this coalescence may occur around the age of 8, when aggression becomes less common among girls than among boys, and accelerate during adolescence, when girls' academic achievement recedes, and reach a peak in the late teens, when "romance" becomes a major preoccupation and gender identity is probably at its zenith.

Some developmental paradigms make allowance for regression; some make allowance for roadblocks that halt further growth; some imply a one-way path; some imply that skipping of stages is not possible, that we have to cover the ground, master the "developmental tasks" at every level along the way before further progress is possible. In the present context a number of questions arise. Do young men and women *have* to go through Stage II—a period of maximized sex-role differentiation—before they can transcend it? Hefner and Nordin do not think so. They believe that "there may be different tracks leading to a transcendent view of sex roles. . . . It may not be necessary for an individual to pass through a stage in which she firmly (or at all) accepted the stereotypes. The fact that children appear to do this over-differentiating may be the result of the milieu only and not a step *required* for transcendence" (Hefner and Nordin, 1974:51).

Although answers to the many questions involved in Stage III—or, for that matter, Stage II—will have to await the completion of the Hefner-Nordin research, we can, in the meanwhile, catch a glimpse of the kinds of young women who even under present-day conditions do achieve at least partial role-transcendence. The data on these young women presented here are drawn from the fifth in a series of annual American Council on Education surveys of entering college and university freshmen.[8]

II. Sex-Role Transcenders

PIONEERS AND TRADITIONALISTS

Two samples of women were selected from the total population of entering women students.[9] One, the Pioneers or Stage III women, consisted of all those who gave evidence of role-transcendence on the basis of five criteria, that is, they did not conform to the stereotyped pattern of feminine behavior on five survey items. They (1) had argued with a teacher, (2) wanted administrative responsibility, (3) wanted to be an authority in their field, (4) wanted not to be obligated to anyone, *and* (5) believed large families should be discouraged. They were, in brief, aggressive, ambitious, achievement-oriented, independent, and not interested in full-time domesticity. The other sample, the Traditionalists or Stage II women, was

8. For details of sampling and the nature of the survey instrument uses, see American Council on Education, 1970:2–12. It should be made clear that the survey was not designed to elicit information on role transcendence. The data do not, therefore, lend themselves to all the analyses that would have been relevant for a study of that topic.

9. All comparisons between role-transcendent women and men are comparisons with run-of-the-mine men, not men who had answered the same way as the women on the five criterion items. If the comparison had been between men who had answered affirmatively on the five items and women who had, the differences might have been less. Engin Holstrom, of the American Council on Education, was co-author of the study of sex-role transcenders.

selected on the basis of those who gave evidence of conformity to traditional sex-stereotyped role conceptions. They (1) wanted to marry within five years, (2) wanted to raise a family, *and* (3) believed a woman's place was in the home. One of the most remarkable aspects of the Stage III women was the fact that they actually did transcend polarity in the values they viewed as very important or essential; they were more "feminine" than other women *and also* more "masculine" than were the men. The supporting data are presented below. There were, incidentally, almost 10 times as many women in the second as in the first category, more Traditionalists or Stage II than Pioneers or Stage III women.[10]

SIMILARITIES

Before noting the differences between these two samples it is well to point out the many similarities between them. As measured in terms of rank in high-school class, the two samples were homogeneous so far as *ability* is concerned (Table 3.1). There were more women than men who had been in the top quarter of their high-school classes, but among the women themselves the distributions for all women, for Traditionalists or Stage II women, and for role transcenders were very similar. Slightly more role transcenders than Traditionalists had been in the top fourth, but the difference (2.5 percentage points) was slight. (Because of the large number of cases, even small differences are "statistically significant," whether or not they are meaningful.)[11] We are not, therefore, comparing bright young women with less talented young women. We can eliminate at the outset, therefore, ability as measured by high-school rank as an explanatory factor in differences.

Table 3.1

Ability as Measured by Rank in High School (in Percentages)

	PIONEERS	TRADI-TIONALISTS	ALL ENTERING WOMEN	ALL ENTERING MEN	ALL ENTERING STUDENTS
Top quarter	49.9	47.4	48.1	37.4	42.2
Second quarter	30.1	31.4	30.6	31.9	31.3
Third quarter	17.2	18.3	18.4	25.5	22.3
Bottom quarter	2.7	2.3	2.9	5.2	4.2

10. The ACE sample consisted of 180,684 cases from a sample of 275 institutions, weighted to represent the total United States population of approximately 1.6 million first-time, full-time freshmen entering the nations' colleges and universities in 1970. Not quite half—45 percent—were women.

11. All of the women in the Pioneer or role-transcending category (6,184 cases) were included, but only a ten percent random sample of those in the Traditionalist category (7,455). National norm data are used whenever comparisons are made to all women, to all men, and to all students.

The *quality of the schools* the two samples of women attended, as measured in terms of the proportion of students who went on to college, was about the same. A third of the schools of both role transcenders and Traditionalists sent up to half of their graduates to college; two-thirds sent more than half. More role transcenders (3.1 percent) than Traditionalists (1.7 percent) went to private nonreligious schools, but the proportions involved were minuscule.

The data on *class background* were so equivocal and inconsistent that the only clear-cut conclusion one can draw is that there were no definitive differences between the two samples. Although more role transcenders than Traditionalists came from low-income families (see below), the occupations of the fathers were homogeneous. Only 19 occupational categories had more than 100 cases and only 3 of these showed differences, and even these were small. More role transcenders (2.8 percent) than Traditionalists (1.7 percent) had fathers who were unskilled workers; more Traditionalists (12.1 percent) than role transcenders (10.8 percent) had fathers who were skilled.

So much, then, for the ways in which the two samples of women resemble one another. In neither ability nor occupational class background is there evidence of superiority or inferiority in either one. On a number of other variables, however, differences do show up.

DIFFERENCES

The differences between the two samples may be categorized as differences in (1) general dynamism or "social metabolism," (2) past achievement, (3) self-confidence, (4) achievement orientation, (5) "transcended polarity," and (6) political orientation.

General Dynamism.   Before discussing substantive differences, the quality of the role transcenders' general approach to life should be recognized. Their "social metabolism" seemed to be higher than that of the Traditionalists. Thus, for example, although practically all of the freshmen were 18 years old, the usual age for entering college, slightly more role transcenders (5.6 percent) than Traditionalists (3.9 percent) were only 17 and slightly more Traditionalists (13.5 percent) than role transcenders (11.5 percent) were 19 or older. In brief, these role transcenders seemed to be running faster. With about the same ability as measured by rank in high-school class, they arrived at college somewhat earlier. In contrast to the role transcenders, the Traditionalists seemed to be less highly motivated, less active, less confident. Fewer expected to be active or to achieve at a high level in college. They seemed to be more low-keyed, subdued. Role transcenders had a more forceful style. They seemed to take stronger positions on issues, whether liberal or conservative. Thus on half of the 18 issues shown in Table 3.6, more role transcenders than Traditionalists—whether pro or con—selected agree "strongly" or disagree "strongly." Mild reactions were not their bag. The role transcenders seemed to be more Dionysian, the Traditionalists more Apollonian. It is possible, though there are no data to corroborate such a conclusion in the present study, that genuine differences in energy resources underlie these differences (Rossi, 1973: 154–155).

Past Achievement. Not unexpected but astonishing in degree is the evidence of general dynamism as shown in past activity and achievement in high school (Table 3.2). The remarkable superiority of the role transcenders in past achievement and activities shows up not only as compared to the Traditionalists but also as compared with all women, with all men, and with all entering students. With the exception of participation in sports and science contests, the role transcenders excelled in all achievements, but most especially in those involving verbal skills such as editing, publishing, dramatics, and speech contests, and in academic honors (honor societies and participation in merit scholarship contests). The Traditionalists tended to fall below all women as well as below role transcenders where most achievements and activities except sports were concerned, but they surpassed even the men in several, including those having to do with verbal skills and—most interestingly—competition, a male-typed activity, in science, a male-typed interest. The mediocre showing of the Traditionalists as compared to the role transcenders and to all women is the more remarkable in view of the relatively high proportion who were in the top fourth of their high-school classes.

Self-Confidence as Measured in Terms of Expected Future Achievement and Activity. The generally high level of self-confidence of the role transcenders is shown by their high expectations of college achievements and activities (Table 3.3). More role transcenders than (1) Traditionalists, (2) all women, even (3) all men expect to graduate with honors, be elected to an academic honor society, write or co-author a published article, and be elected to a student office. Although the proportions are small, they are still higher than for other students. It is interesting to note that more role transcenders than Traditionalists or all women also expect to fail one or more courses. This expectation might be related to the relatively hard courses they expected to take. Of the 49 fields of study dealt with here, only 26 had at least 100 cases and of these, 8 showed seemingly meaningful differences. Role transcenders exceeded Traditionalists in 6 of these 8: journalism, speech, prelaw, premedicine, political science, and business administration, all but one of them sex-typed as male interests. Only in the female sex-typed fields of education and secretarial courses did Traditionalists exceed role transcenders.

Table 3.2

High-School Achievements and Activities (in Percentages)

	PIONEERS	TRADITIONALISTS	ALL ENTERING WOMEN	ALL ENTERING MEN	ALL ENTERING STUDENTS
Was a member of a scholastic honor society	33.4	29.9	30.8	20.2	25.0
Was elected president of one or more student organizations (recognized by the school)	27.4	21.0	18.8	19.1	19.0
Edited the school paper, yearbook, or literary magazine	25.3	13.6	14.6	8.2	11.1
Had poems, stories, essays, or articles published	23.9	13.3	18.2	13.2	15.5
Had a major part in a play	21.7	13.6	15.5	14.8	15.1
Won a varsity letter (sports)	17.4	18.0	13.6	44.7	30.6
Won a prize or award in an art competition	10.7	6.0	6.3	4.8	5.5
Won a Certificate of Merit or Letter of Commendation in the National Merit Program	10.7	4.1	7.5	7.5	7.5
Participated in a state or regional speech or debate contest	8.5	4.2	5.5	6.5	5.0
Placed (first, second, or third) in a state or regional science contest	2.8	3.1	2.1	2.4	2.3
Voted in a student election	97.7	95.6	71.9	64.9	68.0
Participated in high-school campaign	61.1	45.5	40.7	37.4	38.9
Participated in other political campaign	21.5	13.5	15.1	13.4	14.1

The self-confidence of the role transcenders revealed itself in career choices also. Although elementary and secondary education were the career choices of a quarter of the role transcenders (and almost two-fifths of the Traditionalists), their other choices were less stereotypically "feminine." More role transcenders than Traditionalists, as expected, selected such male-typed occupations as medicine, engineering, law and scientific research. Many more Traditionalists, on the other hand, chose housewife as their probable occupation.

In role-transcenders, then, we see young women who seem to know what they are capable of doing and taking it for granted that they will do it. Their past dynamism is expected to have a momentum of its own.

Achievement Orientation. The students' goals or objectives were elicited by asking them which among a list of 18 achievements they considered very important or essential. A veritable chasm in achievement orientation seemed to yawn between role transcenders and all other students, male or female, as measured by these life goals. They exceeded others to such an extent as to constitute a separate statistical universe. If the responses of nine other samples of women reported in the survey from nine types of institutions[12] are viewed as separate samples of entering women, the role transcenders are at least three standard deviations away from the average of these nine samples in the case of 10 of the 18 items,[13] and more than two

Table 3.3

Expected College Achievements and Activities (in Percentages)

	PIONEERS	TRADI- TIONALISTS	ALL ENTERING WOMEN	ALL ENTERING MEN	ALL ENTERING STUDENTS
Graduate with honors	8.4	2.1	3.8	5.6	4.8
Be elected to an academic honor society	5.5	1.6	2.5	2.5	2.5
Author or co-author a published article	8.0	1.9	4.5	4.9	4.7
Be elected to a student office	4.6	1.1	1.3	2.2	1.8
Achieve at least the B.A. degree	91.4	85.7	87.0	93.0	99.3
Join a social fraternity, sorority, or club	30.0	22.6	21.8	19.1	20.4
Fail one or more courses	3.5	2.5	2.3	3.9	3.2

12. Public two-year colleges, private two-year colleges, technical institutions, public four-year colleges, private nonsectarian colleges, Protestant colleges, Catholic colleges, public universities, private universities.

13. Obtain recognition from peers, influence political structures, influence social values, have active social life, be an expert in finance, be very well off financially, become a community leader, write original works, succeed in own business, and participate in community action programs.

standard deviations away in 3.[14] The Traditionalists differed from the average of the nine samples on only 2 items.[15]

The Pioneers or role transcenders seem greedy for activity and achievement (Table 3.4). At least half consider it important or essential to achieve recognition from peers, to help others in difficulty, to participate in community action programs, to influence social values, to keep up with political affairs, to succeed in their own business, to be well-off financially, to have friends different from themselves, and to develop a philosophy of life—all this and an active social life to boot! Only four goals seemed very important or essential to as many as even half of the Traditionalists: to develop a philosophy of life, have friends different from themselves, have an active social life, and help others in difficulty. These life values are, however, even more illuminating as indicators of "androgyny" than of achievement orientation.

"Polarity Transcended." If the values or achievements shown in Table 3.4 are categorized as those involving (1) the arts, science, and philosophy (items 1–5); (2) power, influence, and success (items 6–14); and (3) humanitarian or "people-oriented" activities (15–18), the first set may be viewed as equally "masculine" and "feminine," that is, equally appropriate achievements for both sexes. The second set of items may be viewed as conforming to stereotypically male achievement values; and the third set, as conforming to stereotypically female achievement values. Table 3.5 shows how the Pioneers differed from the Traditionalists, from all women, and from men.

The most significant finding, already noted earlier, is that the role transcenders were more "feminine" than both Traditionalists and all women, and more "masculine" than men. More of the role transcenders than of the others considered all 18 of the life achievement goals as very important or essential. On the average, more of the role transcenders than of the men considered power, influence, and success important achievement values; but more role transcenders than of all women considered humanitarian or "people-oriented achievement values essential. The role transcenders did, indeed, thus combine the sex polarities. Both the stereotyped male and female achievement values could coexist in the same individuals. Having "feminine" achievement goals did not preclude having "masculine" goals also.

Relevant here also is another interesting apparent violation of sex stereotypes. In high school, more of even the "feminine" Traditionalists than of men had competed successfully in science contests (Table 3.2),

14. Achieve in the performing arts, have friends different from me, and keep up with political affairs.
15. They deviated more than three standard deviations on wanting "an active social life" and "wanting to be an expert in finance"; they were more than two standard deviations away on one item: influencing political structure.

Table 3.4

Values: Objectives Considered Essential or Important (in Percentages)

	PIONEERS	TRADITIONALISTS	ALL ENTERING WOMEN	ALL ENTERING MEN	ALL ENTERING STUDENTS
Becoming accomplished in one of the performing arts (acting, dancing, etc.)	23.7	10.3	14.8	11.1	12.8
Making a theoretical contribution to science	18.6	3.8	6.2	13.4	10.2
Writing original works (poems, novels, short stories, etc.)	28.3	10.4	15.9	12.4	14.0
Creating artistic work (painting, sculpture, decorating, etc.)	28.5	18.2	21.4	11.9	16.2
Developing a meaningful philosophy of life	89.3	76.8	79.1	72.6	75.6
Influencing the political structure	28.9	9.2	14.0	21.8	18.3
Influencing social values	54.5	34.5	36.2	32.3	34.0
Keeping up to date with political affairs	64.6	45.5	50.6	54.7	52.8
Becoming a community leader	36.4	12.1	11.5	18.3	15.2
Participating in a community action program	51.4	30.1	32.3	27.0	29.4
Being very well-off financially	55.6	34.3	28.0	48.3	39.1
Becoming an expert in finance and commerce	34.1	30.6	8.6	21.7	15.8
Obtaining recognition from my colleagues for contributions in my special field	65.9	34.7	33.4	45.3	39.9
Being successful in a business of my own	60.9	32.7	31.9	53.9	43.9
Having an active social life	69.7	66.6	53.7	58.7	56.5
Having friends with different backgrounds and interests from mine	79.9	64.8	65.7	58.2	61.6
Helping others who are in difficulty	81.2	75.0	74.0	57.4	64.9
Participating in an organization like the Peace Corps or Vista	35.3	19.8	26.1	14.3	19.6

presumably a "masculine" activity (competition) in a "masculine" field of interest (science). The proportions were small, to be sure, but not the relevance as an indication that both "femininity" and "masculinity" could exist in the same individuals.

Political Orientation: Who's Deviant? The students were asked whether they agreed or disagreed on a number of issues. The responses to 18 of the issues are presented in Table 3.6. Expectably, more Pioneers than Traditionalists gave liberal responses on all three categories of issues— civil-rights-campus,[16] libertarian,[17] and feminist[18]—most especially on feminist issues. In Table 3.7 the differences in the average proportion of respondents giving liberal or conservative responses on the three categories of issues are shown, positive differences indicating a liberal direction and negative, a conservative one.

Table 3.5
Average Deviance of Pioneers in Specific Categories of Values

VALUES DEALING WITH	FROM TRADITIONALISTS	FROM ALL WOMEN	FROM MEN
Arts, science, philosophy (1-5)	13.8	10.2	13.4
Power, influence, success (6-14)	21.5	21.8	14.3
Humanitarian or "people-oriented" activities (15-18)	10.0	11.7	19.4

Since there is no set sex-role pattern with respect to position on civil-rights-campus issues, there is little to be made of the differences between Pioneers and Traditionalists on such issues. If issues relating to disadvantaged students, equal opportunity, the rights of criminals, and the death penalty are viewed as, in general, "humanitarian," they may be viewed as conforming to the female sex-role stereotype. On these four "feminine"-type issues, the role transcenders were "more feminine" than Traditionalists, than all women, and all men. The Traditionalists were less

16. Students should have a major role in curriculum; college officials have right to regulate student behavior off campus; faculty promotions should be based in part on student evaluations; college grades should be abolished; student publications should be cleared by college officials; college officials have the right to ban persons with extreme views from speaking on campus; most college officials have been too lax in dealing with student campus protests.

17. Students from disadvantaged social backgrounds should be given preferential treatment in college admissions; everybody should be given an opportunity to go to college regardless of the possible consequences; marijuana should be legalized; there is too much concern in the courts for the rights of criminals; the death penalty should be abolished; only volunteers should serve in the armed forces.

18. Divorce laws should be liberalized; abortions should be legalized under some conditions; women should have equal salary and opportunities for advancement as men in comparable positions; women should be subject to the draft.

Table 3.6
Differentiating and Nondifferentiating Issues (in Percentages)

	PIONEERS	TRADITIONALISTS	ALL ENTERING WOMEN	ALL ENTERING MEN	ALL ENTERING STUDENTS
CIVIL RIGHTS AND CAMPUS ISSUES					
Most college officials have been too lax in dealing with student protests on campus*	41.2	49.7	44.5	39.0	41.5
Students should have a major role specifying the college curriculum	92.8	91.8	92.9	90.1	91.4
College officials have the right to regulate student behavior off campus*	80.5	79.6	83.2	82.8	83.0
Faculty promotions should be based in part on student evaluations	70.8	71.4	70.6	71.8	71.3
College grades should be abolished	44.5	44.5	46.2	42.9	44.4
Student publications should be cleared by college officials*	58.2	47.3	57.4	57.0	57.2
College officials have the right to ban persons with extreme views from speaking on campus*	66.4	62.1	69.5	64.6	66.8
LIBERTARIAN ISSUES					
Students from disadvantaged social backgrounds should be given preferential treatment in college admissions	44.0	43.3	41.9	45.7	44.0
Everybody should be given an opportunity to go to college regardless of past performance or aptitude test scores	63.3	65.0	63.6	59.6	61.4
Scientists should publish their findings regardless of the possible consequences	63.5	60.9	58.4	63.6	61.2
Marijuana should be legalized	40.8	24.7	35.2	41.0	38.4

Table 3.6 (Concluded)
Differentiating and Nondifferentiating Issues (in Percentages)

	PIONEER	TRADITIONALIST	ALL ENTERING WOMEN	ALL ENTERING MEN	ALL ENTERING STUDENTS
There is too much concern in the courts for the rights of criminals*	51.9	48.9	55.5	42.5	48.4
The death penalty should be abolished	55.8	53.9	59.8	53.4	56.3
Only volunteers should serve in the armed forces	60.8	56.0	58.3	70.6	65.3
FEMINIST ISSUES					
Divorce laws should be liberalized	53.1	34.2	46.9	55.2	51.5
Under some conditions, abortions should be legalized	92.0	80.6	82.1	84.4	83.4
Women should receive the same salary and opportunities for advancement as men in comparable positions	87.4	80.3	87.1	76.5	81.3
Women should be subject to the draft	19.4	7.7	15.6	26.6	21.7

*All responses have been cast in a form such that the higher the figure the more libertarian they are; that is, the respondents did not agree with the starred items.

"feminine" than all women, more "feminine" than the men. On the other three items, more Pioneers than Traditionalists were on the liberal side—especially with respect to the legalization of marijuana. But more of both Pioneers and Traditionalists than of all women were on the liberal side and fewer of both than of men were.

The four feminist issues define aspects of a non-traditional concept of the female role. The stereotyped female should not want divorce laws liberalized, not want abortions legalized, not insist on equal opportunities for women, and not want women subject to the draft. On these issues, the Pioneers show up as genuine role transcenders and the Traditionalists as far more conformist to the stereotype.

But it is interesting to note that on all three sets of issues the role transcenders are more like all women than the Traditionalists are. And in this sense they may be viewed as less "deviant" than the Traditionalists. This relatively greater "deviance" on the part of the Traditionalists is interesting because more of them (83.3 percent) than of Pioneers (64.9 percent) saw themselves as conformists. That is, they replied affirmatively to a question that asked whether they felt their beliefs were similar to those of others. In this they were like members of an ancient regime who have not yet noticed that others had passed them by. They thought others agreed with them.

On the other hand, almost twice as many role transcenders (22.5 percent) as Traditionalists, (12.8 percent) felt that there was a generation gap between themselves and their parents. More Traditionalists, in brief, felt in tune with both their own generation and their parents' generation; more role transcenders, relatively, saw themselves as different from both generations.

Political Orientation: Whither Bound? When the students were asked about their current political position on a 5-point scale—far right, conservative, middle-of-the-road, liberal, far left—as they felt it to be today and as they expected it to be after four years of college, a tendency toward convergence showed up (Table 3.8). The differences between Pioneers and Traditionalists were expected to be smaller in four years than they were today. The shift was in the direction of greater liberalism at the expense of a middle-of-the-road position, and it was thus in the direction of the Pioneers.[19]

Women as a whole as well as Traditionalists seemed to be moving in the direction of the Pioneers. The differences between them were expected to be smaller in four years than they were today. In this sense the role transcenders may be viewed as prototypical of the future.

19. Differences were estimated by averaging the differences between proportions responding at each point on the scale.

Heterogeneity. Before leaving the topic of differences, note should be taken of the hints that—perhaps precisely because they were sex-role transcenders—the Pioneers seemed to be more heterogeneous in their replies to some of the items on the questionnaire. For example, more role transcenders (22.2 percent) than Traditionalists (19.9 percent) said there

Table 3.7
Differences among Average Proportions of Respondents on
Specified Categories of Issues*

ISSUES	DIFFERENCES BETWEEN PIONEERS			
	AND TRADI-TIONALISTS	AND ALL WOMEN	AND ALL MEN	AND ALL STUDENTS
Civil-rights-campus (7)	+ 4.1	− 1.5	+ .9	− .2
Libertarian (7)	+ 3.9	+ 1.1	+ .7	+ .6
Feminist (4)	+ 12.3	+ 5.1	+ 1.3	+ 3.5
	DIFFERENCES BETWEEN TRADITIONALISTS			
	AND PIONEERS	AND ALL WOMEN	AND ALL MEN	AND ALL STUDENTS
Civil-rights-campus (7)	− 4.1	− 2.8	− .3	+ .2
Libertarian (7)	+ 3.9	− 3.0	− 3.4	− 3.2
Feminist (4)	− 12.3	− 6.2	− 9.9	− 8.8

*SOURCE: Table 3.6. Negative difference indicate conservative direction, positive, liberal.

Table 3.8
Current Political Position and Expected Position after Four Years

	PIONEERS	TRADI-TIONALISTS	ALL WOMEN	ALL MEN	ALL STUDENTS
CURRENT POSITION					
Far left	3.6	1.7	2.4	3.7	3.1
Liberal	34.4	21.9	31.5	35.1	33.5
Middle-of-the-road	41.0	53.8	49.4	42.0	45.4
Conservative	20.5	22.4	16.1	18.0	17.1
Far right	.5	.2	.6	1.3	1.0
FOUR YEARS LATER					
Far left	3.2	2.1	3.2	4.6	4.0
Liberal	43.4	36.9	42.1	39.3	40.6
Middle-of-the-road	28.1	31.8	31.1	31.4	31.3
Conservative	23.2	26.2	21.7	22.3	22.0
Far right	2.1	3.0	1.8	2.4	2.1

was little chance they would change their major in college; but more also said the chances that they would change were good (17.7 percent and 14.6 percent). Similarly, more Pioneers (22.4 percent) than Traditionalists (19.4 percent) said there was little chance they would change their career choice; but more also said that chances were good that they would (19.5 percent, 14.8 percent). More Pioneers (6.1 percent) than Traditionalists (2.0 percent) did not discuss their future with their parents at all; but more also frequently discussed their future with their parents (53.7 percent, 51.8 percent). Pioneers were more likely than Traditionalists to have both a small number—none or one—of close friends (5.7 percent, 3.5 percent) and also a large—more than 21—number (12.3 percent, 10.3 percent).

Pioneers seemed also to come from more heterogenous backgrounds. Thus more Pioneers (12.8 percent) than Traditionalists (6.8 percent) had graduated from lower- and working-class high schools; but more had also graduated from upper-class high schools (5.6 percent, 3.3 percent). More Pioneers (13.7 percent) than Traditionalists (11.5 percent) came from lower- and working-class neighborhoods but also more came from upper-middle- and upper-class neighborhoods (42.4 percent, 41.9 percent).

Some of the seeming inconsistency in findings on class background is undoubtedly related to the fact that twice as many role transcenders (15.1 percent) as Traditionalists (7.7 percent) were black.[20] Black women, it might be noted in passing, show up as remarkably high in aspirations and achievement orientation. They are in many ways prototypes of Stage III human beings.

It is not the size of any of the differences in these indexes of heterogeneity so much as the frequency of their occurrence that is interesting. Heterogeneity is compatible with the Hefner-Nordin statement that "there may be different tracks leading to a transcendent view of sex roles," different for different types of young women, different for young women with different backgrounds.

BACKGROUND DIFFERENCES

Community Background. Although about the same proportion of both role transcenders and Traditionalists were reared on farms (9.6 and 9.5 percent respectively) and in suburbs (25.0 and 22.0 percent), twice as many role transcenders (17.2 percent) as of Traditionalists (8.6 percent) were reared in large cities.

Family Income. Although, as noted earlier, the occupations of fathers did not show great differences, family income did. More role transcenders (16.9 percent) than Traditionalists (12.3 percent) came from families with

20. Engin Holmstrom is pursuing further the extraordinary showing of black college women.

incomes under $6000 (as of 1970). Fewer role transcenders (63.6 percent) than Traditionalists (73.3 percent) therefore expected to rely on their parents as a major source of financial support. Role transcenders were thus more likely to rely on scholarships as a major source of financial support than Traditionalists (28.7, 17.7 percent) and part-time work was going to be a major source of financial support among more role transcenders (26.6 percent) than among Traditionalists (20.9 percent). These differences may reflect greater dynamism or drive to achieve a college education.

Religion. More role transcenders than Traditionalists professed no religion at all (10.2 and 2.4 percent). Among those who had religious preferences, more role transcenders than Traditionalists tended to be members of structured denominations: Episcopalians (5.2 and 4.5 percent); Lutheran (6.7 and 4.6 percent); Roman Catholic (30.5 and 27.2 percent); and Jewish (4.5 and 3.6 percent). More Traditionalists than role transcenders were Baptist, Methodist, Presbyterian, other types of Protestant, and adherents to other religions.

Family Relations. More Traditionalists (87.2 percent) than role transcenders (77.8 percent) came from intact families. Almost twice as many role transcenders (11.6 percent) as Traditionalists (5.9 percent) came from families in which there was a divorce.[21] Quite in line with the Dionysian character of the role transcenders was their independence from their families as indicated by their distance from home. More (42 percent) of them than of the Traditionalists (36.8 percent) were farther than 100 miles from home; more (12 and 9.6 percent) were farther than 500 miles from home.

Mothers. Almost 60 percent of the Traditionalists had mothers who were housewives; fewer than half (47.8 percent) of the role transcenders did. The mothers of the role transcenders seemed to be prototypical role transcenders themselves. Very few had graduate degrees, but almost twice as many mothers of the role transcenders (3.7 percent) as mothers of Traditionalists (2.0 percent) did. The occupations pursued by mothers of both samples of women were the traditionally sex-typed female professions of teaching and nursing.

It would be difficult to tell from a vignette of a modal Pioneer what sex she was. Except for career choices, which tended in the female-typed direction, her values and political positions, except on feminist issues, were not especially feminine or masculine. Indeed, her values were both masculine and feminine. Even under present sex-role socialization, then,

21. More role transcenders (10.6 percent) than Traditionalists (6.9 percent) came also from families in which one or both parents were dead.

some young women manage to transcend polarities. And, so far as we know, their gender identity does not suffer.

Not all human beings with female gender identity are so fortunate; nor, for that matter, human beings with male gender identity. The emphasis in the discussion so far has been on the acquired, culturally determined nature of gender identity and we have assumed that all have accepted the gender identity assigned to them. Emphasis on the cultural and acquired nature of gender identity encourages us to accept the possibility of extensive change.

But it is the part of wisdom to face the possibility of limitations to change also. Not everyone accepts the gender assigned to him or her. Robert J. Stoller reminds us that "while gender, gender identity, and gender role are almost synonymous in the usual person, in certain abnormal cases they are at variance" (1968:xiii). We cannot ignore the relevant research on gender identity.

Anomalies in Gender Identity

It would be diversionary to attempt to review the literature on "errors of the body,"[22] however much they can teach us. But even among men and women who do not suffer from such "errors of the body" there are anomalies that should give us pause.

If sex refers to biological differences, gender refers to a subtler kind of difference, differences in identities. The sexes are male and female; the genders are masculine and feminine. Stoller places great emphasis on the culturally determined and learned nature of gender identity and certainly of gender role, but he does not rule out a biological component not yet adequately understood. "If the first main finding" of current research, he tells us, "is that gender identity is primarily learned, the second is that there are biological forces that contribute to this," that gender identity "is augmented, or interfered with, by certain biological forces" (1968:xiii). Sometimes, that is, despite all our efforts to instill the correct gender identity in a given individual, we fail. Despite female genes, female internal anatomy, external anatomy, and even gender assignment, the woman "feels like a man"; in her own mind and heart, she "is" a man. And, of course, vice versa. They are not androgynous—or "gynandrous"[23]— because they are as polarized as conventional women and men, but "erroneously" polarized. Stoller describes some such cases he has known of women with male gender identities.

These people, living permanently as unremarkably masculine men, are biologically   normal   females   and   were   so   recognized   as

22. Ehrhardt, Epstein, and Money, 1968; Ehrhardt, Evers, and Money, 1968:115–122; Money and Ehrhardt 1972: Chapter 6. For a table of some such cases, see Bernard, 1971:18.

23. In the English language, adjectives precede nouns. Thus, according to the logic of our language, *androgyny* refers to a female body housing a male gender identity and *gynandry* refers to a male body housing a female gender identity.

children. . . . Among those I know one is an expert machine tool operator, another an engineering draftsman, another a research chemist. Their jobs are quiet, steady, and unspectacular; their work records as men are excellent. They are sociable, not recluses, and have friendships with both men and women. Neither their friends nor their colleagues at work know they are biologically female. They are not clinically psychotic (Ibid.: 194, 196).

Until recently, however, we have never had inside accounts by skilled reporters of such cases of gender "misidentity" in genetically, hormonally, and anatomically normal individuals. Now Jan Morris (1974) has given us such an account in her book *Conundrum*.

James Morris was a perfectly normal male. He lived the life of an ordinary male. He was dealt with as a man. He married and fathered five children. There was nothing exceptional in his appearance or behavior. But James knew the body was wrong; the identity that inhabited the body was that of a woman. In nonscientific but quite poetic terms—the author is a professional writer—the nature of gender identity is described.

> To me gender is not physical at all, but is altogether insubstantial. It is soul, perhaps, it is talent, it is taste, it is environment, it is how one feels, it is light and shade, it is inner music, it is a spring in one's step or an exchange of glances, it is more truly life and love than any combination of genitals, ovaries, and hormones. It is the essentialness of oneself, the psyche, the fragment of unity . . . sex . . . and gender, though they . . . obviously overlap, are far from being synonymous. (Morris, 1974:57)·

Though James' sex was male, his gender was not; the woman inside did not want the public success available to the male gender role. "I deliberately turned my back on it, as I set my face against manhood."

Some societies make provision for such sex-gender anomalies. The Comanche Indians, for example, recognized the *berdache*. This was the biological male who preferred to live the life of a woman, or the biological female who preferred to ride with the warriors. Among the Nuer of Africa, biological females who wish to may accumulate property, acquire a wife, and become heads of families. Our own society is less permissive. We force secrecy, even shame, on such body-gender mismatching or biological change. When the mismatching became intolerable for James Morris, a long sex-change treatment was entered into, ending finally in surgical procedures.

This was no frivolous spur-of-the-moment, heedless, impulsive gesture. All the consequences were weighed:

> To myself I had been woman all along, and I was not going to change the truth of me, only discard the falsity. But I *was* about to change my

form and apparency—my status too, perhaps my place among my peers, my attitudes no doubt, the reactions I would evoke, my reputation, my manner of life, my prospects, my emotions, possibly my abilities. I was about to adapt my body from a male conformation to a female, and I would shift my public role altogether, from the role of a man to the role of a woman (Ibid.:60).

James became Jan and finally felt at one with herself. Her gender identity and her body were now in harmony.

So far the story of Jan highlights the unlearned, perhaps biological, component of gender identity, in her case a female gender identity in a genetically and hormonally normal male body. But her story after the sex-change emphasizes the enormous influence—which John Money's work has also shown—of role expectations on personality. When she was dealt with as a woman, treated as a woman, she began to acquire the characteristics considered feminine:

> The more I was treated as a woman, the more woman I became. I adapted willy-nilly. If I was assumed to be incompetent at reversing cars, or opening bottles, oddly incompetent I found myself becoming. If a case was thought to heavy for me, inexplicably I found it so myself. Thrust as I now found myself far more into the company of women than of men, I began to find women's conversation in general more congenial. Women treated me with a frankness which, while it was one of the happiest discoveries of my metamorphosis, did imply membership in a camp, a faction, or at least a school of thought; and so I found myself gravitating always toward the female, whether in sharing a railway compartment or supporting a political cause. Men treated me more and more as a junior—my lawyer, in an unguarded moment one morning, even called me "my child"; and so, addressed every day of my life as an inferior, involuntarily, month by month I accepted that condition. I discovered that even now men prefer women to be less informed, less able, less talkative, and certainly less self-centered than they are themselves; so I generally obliged them (Ibid.:64).

As significant as what this case teaches us about gender identity and potential limit to change is the fact that even in such anomalous situations, gender identity is still *polarized*. It is a reversal of gender, not a transcendence of it.

III. Some Implications of Role Transcendence

In reply to the questions raised at the beginning of this paper, my own answer would be that the change we should aim at is role transcendence.

What could we expect from such changes? What could we expect, for example, in Heilbrun's world "in which individual roles and the modes of personal behavior can be freely chosen?" or in the Hefner-Nordin world in which we permitted "individual behavioral and emotional choice that was based on the full range of possible human characteristics?" We really do not know. We do not know what either men or women would be like under conditions that did not impose stereotyped role patterns on them. Their bodies would still remain different. Their qualities, however similar, would still be packaged differently (Bernard, 1964: 168–169). For, after all, it is *role* transcendence, not *sex* transcendence we have in mind. Neuters are not in the future.

First a word about our fears. Would sex-role transcendence eliminate sex appeal? Love? Romance? If individuals were complete, whole entities, why would they ever want one another? With both male and female strengths, why would they ever experience the dependencies that constitute such a large component in loving relationships? Would we not become coldly atomized and hence alienated entities? Actually even under our system of stereotyped sex patterns we permit dependencies even in the male model, however much disguised the form it takes may be. Men, for example, are as dependent on women as women on men.[24] Dependencies are part of the human condition. Sex-role transcendence would not obliterate them.

My own answer to the questions raised above is that we could expect for an indeterminate number of human beings the choices would remain as they are now. For another indeterminate number of human beings—like Jan Morris or like the Comanche *berdache*—I think we could expect the choices would be the reverse of what they are now. But we would not demand that those who made such choices alter their bodies if their bodies did not conform to our preconceptions as to which body should live which way. Polarities in both of these kinds of cases—traditional or reversed— would remain. We would have both men and women, in whatever ratio, at both ends of a rather flat bell-shaped curve following, at one end, a specialized "feminine" lifestyle and, at the other, a specialized "masculine" life style.

In between we would have an indeterminate number of men and women, in whatever ratio, who—like the role transcenders here described—had the dynamism associated with maleness harnessed to the people-oriented, humanitarian achievement values associated with femaleness. Not at all a frightening prospect.

24. Bernard, Chapter 2, documents the greater dependency of men on marriage as compared with women.

References

American Council on Education, Staff of the Office of Research. 1970. *National norms for entering college freshmen, Fall 1970.* ACE Reports, vol. 5, no. 6 (December).

Bernard, Jessie. 1964. *Academic women.* University Park: Pennsylvania State University Press. New York: Meridian, 1966, 1972, 1974.

————. 1971. *Women and the public interest, An essay on policy and protest.* Chicago: Aldine.

————. 1972. *The future of marriage* New York: World. New York: Bantam, 1973.

Ehrhardt, Anke A.; Epstein, R.; and Money, John. 1968. Fetal androgens and female gender identity in the early-treated androgenital syndrome. *Johns Hopkins Medical Journal* 122:160–167.

Ehrhardt, Anke A.; Evers, K.; and Money, John. 1968. Influence of androgen and some aspects of sexually dimorphic behavior in women with the late-treated androgenital syndrome. *Johns Hopkins Medical Journal* 123:115–122.

Hefner, Robert; Nordin, Virginia Davis; Meda, Rebecca; and Cleshansky, Barbara. 1974. A model of sex-role transcendence: Role polarity and sex discrimination in education. University of Michigan Technical Proposal to National Institute of Education, Contract NIE-C-74-0144, May, 1974.

Heilbrun, Carolyn. 1973. *Toward a recognition of androgyny.* New York: Knopf.

Lipman-Blumen, Jean. 1971 Role de-differentiation as a system response to crisis: Occupational and political roles of women. *Sociological Inquiry* 43:105–129.

Money, John, and Ehrhardt, Anke A. 1972. *Man and woman, boy and girl.* Baltimore: Johns Hopkins University Press.

Morris, Jan. 1974. *Conundrum.* New York: Harcourt Brace Jovanovich. Citations from abstract in *Ms*, July, 1974.

Neumann, Erich. 1963. *The great mother.* Princeton: Princeton University Press.

O'Reilly, Jane. 1972. The housewife's moment of truth. *Ms* 1 (Spring):54–59.

Rossi, Alice. 1973. Maternalism, sexuality, and the new feminism, in Zubin, Joseph, and Money, John, eds. *Contemporary sexual behavior: Critical issues in the 1970s.* Baltimore: Johns Hopkins University Press.

Schlossberg, Nancy K. 1974. The right to be wrong: Women in academe. Paper presented at 1974 Presidents Institute, June.

Stoller, Robert J. 1968. *Sex and gender.* New York: Science House.

FOUR

Adolescence and Socialization for Motherhood

This paper consists of four parts. The first presents a descriptive statement of current changes in adolescence and motherhood and a critique of the way girls have been socialized for motherhood in the past. The second part, using the concepts of tipping points and turning points, attempts to pinpoint the time when certain changes relevant in the present context have occurred or will occur, namely, the time when the institutional structures of our society dealing with basic aspects of marriage and motherhood have titlted or will tilt, restructuring the three fundamental roles of women—worker, wife, mother. The third part deals with the critical turning point in the lives of adolescents that occurs with sexual initiation. The final part tries to assess the impact of feminism on adolescents today.

I. Three Key Concepts: Adolescence, Motherhood, Socialization

The young women who are adolescent today, say 13 to 19 years of age, were born in the period 1954 to 1960, just at the crest of the so-called feminine mystique era. They were under 10 when Betty Friedan (1963) analyzed that mystique for us and stimulated the recrudescence of feminism. They are among the first adolescent generations to vote for a president; see abortion as a political issue; confront a drug culture; know that there were

69

communes or pads to which they could escape from home if they wanted to; have free access to contraceptives; be exposed to the environmental or ecological movement; learn of zero-population growth; see their older sisters deciding where to live on the basis of the quality of the air as well as the quality of the schools.

During the lifetime of these adolescents, new life styles have been adopted by their mothers as well as by their peers. Their mothers have less elaborately coiffed hair; their lip makeup, if they wear any at all, is more subdued. Their clothes are more casual and comfortable—they wear slacks instead of skirts a good deal of the time—stiletto heels are uncommon, and entertaining is less formal. If their mothers are in the 35 to 44 or the 45 to 54 age brackets, over half (52 and 54 percent, respectively) were in the labor force in 1972 (President's *Manpower Report 1973*: Table 2). Rather than encouraging the coquettish arts, many of these mothers are disappointed when they find their daughters still reluctant to take the initiative in asking boys to dance with them at high-school parties. They are more feministic than their daughters. They cry as well as laugh when their 5-year-old daughters say they want babies of their own to play with.

They are the first generation of adolescents to find their textbooks challenged for the sexism of their contents, their school boards challenged for the disparity in funds expended on boys' and girls' athletic programs, their schools challenged for not permitting girls to take shop courses.

They are among the first adolescents to be exposed to the new feminist movement of the late 1960s and early 1970s, to hear about respectable women who deliberately have children outside of marriage because they want motherhood but not marriage (Klein, 1973). They are the first young women to see the ideal to which young women used to look forward—marriage to an affluent husband who could provide a life of leisure—in process of devaluation to the status of a luxury that should be taxed. They are among the young women who have since 1958 been showing less and less interest in marriage.[1]

They are the first adolescents to arrive on the scene at a time when there is a rebellion in process against motherhood as we institutionalize it in our society, when a spate of books appears shouting that *Mother's Day Is Over!*(Radl, 1973). They are the first generation to hear of *The Baby Trap* (Peck, 1972), to read of happily married mothers who "regularly feel like screaming" (McBride, 1973:xi). And, be it noted that they hear these things not only from radical feminists, but from conventional women as well. Women have protested motherhood in the past, to be sure. But it was

1. "During the 12 months ending with August 1974, 2,233,000 marriages were reported. This was 68,000 fewer than the number for the 12 months ending with August 1973, a 3.0 percent decline. The marriage rate for that period was 10.6 per 1,000 population, a decline of 3.6 percent. Cumulative data for the first 8 months of 1974 show a 2.9 percent decline in the number of marriages and a 3.6 percent decline in the marriage rate from the comparable figures for 1973" *(Monthly Vital Statistics Report* 23, October 24, 1974:1).

protest against excessive motherhood—against fifth, sixth, seventh babies they could not prevent. Now it is mothers of one or two, even of no, children who are protesting, mothers who love children but not motherhood as it is institutionalized in our society today. And in public! In the past, such protests were secret, woman-to-woman so that on the surface the illusion of the happy, self-fulfilled mother could be maintained. Now the protest is open, unashamed, and issued without guilt. Earlier adolescents did not hear such protests.

They are the first adolescents to arrive on the scene when the protests of the mothers are supplemented by a strong antinatalism in the media as part of the environmental movement; when young women expect kudos rather than sanctions when they say they do not want to have babies; when a National Organization for Nonparenthood has arisen to help women make motherhood truly voluntary (Bernard, 1974: Chapter 3), and to make the choice to remain "child-free" an acceptable option. A great deal of the research on which our knowldge of adolescence rests does not, therefore, fit this new generation.

Motherhood as it is currently institutionalized is, historically speaking, new and unique and, like adolescence itself, a product of affluence (Bernard, 1974: Chapter 1). Until recently and even now in most parts of the world, able-bodied adult women have been too valuable as workers to be spared for the full-time care of two or three small children. Communes today are learning the same lesson; some will accept no children because their care is too costly in terms of labor-hours. Only those that are relatively affluent or subsidized can afford them. Our own society has been able to spare women for the full-time, exclusive care of children for only a historically brief period of time. This allocation of adult time is good for neither mother nor children, psychologically and economically. Questions about it are now being raised.[2]

Quite aside from any economic argument is the current antinatalist argument that women should be encouraged to enter the labor force in order to discourage them from having the third or fourth child, or for that matter, the second. Or first, for there is even a nascent movement to encourage childlessness. Its message is being heard. Although the proportion of young women who say they want no children is still small— 3.9 percent as of June, 1972—it had tripled in the three previous years, and may conceivably rise higher (Bureau of the Census, 1972). In the same year, 7 percent of a sample of adolescent girls replied "false" to the statement "someday I will probably want to get married and have children" (Sorensen, 1973, 502). Although it is probably safe to say that at least 9 out of 10 girls who are adolescent today are going to be mothers, it is probably also safe to say that they are not going to have many babies.

The role of mother is no longer being defined as monopolizing a

2. The supporting data for the discussion of motherhood are presented in Bernard, 1974.

woman's whole life or, even when her children are in school, her exclusive attention. The mother of school-age (but not preschool) children who is not in the labor force is today becoming the exception rather then the rule, a point to be elaborated in greater detail below.

When we speak of the socialization of adolescents for motherhood we have to ask, socialization for what stage of motherhood? For motherhood is by no means a unitary or homogeneous phenomenon. At least four stages can be delineated: (1) early motherhood, when the children are preschoolers and the mother is, let us say, 25 to 34 years of age; (2) middle motherhood when the children are of school-age and the mother is in the 35 to 44 or 45 to 54 age bracket; (3) late motherhood when the children are 18 years of age or older and the mother is 55 or over; and, for some long-lived women, (4) when mother-child roles are reversed.

So far as *socialization* is concerned, a growing literature documents the way we have bent the female twig for motherhood. As long ago as 1916, Leta Hollingsworth (1916) was pointing out the many techniques used to impress upon girls the importance of bearing children; Judith Blake Davis (1972) has reminded us again. And the many studies of sex-stereotyping from the primer on up have documented how insistently, almost coercively, and pervasively we have socialized girls to believe that the primary lifetime role for them was that of mother. Only recently has the coercive nature of this socialization come under challenge. Only now is there a concerted effort on the part of at least some to counteract this pressure and make motherhood genuinely voluntary.

Not only has socialization for motherhood been all-pervasive, it has also been counter-productive, structured in such a way as to produce precisely the characteristics in girls that were dysfunctional for motherhood. Girls were socialized for dependency rather than for the strengths required for the role of mother (Newton, 1955). In Erikson's schema the young woman at marriage moved from one dependency to another, that of the parental family to that of her husband. She might, Erikson conceded, have a brief moratorium between the two dependencies, but for the most part, "such women . . . assumed that, after college, they need not make a life of their own but could live their lives through boyfriends and, later, husbands." They agreed with the young woman who said: "I had always been taken in by the myth that all you have to do is find a man and you'll be happy." If they were to find a man they must not be too self-assertive (Carden, 1973:18). And this is how it looked to the young women:

> I had always been told that men wouldn't like me because I was too aggressive. I thought I had gotten over that. I had, to a large extent, but . . . in my senior year, when lots of women were getting married, I worried about not being married and about there being no position in

this society for a single woman. Until I left [college] I accepted the myth that women are submissive, not speaking at SDS meetings, sitting in the dorms waiting to be asked out (Ibid.:26).

Surely not the caliber required for effective motherhood.

Not only has the model for socializing girls for motherhood been counterproductive so far as dependency was concerned, it has also become increasingly inadequate for socializing young women for motherhood in the world they live in today, in a world, that is, where, as documented below, the norms of virginity which in the past protected against irresponsible motherhood are in process of dissolution. They are not being adequately socialized for responsible as well as for voluntary motherhood.[3]

In the past a major component of the socialization for motherhood consisted of the maintenance of virginity as a first line of defense against involuntary or irresponsible motherhood. Virginity is an absolutely certain way to avoid motherhood. (There is a folk saying that the best contraceptive is 10 feet of space.) In a society that makes so little provision for infants born outside of marriage, a sense of responsibility includes involving the father as well as the mother in a serious commitment if motherhood is undertaken. For teenagers (if not for mature women) in our society, therefore, this responsibility still precludes premarital motherhood. If virginity is not to serve as the first line of defense against irresponsible motherhood, there must be other defenses, including care to prevent conception in the first place.

Such second-line defenses are far from normative today. Responsible use of contraception has not yet achieved even the limited success of the mores of virginity as a defense against irresponsible motherhood.[4] How to socialize adolescents for the prevention of irresponsible motherhood in a

3. This harsh judgment should be tempered by recognition that young people are increasingly viewing parenthood with concern for the environment. Thus, overall, half (49 percent) of all the young women surveyed in 1972 (Sorensen, 1973: Table 296) agreed that it was immoral to have an unwanted child in our overpopulated world, especially since abortion is so available. More of the older (54 percent) than of the younger women (43 percent) agreed. There is also recognition of the dysgenic effects of drug use (see vignette number 8).

4. Although 70 percent of the initiated adolescents worry about becoming pregnant, fewer than half (44 percent) are inhibited by fears of becoming pregnant and an almost equal proportion (45 percent) consider contraception (except the pill) too much trouble. Fewer than a third (31 percent) use the pill. Understandably, in view of such irresponsibility, almost a fourth (23 percent) have had a pregnancy. Among all the initiated adolescents, 14 percent feel the availability of abortion relieves them of worry about pregnancy and if they had become pregnant, 18 percent would seek an abortion; almost a third would marry the father. It is true that the older teenagers show more responsibility than the younger ones do, and that young women with current sexual experience show more responsibility than others; still even they seem less than prudent in their behavior (Sorensen, 1973: Tables 451, 452, 385, 507, 311, 481, 503, 457, 458, 386, 476, 308, 507, 505, 330, 479, 480).

Another study of unmarried women 15 to 19 years of age found that "less than half of the sexually experienced used any method of contraception at last intercourse and less than one-fifth have always sought to protect themselves" (Kantner and Zelnik, 1973:34).

world where the mores of virginity can no longer hold the line against it remains an unsolved problem.[5]

In brief, socialization for a new kind of adolescent in a new kind of world for a new kind of motherhood calls for a thoughtful new look.

II. Tipping Points and Turning Points

Daniel Patrick Moynihan (1973) has interpreted the eruptions of the 1960s in terms of what might well be called a societal "quake" theory. The eruptions were brought about by demographic forces. In that decade the children born during the era of the feminine mystique "rushed" our society. We were quite unprepared for their assault on our institutions. Our fifteen-year-old adolescent girl—taken here to represent her generation— was a bit too young to participate in those eruptions, but not too young to be exposed to their reverberations.

To say that our society is undergoing the throes of rapid change is banal. But to say that we can now pinpoint the exact moment when an entire institutional structure, like a geological one, tilts is not banal. And that is what we can now do for at least some components of the institutional structure dealing with marriage and motherhood. If we had a Richter scale for societal quakes, the present one would surely register at 9. (The highest recording on the Richter scale for earthquakes, recorded in Columbia and in India, has been 8.6.) We cannot pinpoint all of these tiltings with precision but within a year or two, more or less, we can zero in on the time when such institutional tilts have taken, or are about to take, place. This very moment may be such a time.

The concept of the *tipping point* comes from the study of urban communities where it refers to the process by which one land-use succeeds another. It has been applid especially to the racial composition of an area. A neighborhood, primarily white, attracts a few black families; their number increases. For a while it remains biracial. But as the number of black families increases the white families become uneasy. One by one they sell their homes to black families until, at the tipping point, there is a kind of panic selling and the whole neighborhood tilts to become all black.

The concept of tipping point as applied here is not identical to this ecological use. It merely denotes the fact that there comes a time when what was formerly typical or modal now becomes "deviant"—in a statistical and nonpejorative sense—or nonmodal and vice versa. As Ruth Hartley

5. Not until 1973, after two years of controversy, did the Board of Education in one of the most affluent and educated counties in the country finally approve of the study of contraception for high-school seniors. Even so, it will require parental approval. And a Local Advisory Committee will decide when each school is ready to offer such study *(Washington Post,* September 12, 1973. Parental disapproval remained strong).

(1970:129) notes, when a pattern becomes modal it tends to become normative, even coercive if not panicky as in ecological tipping.

In the present context the societal tipping point is defined as the moment when the 50 percent level is reached. When half of the members of a society do or accept or believe something the chances are that it will tend to become normative.

The moment when a 50–50 balance has been reached may be viewed as a time of true normlessness, in the sense that two different norms cancel one another out. Rather than leading to a different normative pattern that then becomes coercive, it may result in the absence of any definitive consensually accepted norm. Such a state of normlessness leaves the adolescent without guidance. He or she does not know which norm to follow; the woman in middle motherhood does not know whether or not to enter the labor force. Anomie results.

In addition to the concept of tipping points I have found it useful to use the concept of *turning points*. Without investing too much time in fine distinctions, I will say only that turning points are here distinguished from tipping points in that they refer to changes in the direction of a curve rather than, as in the case of tipping points, simply a level in a continuing trend in a given direction. A turning point is countertrend, a tipping point is trend-conforming and trend-confirming.

It is admittedly not always easy to distinguish between a tipping point and a turning point. A curve may turn when its tipping point is reached; any curve may hit an asymptote at the tipping point. Birth rates and marriage rates and divorce rates commonly show turning points; they may also show tipping points. The proportion in the labor force of mothers of school-age (but not preschool) children appears to be approaching a ceiling. The upward trend in labor-force participation by women in middle motherhood since 1948 may be interpreted simply as the fancy of one cohort or generation of women, as the feminine mystique was for the generation of the 1950s. There are always pitfalls in projecting statistical trends and always numerous ways to interpret them.

The question arises also, can we prevent a tilt if we wish to do so? Or can we reverse it? Have we turned the tide against the heroin "epidemic"? Did Nixon reverse the trend toward centralized government? Have we reversed the trend toward violence in the cities, as John Spiegel (1973) thinks we have? For him, the Chicago convention and the Kent State shooting "represent the cutoff [turning] point of the old era and the entering point for the new era which we are entering or already have." Is the so-called equilibrium theory correct in the sense that there is a kind of homeostatic mechanism at work that tends to maintain a system and prevent tilts, which puts corrective processes to work when or if it is disturbed so it returns to its original balance or achieves a new one? Will sex roles return to pre-"quake" definitions? I believe not.

TWO SOCIETAL TURNING POINTS

Two turning points relevant for our discussion here have to do with the birth rate since 1957 and the first-marriage rate since the late 1940s. Both will now begin to have important implications for the 15-year-old adolescent girl we are thinking about here as she approaches marriage or motherhood.

The young woman who is 15 years old today was born in 1958, the turning point that marked the end of the era of the feminine mystique. The birth rate, which had crested the year before she was born, now resumed its long-time secular trend downward. She belongs therefore to the first female cohort since World War II not caught in Paul C. Glick's marriage squeeze; there were more boys born in 1956–1957 than girls born in 1958. Young women born during the 1950s with its rising birth rate were caught in the marriage squeeze; there were not enough young men born in the year or two before they were born to become their husbands 20 years later. By 1977, when the present generation of adolescents is age 20, young men a year or two older than they will outnumber young women, who will therefore not be so vulnerable to panic about "getting their man." There will be enough young men of the right age to go around. Indeed, the very concept of getting one's man is, I believe, becoming anachronistic for this generation of adolescents.

The current marriage squeeze, reflecting the rising birth rate of the 1950s, will continue until 1977; young women have been waiting for the young men, with a consequent slight rise in age at marriage. One might expect a return to the lower age at marriage when the squeeze reverses itself to fall on the men rather than on the women. But there is, I believe, reason to anticipate a somewhat different pattern.

In the past, when a young woman—"wired for marriage" by the socialization she had undergone—went to a young man in the marriageable years, what she proposed in effect if not in words was something like this. Please father the two or three children I need for my self-fulfillment; support me while I bear them; support them until they are about 18 years old and me for the rest of my life. In return I promise to take care of your personal needs as long as you live or until you can afford to relieve me and hire others to do so. That was the image of life which formed her mentality, her sexuality, her emotionality. She was set in that course or in the literal sense, career from the moment of birth.

That proposal looked quite reasonable in view of the way roles were structured in the past. It took into account the enormous disadvantage women labored under in the work force; it anchored them safely within the bonds of marriage. It was about the best they could hope for. They got what they were socialized to want, even though in some cases they got it at enormous cost.

Our fifteen-year-old adolescent is not likely to view marriage in this light. She is less likely to think of herself as forever "taken care of" by the man she marries. Her proposal may now take some such form as this: Give me a baby or two for self-fulfillment and help me also in my career or job by sharing with me the costs of motherhood, including any time out from career or job required; in return I will share with you the provider role for the family and help you also in your job or career. The young man—who needs marriage more than she does (Bernard, 1972:Chapter 2)—will feel less reluctant about the financial obligations when they are to be shared. And since the young woman is not necessarily asking for lifelong support nor, for that matter, in a growing though still smaller number, even for children, she is less likely to consider marriage the *ultima Thule* of her life. There are, further, extramarriage life styles available as the rapid increase in female-headed households shows (Bernard, 1968). Marriage itself will seem less important to her.

Thus we might well ask if marriage will have the same urgency for these young women as it had for young women in the past. Will they feel pressured to "get their man" while the getting is good, in the prime years of the late teens and early twenties? If there are going to be agreeable alternatives to marriage, will that make a difference?

We are beginning to get data to help firm up our knowledge and help answer such questions. They come from the analyses of the marriage rate by Paul C. Glick and Arthur J. Norton, who report a strange but interesting downward trend in the first-marriage rate since a turning point in the late 1940s, as shown in Figure 4.1.

I had been watching the overall marriage rate with a great deal of interest for several years. After a steady rise during the early 1960s, it had begun to waffle, leveling off in 1969; it began to show declines from time to time. For the first eight months of 1974, for example, both the number of marriages and the rate were lower than in 1973, indicating a possible reversal of the long upward trend. The 1970 census had shown a smaller proportion of young women 18 to 24 married than the 1960 census. Something, clearly, was happening, but exactly what did not become apparent until the work of Glick and Norton (1973) clarified it. They found that a downturn in the *first*-marriage rate compensated for by the rising *re*marriage rate, suggesting a lessening of enthusiasm for marriage among the young women.

If the downward trend in the first-marriage rate was due to delayed marriage resulting from the marriage squeeze or from such historical war-generated influences as "pressures among young men to continue a college education to ensure draft deferment," it had not been compensated for by 1970 (1973a:306). This leads Glick and Norton to ask whether "a decline in eventual marriage is developing?" (Ibid.:305). They are cautious in their reply. It is "too early to assert with confidence that there is an impending

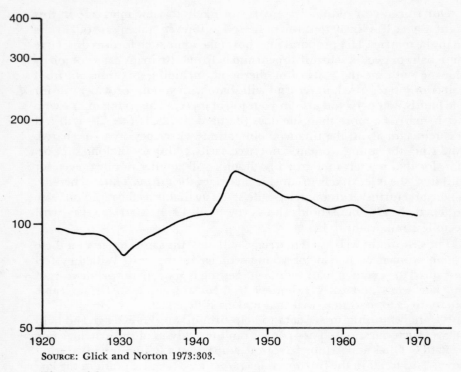

Source: Glick and Norton 1973:303.

Figure 4.1
First-Marriage Rates per 1000 Single Women: United States, Three-Year Averages, 1921 to 1971.

upsurge in lifetime singleness" or, stated more relevantly for our purposes, an impending decline in marriage for oncoming teenagers.

So much, then, for two societal turning points—the decline in the first-marriage rate since the late 1940s, and in the fertility rate since 1957— which, 20 years later, have major implications for today's adolescent girl. They affect the marital matrix in which motherhood as she will know it will be embedded. Both are related to equally relevant tipping points, one having to do with the redefinition of the role of mother now in process and one with the norm of virginity.

TWO SOCIETAL TIPPING POINTS

Figure 4.2 presents a tipping point I consider of major significance for our concerns here. It deals with the proportion of mothers with school-age (but no preschool) children who were in the labor force from 1948 to 1972. In 1972 for the first time the proportion of these mothers who were in the labor force reached a tipping point. To be sure the tilt was not great. (It would

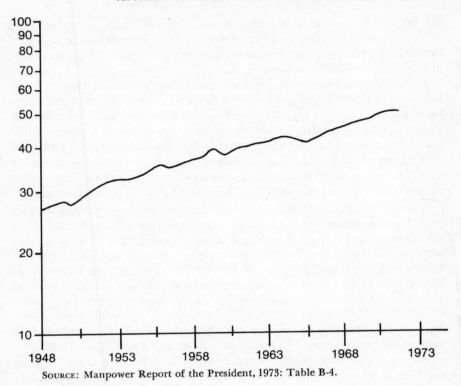

SOURCE: Manpower Report of the President, 1973: Table B-4.

Figure 4.2
Proportion of Mothers with School-Age (but not Preschool) Children in
Labor Force, 1948-1972.

have been greater if it had included mothers who were in the labor force for
as much as a week.) Nor was it rapid. By 1990, when our teenagers will be in
their early thirties, the proportion of women in the age brackets 35 to 44 and
45 to 54—who are most likely to be mothers of school-age (but not
preschool) children—is projected to be still only 55 and 58 percent
respectively (President's *Manpower Report 1973*: Table E2).

These data suggest nevertheless that the role of mother into which
adolescent girls today are to be socialized is in process of redefinition to
involve labor-force participation as well as child rearing. When we face the
adolescent girl we see a young woman who is likely to be simultaneously
both a mother and a labor-force participant for a good many years of her
life. We can no longer socialize her for motherhood without socializing her
also for a serious worker role as well. We have long been thinking of this in
connection with women in the late—or, as sometimes called, the "empty-
nest"—stage of motherhood when their children are over 18 years old. And

the labor-force participation of women in the 45 to 54 age bracket is, indeed, already fairly high—54 percent since 1970. But we must now begin to think of labor-force participation among mothers with school-age children still in the home as well.

A considerable amount of "motherwork" already includes a job, as Ruth Hartley (1959–60) found in her interviews with working mothers some years ago. Adolescent girls can, as noted earlier, no longer assume as a matter of course that they will be taken care of for the rest of their lives once they become mothers. Nor can we any longer encourage a casual attitude toward their work history. The socialization of adolescents for motherhood as it is now coming to be institutionalized calls not only for the acquisition of marketable vocational skills, but also, seriously, for their maintenance.

A second great tipping point has to do with female virginity. Researchers have been watching with a kind of near-voyeurism the changing mores with respect to premarital sexual relations, especially among women— understandably so, for premarital virginity was one of the bedrocks of traditional marriage. Because of the centrality of female virginity, it became one of the major strains in research on marriage and the family as soon as this field was opened up for study. Kinsey and his associates (1953:Table 37) startled an incredulous world with their finding that about half of all the women in his sample—49 percent—had engaged in premarital intercourse. The bald fact was softened when the details were examined. The proportion varied from only 4 percent if the woman married at 14 to as much as 56 percent if she married at age 28. Also mollifying the impact was the further finding that for the most part, the premarital relations were nearly always with the future husband.

Our concern here is not with marital status at first intercourse but with age, for the most recent survey finds the concept of premarital intercourse of only marginal interest. Sorensen (1973:341) tells us, in fact, that the concept of "premarital sex" is becoming "increasingly outmoded, because young people are not scheduling marriage on their life agenda simply to gratify their sexual needs or in order to legalize their sexual relationships." Marital status at sexual initiation is thus becoming increasingly irrelevant. The discussion here deals only with teen-age, not with premarital, intercourse. (Actually only 2 percent of the respondents in the Sorensen sample were married, so, in effect, the data deal almost entirely with premarital sexual relations; the Kantner-Zelnik data deal only with never-married young women). And here the tipping point for teenage young women is shown in Figure 4.3. In 1971, 46 percent of a sample of 4,240 young women had had coitus by the age of 19; in 1972, 45 percent of the Sorensen sample of 181 young women had had sexual intercourse by that age. For young women born in the 1950s the tipping point, 50 percent, will probably be reached around 1976 or 1977.

It will be recalled that during the 1960s there was considerable

Table 4.1

Behavior and Attitudes of Adolescents as Related to Sexual Responsibility, by Age and Experience

ATTITUDE OR BEHAVIOR	NON-VIRGINS			WITH CURRENT INTERCOURSE EXPERIENCE	WITH NO CURRENT INTERCOURSE EXPERIENCE
	ALL	13-15	16-19		
Sometimes worry about becoming pregnant (Tables 451, 452)	70	61	72	71	68
Used contraception first time (385)	19			29	3
Used contraception most recent time (507)				40 (13-15,23; 16-19,46)	
Do not know where to secure contraceptive information (301)	16	32	9		
Precaution taken in past month (481)				62	
Never trusted to luck in past month (503)				63	
Would have abortion if became pregnant (457, 458)	18	2	23	23	3
Would get married if became pregnant (458) a	31			31	30
Have used pills (386)	31	10	39		
Fear has prevented intercourse (476)	44			38	58
Contraception (except pill) too much trouble (308)	45	35	49		
Did not use contraception last time (507)	40	45	38		
Have not thought about getting pregnant in last month (505)				82	
Don't worry because abortion so available (330)	14	21	11		
Have been pregnant (479, 480)	23	11	28	28	7

SOURCE: Sorensen, 1973. Figures in parentheses refer to Sorensen's tables.
a The young man said he would marry the young woman in 27 percent of the cases; he would maybe marry her in 46 percent of the cases (Table 472).

controversy with respect to trends in premarital coitus. There were those who argued that there had been no increase since the 1920s when the great revolution had occurred; there was only more talk about it since then. But there were others who, observing the current scene, could hardly accept this conclusion. They could not prove it but they felt that premarital intercourse had increased (Packard, 1968:124–126).

The research finally corroborated their hunch. Yes, there had been a second wave of change. In 1938, L. M. Terman (1938) had predicted that if the trends he had traced were to continue, no girl born after 1940 would enter marriage a virgin. He was wrong. The sharp rise in the 1920s abated

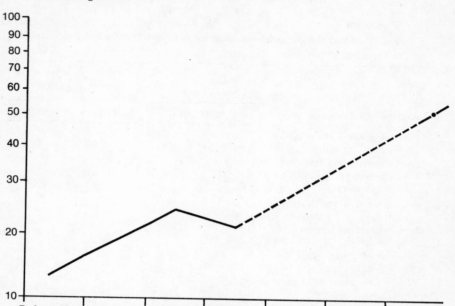

SOURCES: For first four decades, Kinsey and Associates, 1953: Table 83. For the 1950s, Kantner and Zelnik, 1972:9, and Sorensen, 1973: Table 404. The Kantner-Zelnik sample yielded the figure of 46 percent for 1971; the Sorensen sample, 45 percent for 1972.

Figure 4.3
Proportion of Young Women Who Had Sexual Intercourse by Age of 20, by Decade of Birth.

in the 1930s. If they married in their early twenties, half of even young women born in 1950 would still be virgins. But not necessarily young women born later.

The reason for the controversy was, precisely, that we were approaching a tipping point in the 1960s. The young people themselves were talking a great deal about the pros and cons of intercourse outside of marriage, the nature of sexual relations, of marriage, of virginity, and a host of other interpersonal relationships. The talk apparently had its effect.

Another tipping point that may be just ahead of us—or just behind us—has to do with the nature of marriage the 15-year-old adolescent girl will face as revealed in several measures of divorce trends. Figure 4.4 presents three such measures. All show tipping points in the 1970s. The period divorce rate for married women 14 to 44 years of age, which was 28 in 1971 (Glick and Norton, 1973b:67) may "tip" in the last year or two of the decade; the percent of all marriages entered into during the last 35 years that have ended in divorce—40.9 in 1970 (Ibid.:69)—may reach a "tip" sometime next year; and the percent of all marriages that end in divorce seven years later—43.2 percent in 1970 (Ibid.:73)—may have "tipped" in

1972. It is not inconceivable that in the lives of today's teenagers the stable lifelong marriage may become "deviant." Glick and Norton project that about 29 percent of women 15 years older than today's teenagers—born, that is, between 1940 and 1944—will end their first marriage in divorce. The projected tipping point on this measure would come for the generation born between 1970 and 1975 (1973a:311).

There is, of course, no reason to believe that the current upward trend in divorce will continue forever. The tipping points may prove to be turning points, for we know that divorce rates fluctuate over time. The rates may level off and even decline. Still, in reply to their own question, "Is the upward trend in divorce 'phasing out?'" Glick and Norton (1973a:311) reply that although "a levelling off or decline in the divorce rate must come sometime . . . such a change is still awaited."

What we may be witnessing is the approximate form which current experiments in life styles are heading for, either the two-step form of marriage that Margaret Mead has predicted or at least some form of experimental or limited or temporary marriage, dissolved when it fails and followed by a more stable and permanent relationship.

The relevance for motherhood and the adolescent girl can be inferred. She will have to be socialized for a form of motherhood which does not have the supports it has had in the past, weak as such supports proved to be all too often. The more fluid kinds of relationships will have to provide for any children that result. Although men are increasingly asking for and accepting a greater share in the rearing of children, for at least the immediate future it will remain easier for men than for women to renege on parental responsibilities. Although more and more women are rejecting custody of children in divorce, still the preconceptions of judges continue to influence them in granting custody to mothers. The general loosening up of sexual relations and the lag in contraceptive practice by young women also increases the probability of mother-supported children. Bennett Berger and associates (1972) in their study of the anarchist communes in the West noted that young women, knowing that ADC support was available, were more willing than young women in the past to engage in transitory sexual relations that might end in conception.

OTHER RELATED TIPPING POINTS

A change with respect to standards—an increase in what Ira Reiss calls the permissive standard—is also related to changes in adolescent practices regarding sexual intercourse. In 1964 I noted that "there was a time when those arguing for premarital virginity could be assured of a comfortable margin of support in the group [NCFR]. This is no longer always true. Especially the younger members no longer accept this code. A more permissive position is emerging" (1964:32). Somewhere along the line a

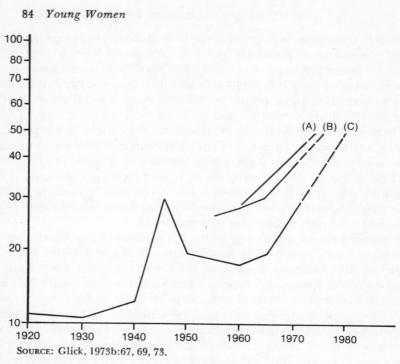

SOURCE: Glick, 1973b:67, 69, 73.

Figure 4.4
Trends in Three Measures of Divorce, 1920 to 1971. A, Period divorce rate for married women 14 to 44 years of age; B, Percent of marriages of at least 35 years of duration ending in divorce; C, Ratio of divorces to marriages seven years earlier.

tipping point had been reached. The work of Ira Reiss (1967), though dealing primarily with college-age students rather than with teenagers, has shown the rise of this more permissive standard. The precise date of the tipping point cannot be pinpointed, however.

One tipping point of interest to our 15-year-old adolescent girl has to do with the man she marries. Among white male high-school graduates 20 to 24 years of age, the tipping point for college entrance came in 1968. Since then at least half of all white male high-school graduates have been going on to college. In 1972, it was 53.3 percent (Bureau of the Census, 1973). This means that the chances are better than ever that at least the white 15-year-old adolescent girl will marry, when or if she does, a man who has had some college education. I do not underestimate the importance of this fact. Several years ago a survey of young people by the Daniel Yankelovich (1969) polling service showed us that the great divide was between college and noncollege youth rather than between the generations. I have noted elsewhere that dealing with any system primarily composed of the college-educated is different from dealing with one with a less educated personnel.

Marriage, we know, is different among the college educated, as is motherhood. Related to this tipping point is another one relevant for our teenager. In 1972 for the first time the proportion of male freshmen entering college who hold to the woman's-place-is-in-the-home ideology fell below half (American Council on Education, 1972). The tilt here is in the direction of a more feminist position. The chances are good that around 1976, when the 1972 entering freshmen are graduated, a larger proportion will be tilted toward a feminist position. A study by Bernice Lott (1973:577) shows that the mean score on a liberation scale of college men is almost as high (18.49) as that of women (20.26).

Yet another related tipping point relevant to the adolescent girl that cannot be located with precision but can be documented in the research literature has to do with the image of the career woman. After a period of denigration, the image of the career woman has been rehabilitated. She is no longer viewed as a deviant eccentric, a misfit, a victim of inauspicious family trauma (Helson, 1972). Indeed, Zella Luria (1972) now warns us against putting sanctions on the college woman who is not career-oriented.

There are doubtless other tipping points at this very moment which we have no trend data to document. But whether there are or not, we know of enough of them to conclude that the years we are now living through, the early 1970s, are witnessing a tilt in the institutional structure of our society of truly spectacular magnitude. Such tilting will surely have profound influence on the motherhood today's teenager will engage in.

Before proceeding to developmental turning points in the lives of the young women themselves, a brief aside on the significance for adolescent girls today of the societal turning and tipping points summarily reviewed above is called for. I believe they will have the effect of giving young women more control over the contingencies which, as Glen Elder has so cogently noted, have dominated their lives in the past. Elder reminds us that:

> A life style dependent on marriage and the husband's career are features of a woman's contingent life. Depending on the man she marries, a young woman's occupational plans and preparations may be invalidated, modified, or receive the support needed for eventual fulfillment. Lacking control over this event, on which everything seems to hinge, most young women have been understandably reluctant "to take their future careers seriously" during the pre-marital years, or even until after the childbearing and rearing phases of marriage (1974).

It seems to me that although for most young women these contingencies still persist, the general tiltings in the institutional structures of our society dealing with work, marriage, and motherhood will give more and more young women increasing control over the contingencies that control their lives. Decisions about marriage and motherhood will be more subject to their own preferences, and the men they marry will increasingly expect them to be. I do not foresee arrogant rejection of husbands' preferences. The young women I know expect to respect them. The vignettes presented at the end of this chapter flesh out these comments.

III. Developmental Turning Points

Although opposed to the concept of development which implies an orderly sequence of changes, the concept of the psychological turning point is old in the folk mind. The best known in the Christian world is the case of Saul on the road to Damascus. The psychology of conversion has confirmed the reality of that kind of experience. The member of Alcoholics Anonymous who recounts his story further confirms the reality of such individual turning points. Most of us have heard people tell of events or experiences that changed them completely from one course to another. The magazine *Ms* (O'Reilly; 1972) has reported the "click" phenomenon among women; it refers to the critical moment when a woman's consciousness suddenly is raised by some remark or incident to the chauvinism in the world about her. In a way such "clicks" constitute turning points. A new definition of reality creates a new reality for her. Her world "tilts" in a new direction.

Parents report their uneasiness as they observe their children teetering between two worlds, fearful that something may happen to "tilt" their lives in the—to them—wrong direction. The son's downfall dates from the moment he met John; the daughter's, from the day she met Mary, or John, as the case may be.

In a study of mother-daughter relations, women college students were asked to write autobiographies. The young women with middle-class backgrounds wrote vaguely and nondramatically of their personal histories. The upwardly mobile young women with working class backgrounds, who showed the psychological malaise that characterizes those we used to call marginal, were different. They frequently noted critical experiences that changed the course of their lives, such as the change resulting from having an ethnic boyfriend, or from a college course. These experiences changed their reality and, they thought, their whole lives (Millman, 1973). In a way the Freudian approach is a form of the crisis concept. One traumatic experience at the age of 4 or earlier, one glimpse of the primal scene, could lead directly to the psychiatrist's couch years later.

But this approach does not lend itself easily to the hard-nosed research techniques so favored today. The crisis that can be subjected to agentic style research must be the garden variety, expectable ones. Adolescence does offer examples of this kind. Sexual initiation, at whatever age, is such an expectable "crisis" that lends itself to the turning-point approach.

An enormous literature documents the sexual initiation of boys. It has been said that almost every first novel is such a document. But though the loss of virginity has been a far more serious turning point for women than for men—loss of virginity in Western cultures almost universally leading to lowered status if not disgrace—few novels deal with it except if it results in pregnancy. When it does, it, too, becomes a major theme. The seduced child, the raped girl, the seducing young woman are—perhaps morbidly—fascinating figures.

It is interesting to note that in all the schema for developmental stages in women, based as they are almost exclusively on childbearing, so little attention has been paid to the importance of sexual initiation. There has been an overwhelming preoccupation with virginity and the importance of preserving it until marriage; the girl's whole life seemed to be centered on protecting it, as did an all-pervasive institutional structure designed for that purpose. Chaperones, restrictions, a thousand little rules of etiquette were devised to keep the girl's virginity intact. In our society it would not have been absurd to label the years in a young woman's development between, let us say, 16 and 20, as the "stage of virginity protection." Be that as it may, the adolescent now entering the scene has had less exposure to the concept of marriage on which the cult of virginity rested. Virginity of women at marriage is important to only 23 percent of young men 16 to 19 years of age (Sorensen, 1973: Table 103).

Sexual initiation does, in fact, constitute a turning point in the development of adolescent girls:

> Once she has had her first sexual intercourse, a girl often feels different about herself—not deprived or bereft of her virginity, but different *within* herself. She seldom feels raped or violated by the experience, although she may feel her first sex partner was insensitive. She does feel more mature and experienced—but in a mildly defensive sense. She sometimes feels the need to rationalize what she has done and to feel more sympathetic with girls who have also had their first sexual experience. This reaction is not diminished even when she continues to have intercourse with the same or other boys. She is, as one girl told us, "now on the other side of the fence," or, as another girl put it, "You're like trying to justify it in your mind . . . so you change your views really drastically." Many girls characterize their first intercourse as a "learning experience;" girls many times more frequently than boys report reactions of guilt, sorrow, and disappointment (Ibid.:190).

Sexual initiation changes an adolescent's relationship not only with herself and her peers but also with her mother. The one and, in many cases, only ground for superior status or claim for authority of a mother vis-à-vis her daughter is sexual experience. She has been initiated; the daughter, according to the mores so far, has not. But sexual experience is a great equalizer. Once the daughter has been initiated, once she, too, shares the adult secret, a major support for the mother's authority is gone. Even "sex education" short of actual experience may add a card to the daughter's hand.

Sexual initiation changes the perception of self among teenagers. "They view their bodies differently. They react to their sexual partners, to their families, and to society in a different way because they perceive themselves differently" (Ibid.:203).

In view of the significance of this turning point, it is of interest to learn that the age at which it occurs among young women as of 1971–1972 is just over 20 years. Among the teenagers who have had intercourse, the modal age at first intercourse is 15, the median, between 15 and 16.[6] A comparison between those 13 to 15 and those 16 to 19 suggests that there may be a movement toward even earlier age at first intercourse, since it had occurred at age 16 among the older girls, but at only 15 among the younger (Ibid.; Table 405).

The crisis nature of pregnancy among teenagers, especially among unmarried young women, needs no elaboration. Inside or outside of marriage early pregnancy—because the earlier the first child is borne the larger the total number of babies borne will be—is not only "demographically disastrous," but also almost determinative of a restricted life history for the mother thereafter. This fact is of interest to educators and social workers who try to head off the dysfunctional results of such early pregnancies, as well as to demographers and those responsible for policy. It would, therefore, again be carrying coals to Newcastle to review the comments of the Commission on Population Growth and the American Future (1972:168) on this point. Their recommendations on the subject were that "(1) states eliminate existing legal inhibitions and restrictions on access to contraceptive information, procedures, and supplies; and (2) states develop statutes affirming the desirability that all persons have ready and practicable access to contraceptive information, procedures, and supplies." But, as we saw earlier, socialization of girls—let alone boys—for the use of such information, procedures, and supplies even when available is quite another matter, a matter we are not now expert in dealing with. Among white young women in the Kantner-Zelnik sample, 10 percent of the sexually experienced had had a pregnancy and more than 40 percent of the black young women (1973:31); in the Sorensen sample, more than a fourth (28 percent) of the nonvirgin teenagers aged 16 to 19 had experienced a pregnancy (1973: Table 479).

6. The data on age at first sexual intercourse are not entirely comparable for the Kantner-Zelnik and the Sorensen data. The first included more black respondents and the second, more younger subjects. The Kantner-Zelnik data show that "the likelihood that a young never-married woman 15 to 19 years of age has experienced coitus rises from 14 percent at age 15, to 21 percent at age 16, to 27 percent at age 17, to 37 percent at age 18, and to 46 percent by age 19" (Kantner and Zelnik, 1972:9). The corresponding figures in the Sorensen sample of young women 12 to 19 years of age were: 25 percent by age 15; 34 percent by age 16; 37 percent by age 17; and 45 percent by age 19 (Sorensen, 1973, Table 405).

The age at sexual initiation is related to the age at menarche, which has been declining for over a century and seems now to have leveled off at the age of 12. The significance for motherhood of a growing spread between age of menarche and age of marriage cannot be ignored in our thinking about socialization for motherhood in adolescence.

IV. Feminism, Motherhood, and Today's Adolescent

As Diana Baumrind notes: adolescence takes on the character of the society that creates it. The adolescent girl today lives in a society in which feminism is exerting an impressive influence. For this reason, when we consider the socializing of adolescents for motherhood we should also consider the way in which feminism deals with motherhood.[7]

The feminist movement is clearly not a disciplined phalanx with a sacred revealed text. It has had to hassle a number of issues. One of the most difficult was that of lesbianism, an issue that for a while looked capable of splitting the movement. An accommodation has now been reached. The movement became secure enough to accommodate lesbians and non-lesbians without insisting that either persuasion obliterate or dominate the other. Feminists can accept choices in the matter of relations between the sexes, provided that the choices be purely voluntary, not coerced.

Now emerges an issue—as yet no larger than a cloud on the horizon the size of a man's fist—dealing not with relations between the sexes but with motherhood. Some of the most talented early feminists were vehemently antinatalist. Not only were they hostile to the maternal role but they also actively propagated the idea of mechanical gestation to minimize women's role as mothers. More recently women with a strongly pro-motherhood point of view have become articulate and active, extolling the joys of motherhood and breast feeding (which they may engage in until the child is 3 years old). For some this cult of motherhood is merely a personal preference; for others it is an almost knee-jerk reaction against the rampant antinatalism evoked by the environmental movement. Any kind of pressure on women—anti- as well as pronatalist—is rejected.

For teenagers, this motherhood issue carries political as well as individual implications. Although there is no official feminist "line" on

7. Only issues relevant to motherhood are commented on here. The most serious issue in the early years was between political and strictly feminist emphases, the politicos, so-called, wished to subordinate strictly female issues to general socialist ones; the feminists wished to emphasize the strictly female issues. That struggle is not pertinent in the present context.

motherhood, the antinatalist feminists—like other antinatalists—have criticized the Movement's support of child-care centers, provisions for maternity leave with pay, and other services for mothers. Because such efforts to help women integrate their roles as mothers and as labor-force participants assume motherhood as an inevitable choice for women, the antinatalist feminists consider them misguided.

If the emphasis on choice, which is a fundamental belief of feminists, is to be achieved—as I believe it will be—there will be no difficulty. Neither a pro- nor an anti-motherhood position will be taken. The emphasis will be on voluntary motherhood, with no hard feelings for those who disagree with one's own preference. OK, have your babies but don't put us down if we don't. Or, conversely, OK, don't have any babies, but don't put us down if we do. The issue of motherhood will certainly be resolved, as was the issue of lesbianism.

Until recently high-school girls showed an apathetic reaction to feminism. Poorly informed, they tended "to see 'women's libbers' as 'a bunch of man-haters and bra-burners.'" They found the "implied rejection of men . . . very threatening." And, at their age they had not yet experienced "the full impact of conflicting values" rampant in our society today, nor could they "anticipate what their lives will be like after graduation" (Carden, 1973:30). Since 1970, however, high-school groups have increasingly asked for speakers on the subject of feminism. Perhaps the hostile antinatalism that characterized some of the early leaders has now been dissipated, rendering the movement more congenial to the young women. In fact, some feminist groups see in "children's liberation" a way to make them better mothers: "a group from New Haven commented: 'although most of us are rejecting the Freudian notion that the only fulfillment of a woman's life is her children, many of us see children as a beautiful and important part of our lives. We want to be able to provide settings which will allow our children to grow and develop happily'" (Ibid.:192). Feminism is seen by these mothers as guides for rearing their children.

Age makes a difference in young women's opinions of feminism. In 1972, although only a third of the 13- to 15-year-olds (32 percent) believed that the women's liberation movement was good for women, almost half (47 percent) of the 16- to 19-year-olds did, the nonvirgins (51 percent) more than the virgins (37 percent) (Sorensen, 1973: Table 268).

Whether or not there is an official rapprochement between feminists and high-school girls, many high-school girls follow the lines delineated by the feminists. For example, a 1970 survey of YWCA teenage leaders indicated that by that time a tipping point had been passed. About 60 percent of the respondents favored child-care facilities outside of the home, believed men should help with household chores, and felt that a man's identity should not be given priority at the wife's expense (Carden, 1973:159). As leaders these respondents are, by definition, ahead of the young women they deal with. But if they are, in fact, harbingers, young women are being socialized for a style of motherhood consonant with the times.

Young women rarely ask the old marriage-versus-career question now. More and more they ask instead, What *else* am I going to do besides being a mother? They take the "else" for granted. Taped interviews with eight high-school seniors, 16 and 17 years of age, recorded by Eleanor Thompson in 1972, show that neither marriage nor motherhood is the sine qua non of a fulfilled life. Only three were unequivocally for motherhood; one would adopt children; two did not plan to have children; and two were equivocal. Certainly early marriage was not their preference. Mid or late twenties was favored among the seven who planned to marry; the one who planned to adopt children wanted to wait until she was close to 40. Late twenties and early thirties were the preferred ages for childbearing. All took some sort of profession for granted (four in science, two in the arts, one in law, one in medicine). The contingencies Glen Elder has noted are recognized: they expect to have husbands who will share their career interests and assume their share of household and parental functions. They do not want to marry men who would not accept such responsibilities. They wish to take care of their children inhhe early years (althoughsome are unrealistic about how long they could take out of their professional careers for this), but they do not wish to become the martyred, self-sacrificing traditional mother. To put flesh on these bare bones, vignettes of these young women are appended.

Eight Vignettes of Contemporary Adolescents

1.

Motherhood "just seems the logical step for me after I've done everything I'd ever want to do. . . . Once I get married, I think I'll just kind of give up on the career and do what I can to keep up with it. . . . I really enjoy biology and there's no way that anybody's going to keep me from doing what I want. . . . [Before marriage] I would like at least to have accomplished a little something. . . . I would like to know I'd done something . . . and that somebody would develop what I started out with". Preferred time to marry, mid twenties; to have children, late twenties and early thirties.

2.

Her future will "possibly include motherhood" despite "anti-feelings due to conditions in society." But recently, "I've been thinking maybe I would [have children] . . . The father will have to take more of a part in the family, will have to be a parent. . . . Hopefully I can pursue both marriage and whatever career I may choose. . . . The mother image isn't the total parental image . . . so she doesn't become the great martyr who gives up everything for her children. . . . I wouldn't start a family until I knew I could function independently on my own. And once I was a mother, I wouldn't give up my whole life. . . . I have images, after I get out of college, of spending a few years *not* settling down—doing something where . . . you had lots of time to travel. . . . [Hopes for] "a very liberated life style, not the kind of thing that one day I'll say to myself, 'I'm in a rut.' Hopefully I'll always be free to make more choices in my life. . . . For a while I thought motherhood was dying. But I think it'll change so that it'll not be the all-inclusive facet of being a woman. But I don't think it will die out. It will continue, but it won't be a woman's reason for existing. That'll change." She wants one or two children when she is in her late twenties. Recognizes she will be influenced by her husband but hopes that will not change her plans.

3.

"When I get married I'm not going to do all the dishes and cook all the food. My husband will help out. . . . The woman who sits around the house all day and mends the clothes and washes the dishes and all that stuff is . . . very boring. Mothers should get out and do things. . . . I'm going to go into architecture, and I'm going to work for a while before I even plan on getting married. . . . When the children are small I could be a draftsman . . . at home. If I went into architecture and the guy I married was going into teaching—well, a lot of times an architect will make more than a teacher. So I might say, 'Look, I can go into architecture and you can stay home with the kids, because I'll be making more money.' . . . He'd probably be upset because the man is supposed to bring home the money; it might be a problem. It would depend on financial need. . . . My mother feels I should go to college and the first week I'm out of college I should marry some guy and have six kids. . . . I'd like to work for a while first. Maybe I'd . . . get good at it, get a decent salary. Then maybe I'd think about getting married. Just so I'd accomplish something. Not just to be a woman so you can have babies and perpetuate life. I would naturally not marry some guy who had completely different views from mine." Wants not more than two children.

4.

"As of now my plans do not include motherhood. Partly because I want to 'save the world' and I plan to be very involved in that, and partly because of my own convictions that this world cannot support an expanded population. I don't see any way I can successfully deal with raising children and with my own career. In the future I may see how this could happen but I don't see it right now. . . . The changes up to now have already affected me. In the future I think it will be easier for me to do what I want to do and not face so much of 'Oh, you haven't had any children yet? Oh, that's sad.' I think people will realize that not to have children is also a sound choice. What I do won't necessarily be what most people do. . . . I assume I will get married eventually, maybe in ten years. . . . I imagine I will spend most of my life working. I can't see myself getting out of my career . . . just to raise children. I can't see that it's that important in our society. It would be unfair to marry someone who wanted to have children . . . but also it wouldn't be fair to me to make me give up my career to have his children. I don't believe I could ever marry a man with whom I could not have this understanding. I just hope it [motherhood] becomes more of a choice for women rather than a foregone conclusion. Then our society will become liberal enough so that any woman who decides to have children—that's fine. And any woman who decides not to have children—that's equally fine, equally good, can be seen to be equally logical and reasonable. I think both choices are equally legitimate."

5.

Motherhood, yes, but "I see a real dilemma, since I want to get a law degree and have a career, and I don't know if I'll have time to raise a family. I love children and I want to get married, but it might be difficult if I were a lawyer, to be a good mother, which is something to think about. . . . You have to combine them [marriage and career]. I just don't see how you could be happy just being a housewife. . . . I wouldn't mind getting married when I was in my third year of law school. But I think I'd want to have a life of my own . . . and just be free, in a sense, and independent because I feel like for the rest of my life I won't be, so why not try to prolong it as long as possible. . . . If I'm a good mother, and a loving mother, I don't know that maybe those hours in the day when I went to work would really matter. I doubt we'll ever get to the stage where men are at home with the children as much as women are. I chose law because of the state of the world. I just felt I wanted to do something. I didn't want to just sit home and watch what was happening or read about it in the newspaper. I wanted to be involved and I wanted to help."

6.

"I want to have a career as a doctor, and I don't think I will have time for marriage because I don't want it. It's just that I was in a family that was very unhappy, and I've seen motherhood with my own mother. It didn't work for her and I don't trust myself that it would work for me. I'm pretty sure I won't change my mind. . . . I would like to be a medical officer on a ship. I want an exciting and dangerous life. I'm an adventurer. That's my problem.''

7.

"I've been thinking that because of the population explosion I would want only two children of my own but maybe adopt some. . . . I notice [changes] in young people, just talking about them. Girls complain about their fathers' male chauvinism toward their mothers, and even boys do. One boy I was talking to at school was complaining about how his father dominated his mother. And if boys take this attitude, then I don't think they'll dominate their wives. . . . If a woman has a career and she's as well educated as a man, she shouldn't be tied down with all the housework duties. And the man shouldn't come home from work and put his feet up and rest for the rest of the evening. The woman has worked all day long, too. . . . I feel that the man should take more part in raising the children. I would force more of the responsibility for the children on my husband. I would definitely not drop my career to raise a family. While taking time out from career to raise children I could be taking courses to back it up and help keep in touch with it without actually working or maybe I could do part-time work. . . . I don't want to be stationary in a suburb. . . . I'd like to get into my career first and then [around 27 or 28] get married. . . . If you just get married after you get out of college chances are you won't get back into your career, You start having kids and you're tied down with them. . . . If my husband doesn't like my career, that's his problem. I'm not going to have my interests changed by my husband. But I imagine if he disapproved of my career then I wouldn't have married him in the first place.''

8.

[Wants no children of her own; she will adopt.] "If I fall in love with someone who has been into drugs, where the genes have even a possibility of having been 'messed up' I don't want to run the risk of having children who would have to live with not being whole. I would be more willing to adopt children anyway. There are plenty of children. . . . For a woman not to have a career while she is married is almost foolish, because she's giving her life away to her children. If I got married at all, I would expect to share the housework and the financial support. . . . I would like to see the mother image changed from the mother who stays at home all the time with the children to the mother who teaches the children, gives herself to her children, and has a life of her own also. And it's very possible because of day care and because of the changing ideas of many men. . . . I could probably work at home [in art, her career choice] and have my children with me a good deal of the time. But it would be a good experience for the children to spend some of their time in a day-care center. . . . I don't really foresee getting married until I'm close to 40. Maybe I would want the emotional security, although right now I don't feel that I need that much. . . . I might adopt an older child rather than a baby. . . . I would try to show my husband that I derive as much pleasure from my career as he does from his."

References

American Council on Education, Staff of the Office of Research. 1972. *The American freshman: national norms for fall 1972.* Washington, D.C., ACE.

Baumrind, Diana. Berger, Bennett M.; Hackett, Bruce H.; and Millar, R. Mervin. 1972. Child rearing in communes, in Howe, Louise Kapp, ed. *The future of the family.* New York: Simon & Schuster.

Bernard, Jessie. 1964. Developmental tasks of the NCFR—1963-1988. *Journal of Marriage and the Family* 26:29–38.

———. 1968. Present demographic trends and structural outcomes in family life today, in Petersen, James A. ed., *Marriage & family counseling, perspective and prospect.* New York: Association Press.

———. 1972. *The future of marriage.* New York: World. Bantam, 1973.

———. 1974. *The future of motherhood.* New York: Dial. Penguin, 1975.

Brandwein, Ruth A. 1973. The single parent family revisited. Paper presented at meetings of the Society for the Study of Social Problems, Fall, New York.

Bureau of the Census. 1972. *Birth expectations and fertility: June 1972.* Series P-20, no. 240 (September).

———. 1973. *Characteristics of American youth: 1972.* Series P-23, no. 94, March).

Carden, Maren Lockwood. 1973. *The new feminist movement.* New York: Russell Sage.

Davis, Judith Blake. 1972. *Coercive pronatalism and American population policy.* Berkeley: International Population and Urban Research, September.

Elder, Glen. 1974. *Children of the Depression.* Chicago: University of Chicago Press. (Present citation from manuscript version).

Erikson, Erik. 1968. *Identity, youth and crisis.* New York: Norton.

Friedan, Betty. 1963. *The feminine mystique.* New York: Norton.

Glick, Paul C., and Norton, Arthur J. 1973. Perspectives on the recent upturn in divorce and remarriage. *Demography* 10:301–314.

———. 1973b. Dissolution of marriage by divorce and its demographic consequences. Liege: International Population Conference.

Hartley, Ruth E. 1959–60. Some implications of Current changes in sex role patterns. *Merrill-Palmer Quarterly of Behavior and Development* 6:153–164.

———. 1970. American core culture: Changes and continuities, in Seward, Georgene H. and Williamson, Robert C., eds. *Sex roles in changing society.* New York: Random House.

Helsen, Ravenna. 1972. The changing image of the career woman. *Journal of Social Issues* 28:33–46.

Hollingworth, Leta S. 1916. Social devices for impelling women to bear and rear children. *American Journal of Sociology* 22:19–29.

Kantner, John F., and Zelnik, Melvin. Sexual experience of young unmarried women in the United States. *Family Planning Perspectives* 4:9–18.

——— . 1973. Contraception and pregnancy: Experience of young unmarried women in the United States. *Family Planning Perspectives* 5:21–35.

Kinsey, A. C., and Associates. 1953. *Sexual behavior in the human female.* Philadelphia: Saunders.

Klein, Carole. 1973. *The single parent experience.* New York: Walker.

——— . 1973. Socialization of the child in voluntary, single parent homes. Paper presented at meetings of Society for the Study of Social Problems, Fall.

Lott, Bernice. 1973. Who wants the children? *American Psychologist* 28:573–582.

Luria, Zella. 1972. Women college graduates. Presidential address, New England Psychological Society, November.

McBride, Angela Barron. 1973. *The growth and development of mothers.* New York: Harper & Row.

Millman, Marcia. 1973. Autobiography and social mobility: life accounts of working-class daughters. Paper presented at meetings of Society for the Study of Social Problems, Fall, New York.

Moynihan, Daniel Patrick. New York. 1973. "Peace"—Some thoughts on the 1960s and 1970s. *The Public Interest* 32:3–12.

National Center for Health Statistics. 1971. Births, marriages, divorces, and deaths for August 1974. *Monthly vital statistics report* 23 (October 24, 1974):1.

Newton, Niles. 1955. *Maternal emotions.* New York: Hoeber.

New Jersey NOW Task Force. 1972. *Dick and Jane as victims.* Princeton: Published by authors.

O'Reilly, Jane. 1972. The housewife's moment of truth. *Ms* 1 (Spring):54–55, 57–59.

Packard, Vance. 1968. *The sexual wilderness: the contemporary upheaval in male-female relationships.* New York: David McKay.

Peck, Ellen. 1972. *The baby trap.* New York: Pinnacle.

President's Commission on Population Growth and the American Future. 1972. *Population and the American Culture.* New York: Signet.

President's Manpower Report. 1973. Washington, D.C., U.S. Government Printing Office.

Preston, Samuel H. 1972. *Female employment policy and fertility.* report of the President's Commission on Population Growth and the American Future. Reproduced.

Radl, Shirley. 1973. *Mother's Day is over.* New York: Charterhouse.

Reiss, Ira L. 1967. *The social context of premarital sexual permissiveness.* New York: Holt, Rinehart, and Winston.

Sanger, Margaret. 1928. *Motherhood in bondage.* New York: Brentano.

Sorensen, Robert C. 1973. *Adolescent sexuality in contemporary America, personal values and sexual behavior ages 13–19.* New York: World.

Spiegel, John. 1973. Quoted in Donovan, Robert J. U.S. said solving violence problem. *Washington Post*, September 3, 1973.

Terman, Lewis M. 1938. *Psychological factors in marital happiness.* New York: McGraw Hill.

Yankelovich, Daniel. Generations apart: A study of the generation gap. New York: Columbia Broadcasting System.

Thompson, Eleanor. 1972. Taped interviews. Unpublished.

PART III

MOTHERS IN TRANSITION

IN THE PAST WOMEN WERE differentiated primarily in terms of childbearing. They were in the prechildbearing stage, in the childbearing stage, or in the postchildbearing stage of their lives; otherwise there was little individuation. In the bloom of youth there was some individuation when men had to choose wives from among them, but when they became wives and mothers they became, except for those they served, nonentities for all intents and purposes. Pretensions to individuality, aside from their families, were frowned upon, at least until the recent past.

Momentous changes are now in process in the role of wife and mother. More and more women are combining labor-force participation with marriage and motherhood, with repercussions that ramify widely through all their other relationships. Old patterns such as those subsumed under the rubric "momism" suffer attrition and finally disappear. New patterns, such as those subsumed under the rubric "returnee"—women who return to school when they are no longer house bound with small children— emerge. Consciousness is raised and women come to see themselves as individuals in their own right; they seek independence of their children. They want new kinds of relationships, with men, with one another, with their children, with the world at large.

The first paper sketches the life patterns of women as they are evolving today;[1] the second sketches some of the options available to women at the

1. For detailed discussion of early motherhood, not dealt with here, see Jessie Bernard, *The Future of Motherhood* (Dial Press, 1974), especially Chapter 5.

present time; and the third offers a reflection of the past as it works itself out among older women. All these women are in transition not only from one stage in their own lives to another stage, but also—all of them—from one era to another. Each generation trails its own past with it into the present, but it also creates a new present to serve as the past for succeeding generations.

FIVE

Ages and Stages of Motherhood

The Idea of Stages

Motherhood, if not childbearing, lasts a long time in the life of a woman. Too long, some people argue. It is not, however, the same throughout its course. It is one thing when it involves a 22-year-old woman and an infant, it is quite another thing when it involves a 37-year-old woman confronting a teenager, and yet another when it is a relationship between a 45-year-old woman and a young married son or daughter, or when it involves an aged woman who has become a charge to her adult sons or daughters in a reversal of roles. The relationship is, therefore, between different people at every moment of time. But the changes do not occur at a steady pace. The woman of 20 has changed less by age 22 than her infant child has in the same two chronological years. The time span between her thirty-second and thirty-seventh birthdays changes her less than it changes her child, now passing through his or her twelfth to seventeenth year. The mother of a small child is always dealing with an individual moving faster than she is. It is hard to keep up; she is always being amazed at the new person she is facing. She has no sooner come to terms with a child than the child becomes someone else. In the "failing years," however, the mother may be changing more rapidly than the adult son or daughter.

The idea of life as a series of stages through which one moves is an old one (Cain, 1964:272–309), and the nomenclature given to the stages reflects the society in which they take place. Latin, reflecting a fairly sophisticated society, distinguished seven stages; as late as the middle of the sixteenth century, French distinguished only three (Ariès, 1962:25). We are all familiar with Shakespeare's seven ages: mewling and puking infant, whining schoolboy, lover, soldier, justice, the old man, and, finally the senile man. Other schemes differentiated the age of toys, of school, of love and sports, of war, of law, science, and learning (Ibid.:24–25). And we know that as our own society becomes increasingly complex we have had to add new stages, such as adolescence and youth.

It is clear, however, that none of these conceptualizations of the ages of— literally—man, with their emphases on male activities, is very helpful in understanding the lives of women.

The Life Cycle of Women

The few existing conceptualizations of the stages in the lives of women have nearly always been in terms of childbearing. A woman's life was divided into premenarchical years, childbearing years, and postmenopausal years.[1] In the past, and even today in some cultures, only one other criterion has approached childbearing as a basis for classifying the critical points in the lives of women; a woman was a maid, that is, a virgin, or she was not, for sociologically if not biologically the sexual initiation of a woman marked one of the most significant transitions of all for her. And even this criterion for demarcating stages was indirectly related to childbearing.

For modern women more is required. At least the childbearing and child-rearing period calls for more differentiation. Helena Lopata has delineated five adult stages in the lives of women in terms of social roles and role-clusters: the stage of becoming a wife and housewife, becoming a mother, a full-house plateau with increasing community involvement, a shrinking circle stage when children leave home, and gradual disengagement (Lopata, 1971:43). Each of these stages involves fundamental changes and requires a good deal of psychological adjustment.

Another study of working-class women delineates five adult life-stages for women: premarital, "a period of dedicated man-hunting"; early marriage, "a relatively trying stage of life"; early children, "a stage in which working-class women have traditionally 'stayed put,' emotionally bogged down, . . . overly busy and tired, demanding and complaining"; late children, a stage when "Working-Class women are beginning to assert or rediscover that they do not need or want to be perpetual mothers and

1. Parenthetically, one might note that there has been a substratum of disparagement for each of the succeeding stages. With the menarche, a woman became periodically unclean. With sexual initiation she lost her chief asset, her virginity. With childbearing she lost her sex appeal. With menopause she lost her reason for being. Every stage entailed a downward step.

housewives"; and post-family, "a focal point [among younger women especially] for much of the independence and flexibility, bounty and liberality which are beginning to appear in the modern Working-Class outlook" (Coup, Greene, and Gardner, 1973:133–135).

Seminal though these characterizations of the several stages of motherhood may be, they are not wholly adequate for modern women. More is required because, as we have been learning, women nowadays are more than bearers and rearers of children. At least two perspectives, therefore, are called for if we want to understand women today, let alone the future. It takes two research streams to supply the knowledge of the life cycle of women today, one dealing with the role of mother and one with the role of worker.

The Interweaving of Roles: Changing Patterns

One research tradition was pioneered by Paul C. Glick and has to do with such major demographic events in the lives of women over their entire life span as birth, marriage, motherhood, and bereavement. The second has to do with work histories and how the mother and worker roles weave in and out.

On the basis of 1950 data, Glick showed us the critical points in the lives of women as of midcentury. Women married on the average at the age of 20, had their last child at age 26, were 48 years old when their last child was married, and 62 when they lost their husbands (Glick, 1955). This seminal work has colored a good deal of our thinking ever since.

But as the worker role began to play an increasing part in the lives of women, it became clear that seeing them solely in terms of the mother role was inadequate. Their lives were far too complex to be encompassed in such simplistic formulations. We had to take some account of both her maternal and her worker roles. Imaginative work by students of the labor force, combined with Glick's research has finally provided us with fairly good models for the stages in the lives of modern women. We now know fairly well the life pattern of women in this century and the part both motherhood and work play in it. We can now, thanks to these studies, catch a glimpse not only of the extent of labor-force participation but also of the changes it has undergone in relation to motherhood.

These changes have been spectacular. In 1957 the National Manpower Council (1957:10) summarized some of them:

> At the close of the last century, about half the adult women never entered paid employment. Now at least 9 out of every 10 women are likely to work outside the home in the course of their lives. Women who

reached adulthood around the turn of the century participated in paid employment, on the average, for 11 years in the course of their lives. Those who reached adulthood just before World War II are likely, on the average, to work over 20 years. Today's schoolgirls may spend 25 years or more in work outside the home.

In 1960, the average number of years of labor-force activity left for a 20-year-old working woman was 45.3 years if she remained single; if she married but remained childless, it was 34.9 years; if she had one child, 25; two children, 22 years; three children, 20; and even if she had four or more children, as many as 17 years (Garfinkle, 1969).[2] In view of these trends, it is unrealistic to think of modern women without paying respects to their role as labor-force participants.

Even more interesting than the mere fact and extent of labor-force participation is the way the timing of paid work has changed in relation to marriage and motherhood. In the past practically all of the labor-force participation of women came before marriage and motherhood. Now most of it comes after marriage and even after motherhood. A variety of patterns have been delineated showing the many ways women have attempted to combine their two roles sequentially and concomitantly (Bernard, 1971: Chapter 4). For the most part, although decreasingly, a sequential-concomitant pattern is typical today. After a drop in labor-force participation in the childbearing and early child-rearing years, the curve of labor-force participation rises dramatically until at the age of 45 to 54—when in the past they were already worn out with childbearing—over half of all women, still vigorous, are in the labor force; over a third of women with children under 18 are.

The changing patterns of labor-force participation over time are shown in Figure 5.1. Each line shows the pattern for a different generation of women, beginning with those born at the turn of the century (1896 to 1905) and including those born between 1936 and 1945. The low point in labor-force participation receded from the ages 35 to 44 in the two older cohorts to the ages 25 to 34 in the lives of women born between 1916 and 1925 and between 1926 and 1935, but among the younger women—those in their late twenties and thirties today—there has been shown no decline from a labor-force participation rate of 45 percent as yet. "Whether the young women now in their twenties have simply postponed having children and will later drop out of the labor force or whether many will continue to work,

2. Michael P. Fogarty, on the basis of Soviet experience, tells us that "it looks as if a professional woman in the Soviet Union might possibly be available for work outside her home for perhaps 13–14 percent less time than a man with a similar qualification" (Fogarty, Rapoport, 1971:76). He cites N. T. Dodge's *Women in the Soviet Economy* (1966) to the effect that the time women lose through having a typical number of children—two—in the Soviet Union is about 6 percent of her professional working life. Other factors, especially earlier retirement, add another 8 percent. All factors combined thus amount to about 14 percent.

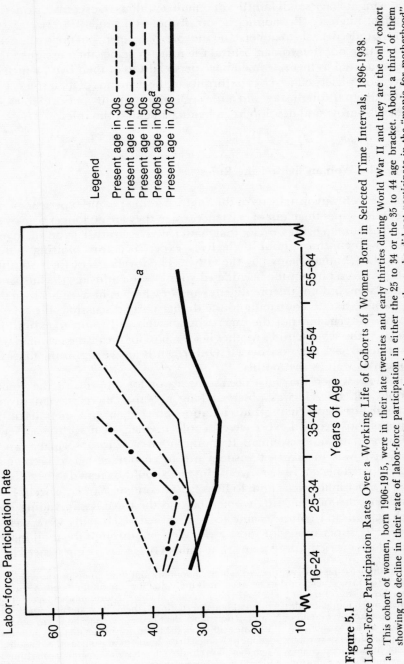

Figure 5.1

Labor-Force Participation Rates Over a Working Life of Cohorts of Women Born in Selected Time Intervals, 1896-1938.

a. This cohort of women, born 1906-1915, were in their late twenties and early thirties during World War II and they are the only cohort showing no decline in their rate of labor-force participation in either the 25 to 34 or the 35 to 44 age bracket. About a third of them were in the labor force during these years. They must have been among those who did not participate in the "mania for motherhood" that characterized the postwar era of the feminine mystique.

choosing to have small families or remain childless is, of course, a question of great interest" (Economic Report of the President, 1973:95).

It is, indeed, basic to understand the roles of women; but not to the extent of blotting out the woman behind the roles. Whether their assigned roles are congenial to them, women have personalities of their own, which are never completely effaced by conformity to the demands of their roles. They not only go through stages in a life cycle, they not only perform roles, but they also grow and develop as individuals behind the roles.

The Woman Behind the Roles

Simone DeBeauvoir tells us of the anguish aging people experience when the Other wipes them out of existence, when they are no longer seen by the Other as human beings, or, for that matter, even seen at all. In an analogous way, women throughout their lives experience this blotting out as individual human beings by the Other. The loveliness of their youthful bodies is seen but not the bewildered young women inside; the husband's wife is seen, but not the intelligent woman who has ideas of her own that she would like to contribute to the dinner party discussion; the infant's mother is seen, but not the eager woman who still wants to exhibit her sketches; the schoolchild's mother is seen, but not the restless woman who wants to go back to school herself. Only recently are we beginning to see the woman as well as the mother.

In the past there may have been some reason for suppressing the woman behind the role. It was observed long ago that there was an inverse relationship between the individuation of women and their fertility.[3] Autonomous women who were people in their own right had fewer children than other women. If motherhood was to absorb the whole woman it was the part of wisdom not to encourage her to become an individuated person in her own right. She should be reared to be satisfied with *Kinder* and *Küche* and, to help her be content, *Kirche* as well. Even when the idea of educating women beyond the three Rs, including even high school and college, came to be accepted, such frills were seen as essentially superfluous for most girls. We went through the motions but the hidden curriculum remained the same. Girls were going to need little

3. In the past the time required to achieve autonomy and individuation was enough to explain the inverse relationship between such individuation and motherhood. A study by Kenneth Keniston (1971) of highly individuated women today reports another factor. These young women found the idea of motherhood threatening to them, alien and unwanted. They wanted control over their bodies and in pregnancy their bodies were acted upon by processes they had no say-so about. All this quite aside from the unvarnished fact that in a cash-nexus society that does not pay for work done by women in the home, most women are economically dependent during pregnancy. When they have children they have, as Francis Bacon reminded us, given hostages to fortune and are dependent on its whims.

beyond a bare minimum. Anything that encouraged independence was a threat to their future "careers" as bearers of children. Under the veneer of equal educational opportunities for both boys and girls, the development of girls was one of preventing or discouraging individuation rather than encouraging it.

It is still true that the most individuated women have fewer children. But as fewer children are going to be wanted, the problem of developing all women for more than reproduction looms large. Until now dependency not, as in the case of boys, autonomy has been the key concept in the development of girls. It cannot remain so in the future.

Developmental Stages

The concept of development was first used in connection with physical growth; it dealt with the maturing of inborn potentials and implied a logical progression from one level to another. One crawled before he or she walked, spoke before he or she wrote. Thus certain changes in the several organs, in growth rate, in neurological and other capacities could be plotted in advance; the mature organism was implicit in the infant and would develop in its own time. In the 1950s the development of behavior in infants was refined by Arnold Gesell and his associates at Yale until it could be specified that such and such behavior was to be expected at six weeks, such and such at nine weeks, and so on. A similar developmental schedule for intelligence tests had already been worked out by Terman, following Binet, in the so-called intelligence tests. And Piaget had formulated another scheme for intellectual development, as Freud had for sexual. So far so good.

But when the developmental concept was extended to include social and moral as well as physical and mental traits the situation became more blurred. Now development was viewed not as the unfolding of a potential inherent in the organism but rather as progress toward some socially approved goal, some character or moral trait that the researchers valued. Role-learning became a major focus. In one set of guide posts for child growth and development, for example, learning one's psychic-socio-biological sex role became a developmental task.[4] Kenneth Keniston delineated five developmental stages; the goals were interpersonal mutual-ity, full sexual genitality, ego autonomy and integration, principled moral

4. Other developmental tasks included: the achievement of an appropriate dependence-independence pattern; achieving an appropriate giving-receiving pattern of affection; learning how to relate to changing social groups; developing a conscience; accepting and adjusting to a changing body; managing a changing body and learning new motor patterns; learning to understand and control the physical world; developing an appropriate symbol system and conceptual abilities; and relating one's self to the cosmos.

judgement, and postrelativistic commitment to a world view (**Keniston**, 1971), clearly role-related.

One of the most influential developmental models was propounded by Erik Erikson. The characterizing aspect of this model was that development was not a more-or-less predetermined process, the surfacing on schedule of certain physical or role dimensions. It was, rather, a sequence of "developmental tasks" which called for "psychological work." Further, there was, at every stage, the possibility of being derailed. In each of the eight stages delineated by Erikson one could go either a desirable or an undesirable route. Thus, for example, during the first two years one could develop either trust or mistrust; during the second or third year, autonomy or doubt; at 4 or 5, initiative or guilt; from 6 to 11, industry or inferiority; from 12 to 18, identity or role confusion; in young adulthood, intimacy or isolation; at middle age, generativity or self-absorption; and thereafter, integrity or despair (Erikson, 1963: Chapter 8).

Especially influential was Erikson's stage of youth with its concepts of identity, role confusion, and crisis. Erikson noted that the study of identity phenomena came only as we entered the industrial age, when identity became a problem; but in these historical circumstances, "the study of identity . . . became as strategic . . . as the study of sexuality was in Freud's time" (Ibid.:282). In the developmental stage of youth, according to Erikson, young men must achieve such identity or suffer role confusion:

> The integration now taking place in the form of ego identity is . . . the accrued experience of the ego's ability to integrate all identifications with the vicissitudes of the libido, with the aptitudes developed out of endowment, and with the opportunities offered in social roles. The sense of ego identity . . . is the accrued confidence that the inner sameness and continuity prepared in the past are matched by the sameness and continuity of one's meaning for others (Ibid.:262).

As in the conceptualization of the life cycle, so here, too, the models have tended to be those suitable for the development of men, not of women, as Erikson himself admitted later on (Erikson, 1968:26).[5] As a result of this neglect we have been less successful in finding suitable models for the developmental stages of women as human beings, as distinguished from merely biological beings on one side or role-performers on the other, than in pinpointing the stages in their life cycle or in their labor-force participation.

True, we do know about the pace of early physical and mental development of girls as compared to that of boys; we know about the

5. Even women scientists have emphasized the pattern of men's lives. Thus Charlotte Bühler (1935), who began a long time ago to study "the curve of life," based her work on biographies of artists, athletes, engineers, business people, doctors, explorers, officers, officials, and salesmen. The only women who appeared in her studies were teachers, nurses, and servants.

synchronization of development or lack of it between the sexes at different ages. Still, a great deal of the story of female development as told by researchers so far seems to be primarily a story of increasing deviation from male patterns and hence of relative defectiveness as measured by male standards. And when we go beyond physical and mental development, the story becomes even more barren.

And so far as "a sense of ego identity" is concerned, there is in the case of women little of the "inner sameness" and "continuity" that Erikson's definition specifies, either within themselves or in relation to others. Rather, we discover a series of discontinuities which subject women to a series of identity crises.

Developmental Discontinuities

Ruth Benedict (1938) has labeled as developmental discontinuities the sharp changes that occur at critical points in life. The stages of biological development are full of such discontinuities: the infant discontinues the breast at weaning; the pubescent girl and boy discontinue their childish activities; age brings its own discontinuities. Role-related stages also show discontinuities, many of them marked by rites of passage. Puberty becomes more than a physical or biological fact; it is also a social or role-related fact.

Among the discontinuities in the lives of girls is one at about the age of 8 when the little girl who has been developing toward independence, as has her brother, is now unlike him, deflected toward the achievement not of autonomy, but of dependency. Another occurs at marriage when the young woman, socialized into accepting dependency, finds that it will not now be indulged, and that she will have to supply the dependency needs of her husband.

Yet another discontinuity—and perhaps the most crucial of all—occurs with motherhood. The physical or biological discontinuities in the woman's body that occur with childbirth are fairly well known; at least there is an old research tradition that can predict such changes. We have long known about some of the mental discontinuities, such as puerperal psychosis. But the potential for serious trauma present for even normal young mothers as they find themselves assigned sole responsibility for the care of a dependent infant is only now becoming subject to fundamental research (Rossi, 1968). Among the many recent movements activated by youth, blacks, women, ethnics, the elderly, and gays, there is now emerging another, this time of young mothers. They are beginning to protest the way the role of mother is institutionalized in our society today (see Bernard, 1974: Chapter 5). The story is far too complex for documentation here but its omission in no way detracts from its significance.

When the last child enters school a discontinuity is precipitated in a woman's life that is new in our history. The woman now has a choice of roles. She has to make decisions. There are options available to her. For an increasing number of women an identity crisis ensues. It is at this point that we pick up the developmental story in Part III.[6]

6. Since the above was written my attention has been called to interesting research now in process on the development of women by Gail Sheehy and Roger Gould. Like me, Gail Sheehy had been frustrated by the fact that a growing and sophisticated corpus of research on human development at both Yale and Harvard, though perceptive and stimulating, did not include women. Women were viewed only, in effect, as props in the development of men. But in the department of psychiatry at the University of California at Los Angeles she found work by Roger Gould that included women. They decided to work together. Their results are not yet available.

References

Ariès, Philippe. 1962. *Centuries of childhood*. New York: Knopf.

Benedict, Ruth. 1938. Continuities and discontinuities in cultural conditioning. *Psychiatry* 1:161-167.

Bernard, Jessie. 1971. *Women and the public interest, An essay in policy and protest*. Chicago: Aldine.

———— . 1974. *The future of motherhood*. New York: Dial. Penguin, 1975.

Bühler, Charlotte. 1935. The curve of life as studied in biographies. *Journal of Applied Psychology* 19:405–409.

Cain, Leonard D., Jr. 1964. Life course and social structure, in Faris, Robert E. L., ed., *Handbook of modern sociology*. Chicago: Rand McNally.

Coup, Roger F.; Greene, Shirley; and Gardner, Burleigh B. 1973. *A study of working-class women in a changing world*. Chicago: Social Research.

Dodge, N.T. 1966. *Women in the Soviet economy*. Baltimore: Johns Hopkins University Press.

Duvall, Evelyn Millis. 1957. *Family development*. Philadelphia: Lippincott. Based on Tryon, Caroline, and Lilienthal, Jesse W. III. 1950. Guidepost in child growth and development. *National Education Association Journal* (March) 39:189.

Economic report of the President. January, 1973. Washington, D.C.: U.S. Government Printing Office.

Erikson, Eric. 1963. *Childhood and society*. New York: Norton.

———— . 1968. *Identity, youth and crisis*. New York: Norton.

Fogarty, Michael P.; Rapoport, Rhona; and Rapoport, Robert N. 1971. *Sex, career and family*. Beverly Hills: Sage.

Garfinkle, S. Work in the lives of women. 1969. Paper presented at the meetings of the International Union for the Scientific Study of Population, London.

Glick, Paul C. 1955. The life cycle of the family. *Journal of Marriage and the Family* 17 (February):3–9.

Keniston, Kenneth. 1971. Themes and conflicts of "liberated" young women. Karen Horney memorial lecture, March, 1971.

Lopata, Helena. 1971. *Occupation housewife*. New York: Oxford.

National Manpower Council. 1957. *Womanpower*. New York: Columbia University Press.

Rossi, Alice. 1968. Transition to parenthood. *Journal of Marriage and the Family* 31 (February):26–39.

SIX

Middle Motherhood

I. Continuing Options

EMOTIONAL BENDS

The stage of early motherhood in which middle-class as well as "working-class women have traditionally 'stayed put,' emotionally bogged down . . . overly busy and tired, demanding and complaining" (Coup, Greene and Gardner, 1973:134) finally passes. For the day finally arrives when the last child has entered school. And middle-class as well as working-class women begin "to assert or rediscover that they do not need or want to be perpetual mothers and housewives" (Ibid.:135). They are in their middle or late thirties or early forties according to the number of children they have had and their age at the birth of the last one. A new stage in motherhood has arrived and will last until their children become young adults. The bondage to the home that they have been held in by the presence of small children is loosened.

The woman at this stage of development may experience a kind of emotional "bends" as she is "decompressed." The urgent demands of pre-schoolers subside; she experiences a kind of euphoria—she is no longer house bound, no longer a "captive housewife." For the first time in many years she is not pushed to keep up with the demands of her children. For the first time in several years she can begin to look around and see what's going on around her. For the first time in many years it begins to dawn on her that she is still a human being with at least a potential identity of her own.

If the psychological work or developmental task of marriage had been to come to terms with the realization that she had to supply the dependency needs of her husband, of early motherhood that she had to bear the entire responsibility for the care of infants and small children, the psychological work of middle motherhood is going to be to achieve a new identity of her own, including lowered dependency vis-à-vis her husband and greater freedom from the demands of her children.

WOMAN'S PLACE AGAIN

At middle motherhood women face the problem of how to reconcile the role of mother with that of productive worker. It is a somewhat different problem now from what it was in early motherhood. In early motherhood the weight of maternal responsibilities was heavier; in middle motherhood it has become attenuated, especially when the children reach adolescence. The pros and cons of labor-force participation are therefore more nearly equal. So nearly equal, in fact, that half of the women living with their husbands and with children of school age—but no preschoolers—elect, for whatever reason, to enter the labor force. The proportion has almost doubled since 1948, from 26 percent in that year to more than 50 percent in 1973. If we include divorced, separated, or widowed mothers, the proportion is even higher—55 percent for those with children under 3 and 73 percent for those with school-age children only.[1]

So long as discussion of career or labor-force participation by women applied primarily to unmarried women, it did not apply to mothers except tangentially. When, in the inexorable wake of labor-force participation by married women—which increased from 16.7 percent in 1940 to more than 40 percent in 1973 *(Manpower Report, 1974:* Table B-2, p. 166)—it turned to working wives, it came nearer and nearer to motherhood. By the late 1960s, for quite extraneous reasons related to women on welfare rolls as well as to the new feminist movement, the focus of interest turned to working mothers. And now, though popular polls still showed the persistence of the woman's-place-is-in-the-home ideology, women themselves were "voting with their feet."

Strange, then, as it may seem, women in their thirties were back again at the old female dilemma, marriage or career. Not as it had been conceived 50 years ago, as a choice for young, especially college, women only, but as we were now learning as an ongoing choice, a choice no longer limited to the stage of youth. Women were now faced with the same choice at any age when they were no longer house bound with small children. They could choose at any point to remain a housewife or to resume their careers.

1. Data for married women living with husbands are from *Manpower Report of the President 1974,* Table B-4:291; data for single, divorced, and widowed mothers are from Dickinson, 1974.

By the time enough of them had voted with their feet so that the ratio between working and nonworking women in middle motherhood approached equality, the temper of popular discussion of women's place began to change. Until now the balance had favored the women who remained out of the labor force. By the late 1960s it was beginning to tip. Now women who did not enter the labor force began to feel on the defensive. In the past, the old "marriage versus career" option had been one in which the choice once made was made for good. Now it was a continuing one, never finally sealed. The permanent availability of a choice precipitated new identity problems.

THE IDENTITY CRISIS OF MIDDLE MOTHERHOOD

The young woman's identity which, according to Erik H. Erikson, had been defined by her attractiveness and by the man she married (Erikson, 1963:283) proved to be a weak reed upon which to build an entire life in the modern world. The physical attractiveness of youth has changed in middle motherhood to a quite different—though, as we are now learning, not a lesser—kind of attractiveness. The man she sought has become a quite different man, too. In any event, neither of these components of female identity is now very relevant for what Erikson calls the core problem of female identity,[2] namely a "biological, psychological, and ethical commitment to take care of human infancy" (Ibid.:266). Where does this leave women when they have fulfilled that commitment, when the care of human infancy is no longer called for? And where is the "accrued confidence that the inner sameness and continuity prepared in the past are matched by the sameness and continuity of one's meaning for others" (Ibid.:262) with which Erikson charactered ego identity? What continuity? What sameness? Certainly not in her relations with her children. Middle motherhood brings as many discontinuities into the lives of women as marriage did, and almost as many as early motherhood did. A new adult identity crisis is now pending.

On the basis of a more-or-less random set of observations, I once placed the critical age for women at 35 or thereabouts. Not until then did they find it possible to free themselves from a triple bind: dependency on mother, dependency on husband, and bondage to their children. It might come a few years earlier or later, but whenever it did come, the light at the end of the tunnel was bright and clear. "If she is not [liberated] by this time, she probably never will be and will remain immature for the rest of her life. Her lingering dependencies are now likely to be severed. . . . She finds herself now or she is probably lost for good" (Bernard, 1956:277–278). Dependency

2. The term Erikson uses is *female fidelity,* but the context makes it probable that he is referring to female identity.

on husbands has been undergoing slow erosion; women have learned that, aside from economic support, husbands do not always supply dependency needs. Bondage to children is not in the same category as dependency on mother or husband, for since children can always claim their mother's help, the woman, though not dependent on them, is not independent of them either. But at least she is free from bondage to their infantile dependencies. A beginning is being made. I gave as illustrations the cases of Elizabeth Barrett Browning, George Eliot, and Eleanor Roosevelt.

Eleanor Roosevelt's identity crisis was an almost textbook example. In her case it was precipitated by her husband's relationship with another woman.

> It was a time for her of harsh self-reproach and depreciation, of desolating conviction that she had failed as a woman. . . . But bitter as the experience was, it also matured her. Slowly she won through to the realization that she could not achieve fulfillment through anyone else. "Somewhere along the line of development we discover what we really are," she wrote in 1941, "and then we make our real decision for which we are responsible. Make that decision primarily for yourself because you can never really live anyone else's life not even your child's. The influence you exert is through your own life and what you become yourself." She buried herself in work. . . . "My experience has been," she wrote in later years, "that work is almost the best way to pull oneself out of the depths." (Lash, 1971:325)

She now ceased to be intimidated by servants. She began to assert more direct supervision over the upbringing of the children. There were costs, to be sure, as there always are in growth. She suffered great weariness, "another manifestation of the conflict within her between a nature seeking to find its true vocation and the life of conformity that the effort to please her husband and mother-in-law had shaped" (Ibid.:333). In time she became capable of losing her temper with her mother-in-law, of refusing to be always available for her mother-in-law's friends and charities, of rejecting a subordinate position. "She did not want to be a name on a letterhead, an ornamental woman, without a job of her own to do. She wanted to be fully involved—with work, with people" (Ibid.:353). And so, indeed, she did become involved. She became as much an individuated human being as her husband was.

Different women emerge from the triple bind—mother, husband, children—at different rates, in different styles, and in different ways. And some, of course, never do it at all. But "the question—'Who am I? Am I merely my husband's wife and my children's mother?" (Lake, 1973:22) still haunts them. It is being asked today by many American women, along with the even harder question, Who do I want to be?

OPTIONS

Closely related to all aspects of the identity crisis of middle motherhood is the decision to participate or not to participate in the labor force. Which identity is more appealing to them? Which role do they prefer? Or what combination of roles? How much autonomy do they really want? And what are the concomitants of their choice for them, for their husbands, for their children?

Of the half who decide to enter or to return to the labor force, some (1) resume careers interrupted by the early years of motherhood if, in fact, they ever left their careers. Others (2) find themselves back in jobs that are below their actual potential, but that are the best they can hope for with old training no longer very valuable in the labor market. Some are back in school for retooling, hoping to return to the labor force in middle-level, people-oriented positions. Some are just trying to get back on the track after being temporarily derailed by marriage and early motherhood.

Among the women who opt to remain at home, at least three situations may be distinguished. In one, (3) although the women do not wish to enter the labor force, they feel conflicted about their choice. In another, (4) the women are satisfied with their status, feeling that they "have a good thing going"—"the price is right" and they do not wish to change it; and in still another, (5) women have surrogate "careers" in the form of community work and volunteerism.

There is no reason to believe that the women who choose any of these ways of meeting the identity crisis of middle motherhood constitute homogeneous "types." In each of the categories there is without doubt a wide variety of temperaments, talents, personalities, and religious persuasions. Like women everywhere and always, they are individual human beings, alike in some ways, different in other ways.

We do know, to be sure, how career-oriented women differ from home-oriented women in the earlier years.[3] But people change with time. The girl who was career-oriented in college may be happily domesticated 20 years later. And the girl who was home-oriented at 20 may be fed up with domesticity at 45.

CAREER MOTHERS

Although women in professional and managerial careers constitute a relatively small proportion of the entire female labor force—about a fifth— they have been the subject of a disproportionate amount of research. The problems they face in combining professional careers with family obligations constitute the subject matter of a burgeoning literature.[4] The

3. Some of these differences are sketched in Bernard, 1971: Chapter 1.
4. Much of the literature is sketched in Bernard, 1971.

so-called dual- or two-career family has been subjected to detailed scrutiny. In general, the same findings lead to the same recommendations, including more flexible work schedules, "parenthood leave" for both men and women, greater involvement of fathers in child care, and child-care centers with staffs including men as well as women (Holstrom, 1972; Rapoport and Rapoport, 1971).[5] An English study adds improvement of all the service occupations on which professional mothers depend, improvement of child-care provisions, and overcoming the common prejudice against career mothers (Rapoport and Rapoport, 1971). Practically all studies comment on the "overload" to which professional mothers are subject since, in addition to their professional obligations they are usually also held responsible for the family's welfare. Almost uniformly the woman's profession is considered less important than her husband's (Bernard, 1974: Chapter 9), and if in a crisis a conflict arises between the obligations as parent and as professional—a child has been injured—it is the mother rather than the father who is required to assume the parental obligation.

As mothers of young children, professional women tend to emphasize the importance of independence and discipline; nonprofessional women the importance of protectiveness and empathy. The professional woman wants her child to be prepared to cope; the nonprofessional, to have emotional security (Von Hering, 1955). Both act according to the way they see the child's best interest.

Career women are among those who countered the forces making for dependency in their early development and have, at least to a feasible extent, achieved autonomy. They have, somehow or other, managed to retain professional interests during the years of early motherhood and are now ready to reenter the mainstream. They have to face all the problems of retooling, of discrimination, of professional recognition, and the like, as well as the problems of their relations with their families. We do not do much to help them (Bernard, 1972: Chapter 5).

MOTHERS WITH JOBS

There are, next, women who, like most men, have jobs rather than careers. They do not wish to make the serious commitment called for by careers but they wish to be in the mainstream. The incentive to enter the labor force may be monetary, and indeed the bias in the past against employment outside the home has been so strong that the only acceptable reason for taking a job was money. Thus when working women are asked why they work they almost unanimously give money as the reason. Formerly, so strong was the disapproval of women who took jobs for any other reason,

5. See also Bernard, 1974: Chapter 9.

that only the necessity of self-support was fully respectable. If their husbands could not supply a good enough income for a respectable standard of living, that might also excuse labor-force participation. (But that was a double-edged sword; it may have exonorated the woman but it denigrated the husband.) Or if a woman had dependents she was responsible for, OK. But any woman living with a husband who had an income capable of supporting her—at even a modest level—should not take a job.

Nowadays some of the monetary reasons given by women workers have been a drop in the husband's income, payment of family debts, payment for credit purchases, help in putting a child through college, hospital bills, music or dancing lessons for the children, and travel. "Pin money," that is, money not in any way committed to the family but available for the woman herself, has also been reported, but even yet it does not loom large (Women's Bureau, 1969:8–9). Since women who work at least in part because they want to be in the mainstream, to achieve at least a modicum of independence, to escape the isolation of the household are even yet disapproved of, they tend not to show up in the research in large numbers. They give more acceptable reasons.

Whether recognized or not, however, more is involved than money. As the satisfactions derived from motherhood face attrition, other sources must be found:

> When the youngest child enters school the mother is left with a day full of housework rather than mothering. . . . Satisfactions from "family inter-relationships," which include the mother role, diminish when the child enters school. While 58 percent of the non-working mothers of preschool children mention this source of satisfaction, only 41 percent of the non-working mothers of school children do so. It is possible that the greater the joys of mothering are for a woman, the more empty the days when the children are all in school. Even women who were satisfied with the housewife role before there were children may not be content to return to it. They have been used to a fuller and, in many ways, a richer day, and the house-cleaning tasks may seem less important and more boring than ever.
>
> The period when the youngest child enters school can therefore be very difficult for many mothers. Not only is the child physically absent from the home, but he is less dependent on the mother, and for some women this is a great loss. Just as many women themselves wish to remain dependent, some also wish to have others remain dependent on them. This is a time when mothers often feel they are no longer needed and their major role is over. They may feel, too, that they are growing old or at least that they have lost the vigor of youth. Thus, the mothers who return to work when their youngest child enters school may be motivated not only by practical reasons—i.e., they are now more dispensable to the household—but also by psychological reasons,

namely, the dissatisfactions that emerge at that time (Hoffman, 1963:29-30).

In recent years, therefore, new reasons for labor-force participation have become acceptable. And as a result an interesting new conceptualization of the role of mother in middle motherhood is beginning to emerge. The woman who had no other raison d'etre than to take care of children is receding. Labor-force participation is increasingly rationalized in behalf of husbands and children. The worker role is interpreted as, in fact, contributing to the welfare of the family. The woman who works relieves her husband of the weight of her dependencies, a weight that may have had a damping effect on the marriage. She also serves the interests of her adolescent children by helping them achieve independence. The worker and the mother role are assimilated, the first becoming, in effect, a component of the second.

Thus a popular journal advocates entering the labor force in order to overcome dependence on husbands. "If years of marriage have narrowed your interests . . . maybe it's time to get a part-time job. . . . Develop another side of yourself. You'll be less dependent on your husband (Brothers, 1972:152). And another woman writes in a Reader's Exchange in a metropolitan newspaper that developing an identity of her own by taking a job will allow her husband to develop interests he has of his own, without suffering guilt (M.G., 1972). This advice reflects a nugget of ancient wisdom. Some years ago a moving picture based on the Blue-beard theme introduced a novel twist to this idea. The wealthy man, instead of destroying his last wife, endowed her with a fortune of her own, thus freeing her from her dependence on him. Thereafter she became a far more interesting and attractive companion to him. She did not lose her appeal, as the earlier wives had, and become an incubus rather than a pleasure. The moral was unequivocal: A woman's dependencies can become a bore, a burden, to her husband. Entering the labor force was a way of pleasing him.

In a family therapy experiment sponsored by the National Institutes of Health, it was found that most of the mothers who took part in it later went to work or back to school. The therapist explained that "the women discovered that they could exist as separate individuals in their own right; they no longer need to live only for their husbands and children" (Tolmack, 1972:8). This proved to be a plus because, having discovered their own potential and having restored their self-esteem, they no longer projected on their families the dislike they had felt for themselves.

Employment is justified also as contributing to the well-being of children. Among the replies evoked by a question on the subject of part-time employment was one that advised women to consider more than the merely monetary factors: "a woman might not think it worth the effort to work [part-time] and pay most of her salary for household help, but perhaps she ought to look forward to the day when her children leave home to lead lives of their own. . . . A job outside the home will help a woman develop her own identity." Then, in true mother-role style, the author demonstrates that developing her own identity is good for her family also; developing her own identity "will help her children gain their eventual freedom more easily" (M. G., 1972).

It is especially interesting to note that the new arguments in favor of labor-force participation by women in middle-motherhood play up part-time employment. The assimilation of the worker and the mother roles is easier if the mother has a part-time job. Among the reasons given for the benign effects of part-time employment are that it reflects less on the husband's presumed failure; it is less likely to produce guilt, it enriches the woman's life and makes the maternal role more gratifying, and it emphasizes independence in the children.

> Thus, part-time employment may help the mother of an adolescent to move from the role of protector and nurturer to that of independence trainer thus enabling both mother and child to adapt more easily to this period of transition before the child leaves the family for adult status. Part-time employment is a less abrupt change for both than full-time employment. And it may be less of a change psychologically for the mother than non-employment since it enables her to fill the void and retain a feeling of contribution to the family (Hoffman, 1963b:198).

The research evidence on the effect of mother's employment on children is reassuring. On the basis of anxiety, adjustment, school grades, and personality, children of employed mothers do not differ from the children of nonemployed mothers. And neither school performance, psychosomatic symptoms, nor affectional relations to the mother seem to be related to the employment status of mothers among adolescents (Ibid.:119–120).[6] In a Canadian study, daughters of employed mothers had memberships in fewer clubs, organizations, and teams and more sons were taking lessons in dancing, dramatics, speech, art, or music (Propper, 1972:419).

For some women, of course, the choice of identities—worker or mother—is not a very real one. It is a matter of enough food on the table. But for an increasing number there is a choice. And, apparently, for an increasing number the choice is made on the basis of achieving an identity in their own right and justified on the basis that it is good for other family members also.

So far so good. There is nothing especially new about these women except in the rate of their increase. They have, presumably, found their identities as both mothers and as labor-force participants and arrived at an

6. See also Ferriss, 1971:106.

accommodation of the two sets of roles. The fact that they are returning to the labor force, either to careers or to jobs, does not, however, mean that the problems of reconciling the roles has been solved. Scores of measures for helping them carry their double load are still called for. Questions are increasingly being raised as to why husbands should not share it. There are many hurdles left to be removed so far as implementing the two roles are concerned. But for these women at least a choice has been made.

This leaves the other half of the mothers with school-age children, but no preschoolers, to be considered. The really tough hassles are among them.

II. The Other Half

AN OLD CONFLICT

There has been a long-standing conflict between women who preferred the sheltered protection of conventional marriage and those who wished to participate freely in the labor force. In the nineteenth and early twentieth centuries the most serious opponents of the women's movement were conventionally married women, secure in their dependence on their husbands. As late as midcentury, career women were still the "bad guys," "castrating females," deviants. Housewives consistently devalued them (Lopata, 1972:51–53). But some began to take the reverse position, that the achieving women were not the villains but that they were, in effect, the victims.

David Riesman, for example, noted that there was a "tacit league of educated housewives accusing working mothers of neglecting their families" (1964:xvi–xvii). And John Eells, Jr., was urging us to "devise honorable and ethical means of protecting our talented women from untalented women" (1964:37). And on a panel of outstanding women achievers, Lillian Hellman in 1972 noted that "the most vigorous [achieving] of ladies always envy the most unvigorous [nonachieving] of ladies," while Carolyn Heilbrun commented on the "envy of those 'unvigorous' women" and noted that it had become apparent to her "early in life how miserable they were" (1972).

Career women and working mothers had been on the defensive well into the twentieth century. The dependent, feminine, home-centered housewife had been the one who received the accolade. The women who insisted on pursuing their own interests, who left the home to take jobs were severely criticized. They were unwomanly. The homebody certainly did not have to defend herself. She was carrying out God's plan.

Not until the middle of this century did a tip in the balance begin. Now it was publicly recognized that women did, indeed, have a right, even an obligation, to participate in the labor force. And not only unmarried women but wives also. And, as time went on, even mothers.

By this time there began a housewife's backlash. Housewives began to complain that they were being put on the defensive, that there was so much acceptance, approval, even honoring of career and working women that they were made to feel denigrated if they did not also enter the labor force. Alva Myrdal and Viola Klein, in a reissue of a highly influential work first published in 1956, were saying in 1962 that "prejudices against employing married women . . . are on the wane, and the practice of going out to work at least part-time has become so widespread among women in their thirties and forties, irrespective of social class, that those who fail to do so now almost have to give an explanation for staying at home" (Myrdal and Klein, 1962:xi).[7]

THE CONFLICTED HOUSEWIFE

The real anguish today may thus occur among the women who do not really want to enter the labor force, who want to remain home, sheltered and protected. They feel put down, denigrated by the emphasis on autonomy among the avant-garde. This is especially likely to occur among women who did well in college. One study comparing them to professional women asked to what extent homemaking and child rearing offered them sufficient satisfaction. It found these women "friendly and compliant" as girls, and avoiding aggressive play. Such a woman "now describes herself as very conventional, dependent and not at all competitive. Her personality style is built on muting of self assertion and aggression and affirmation of love, nurturance and self-sacrifice. Fearful of attenuating family relationships, she avoids employment. Motherhood is her focal life role and she derives a sense of purpose and vitality as well as some vicarious achievement satisfaction from her large family" (Birnbaum, 1971). Despite all these apparent pluses, however, "she currently is experiencing some distress, has low self-esteem and perceives herself as neither attractive to men nor especially competent" (Ibid.).[8]

It is doubtless among these women that a great deal of the distress that characterizes women is found. They do not show it. Since they believe in the norms they have sacrificed so much for, they have to cherish them (Boulding, 1969:5). They put up a charming front, smiling, cheerful,

7. See also the rehabilitation of the image of the career woman in Helsen, 1973.

8. The married professional woman in Birnbaum's study—who was not necessarily a mother—tended to be unconventional, competitive, and not self-sacrificing, to be pleased with herself, to have high self-esteem, and to feel attractive and personally competent. Other studies also show more housewives than women in the labor force exhibiting symptoms of psychological distress (National Center for Health Statistics, 1970, Table 17:30–31).

unassuming, self-deprecating, unthreatening. They never dream of "demanding" anything. Certainly not freedom.[9]

Quite different is the conflicted woman in middle motherhood who would like to enter the labor force but who, for one reason or another, is prevented from doing so.

> I have spent the last two years rationalizing all the problems away. I have joined committees that meet during the three hours the children are now in school. I have used up countless hours sewing clothes I don't need and probably will never wear, but it fills the time. I read endlessly, can even recite from memory the ingredients on the "King Vitamin" box. I take an occasional day off and haunt the museums, art galleries, movie theaters. I am, as they say, "up on things."
>
> But let me tell you, I'm lost. And I was probably lost . . . long before I ever agreed to give up my career plans. . . . I am definitely *not* one of the Pepsi generation, or the liberated generation; I belong, most certainly, to the last of the schlapp generation—two years too old for the pill, the Peace Corps, real liberation.
>
> I don't know what the answers are. If I did, I wouldn't find myself wondering, in near-terror, what to do with myself on days when both my children are invited to friends' houses after school on the same day, and being furious that I have allowed myself to be lured into this trap; that I've let my life become so circumscribed that I have nothing to do some days. What I do know is that there will have to be major changes in the way we all live before anything changes. . . . The women of my generation were not prepared for life. The realities of existence were not part of our training and education. We're not equipped to function in the lives we live (Kaufman, 1972).

This cacophony of misery has a strange ring. A few years earlier the author had been happily engaged in a part-time job, enjoying both her work and her motherhood. Then, at her husband's insistence, they had moved to a different city where his—but not her—career opportunities were better. Since in our society women are expected to live where their husbands live, they went. Pursuing her career became impossible. She rejected the housewife, if not the maternal, identity. She was miserable.

Some housewives prefer to remain home but would like to add to the family income.[10] Comments made by them in one study "indicate a

9. Paulo Freire is quoted as saying of the poor in northeast Brazil that they "prefer this security of conformity with their state of unfreedom to the creative communion produced by the pursuit of freedom. . . . Self-depreciation is . . . characteristic . . . deriving from their internalization of the opinion the oppressors hold of them (McCarthy, 1972).

10. The counterpart of the conflicted housewife is the woman in the labor force who would prefer to run a household. A survey of 1209 adult men and women in the Washington Metropolitan Area in August, 1973, found that although more than half of the women in the area were actually in the labor force, 43 percent of those queried in this study said they considered running a household more rewarding than a full-time job (Mathews, 1974).

definition of outside employment not as a source of self-expression, but as an imposition brought about by a shortage of money" (Lopata, 1972:178). They would like to relieve their husbands from having to work so hard, but they are not very clear just how they could do so (Ibid.).

"THE PRICE IS RIGHT"

In the past, the apologia for the woman's-place-is-in-the-home ideology rested solidly on high-level moral, even theological, grounds. It was clear that God's design called for women to stay home. And in the nineteenth century world of early industrialization, the woman in the home could preserve humane values severely banished from the dog-eat-dog outside world. But those circumstances had passed. And little by little other arguments against the employment of women had begun to suffer attrition. One, in particular, was undergoing modification. It had to do with a so-called latent, not an openly advocated, function of women.

In 1899 a wryly perceptive economist wrote a treatise on the theory of the leisure class. It contained a great deal of interesting material on the nature of work and of conquest, but it came to be known primarily for its concepts of "conspicuous consumption" and "vicarious leisure" (Veblen, 1899). Since in our industrialized society men could no longer get out of dull productive work by conquest, forcing others to do it for them and thus releasing them for leisure themselves, women were pressed into that service. Wives and daughters "performed" leisure for men to show that they did not have to work. And a large part of the work of performing vicarious leisure consisted of conspicuous, preferably wasteful, consumption. On a lower economic level an analogous situation occurred when a wife could stay home rather than enter the labor force, again giving evidence of her husband's earning power. The Victorian "lady" sheltered from the harsh outside world found her counterpart in the wife who did not have to "work" (Myrdal and Klein, 1962:8–9).

Charlotte Perkins Gilman was a contemporary of Veblen's. In a biting critique of the—to her—parasitical status of the nonworking wife, she had pointed out that to the extent that a wife contributed useful labor in the household she was entitled to recompense. But the woman who was not contributing such services was simply a kept woman, paid for her sexual favors (Gilman, 1898). And as for pleading the case that motherhood was a full-time occupation, she asked proof. And, further, women were doing a very poor job, turning out adults who were tired, timid, selfish, and unprogressive. Rearing children should become an independent profession.

Neither Veblen nor Gilman had much immediate impact on the "working mother" controversy. The "lady" remained an honorable character until well into the twentieth century. Only recently has the absurdity of conspicuous consumption and vicarious leisure become evident to all. The man who had enjoyed the envy of his peers for his ability to shower jewels and mink coats on his wife came to look rather puerile and the woman who made a career of displaying them, trivial.

The fall, 1972, issue of *The American Scholar,* journal of the Phi Beta Kappa Society, carried the discussion of a panel of top-flight women achievers in reply to the question, "If we win, what will we lose?" In it Lillian Hellman, echoing Charlotte Perkins Gilman, noted that "the upper-class lady, or the middle-class lady, has made out very well as the weaker and the more fragile of the pair, husband and wife. . . . There is still a good living and a great many mink coats to be earned by pretense. Respectable whoredom. Marx wrote about it. I think it's been quite deliberately done by women and quite deliberately kept alive" (1972:603). And women who made a "good living"—including mink coats—by traditional life styles were not likely to welcome changing role conceptions.

So long as the woman's-place-is-in-the-home ideology had secure support all around, even theological support, the women themselves did not have to bestir themselves. But when women who selected the housewife identity in middle motherhood felt themselves on the defensive, and were no longer automatically accorded kudos for their choice, the argument of at least some of them became crasser; brass knuckles appeared. The backlash was directed against feminists. Didn't they know they were upsetting the apple cart? Arguments that had seemed better unarticulated in the past now came to be verbalized, namely that there were rich rewards in the traditional role. It was a bargain, whatever the price. Who wanted equality when women were doing so much better than that as housewives? Women really had it made. "Women libbers" were rocking a very comfortable boat. "Unless we stop making equality noises, men might wake up and realize what they have been missing. God help us then!" (Thrope, 1972).

And husbands were, indeed, beginning to wake up and realize what they had been missing. Why shouldn't men have the same options as women? A Harris Poll taken in the fall of 1972 had reported more married men than married women enthusiastic for women's liberation, more working-class then upper-middle-class women. Little by little it was becoming clear that the income contributed by women in the labor force was liberating to husbands. And there was no disgrace or humiliation associated with it.

> The worker who loses his job will not feel the pressure to get work immediately if his unemployment compensation can be supplemented by his wife's earnings. The worker facing a cut-back in overtime may be less eager to moonlight if his wife can bring in additional income from part-time work. In fact, over the past two years the duration of unemployment among married men has averaged significantly longer

than among single men; and the percentage of married men who have remained unemployed for over 15 weeks has consistently exceeded the figure for single men. Clearly, the family can withstand economic hardship, despite unemployment for the "breadwinner," by means of the earnings of working wives (Bell, 1973:83).

So far, then, from the past when working wives reflected failure of husbands, the present day employment of women spares him humiliation. It does even more. The man who wishes to change his job or even career feels freer to do so when there is a wife's income to backstop him! "working women have enabled men to drop in and out of the labor force when . . . educational opportunity presents itself or seems reasonable to pursue" (Ibid.:85). And when half of all male earners have wives contributing to the family income, it can't be all that disgraceful. The women spearheading the backlash were justified in their concern.

VOLUNTEERISM AS SURROGATE CAREER

A third way of dealing with the identity crisis of middle motherhood outside of labor-force participation is a kind of compromise between that and the role of mother, ranging from an extension of the maternal role at one extreme to interpersonal service at the other. It involves a major commitment to the home but also a commitment, of varying degree and extent, to an outside activity—church related, school related, community related. Such a commitment may supply much of the satisfaction that the woman in the labor force receives from job or career. It does not, however, supply income and hence a modicum of autonomy. The work itself may be simply an extension of the mother role, as when a woman becomes a teacher's aid, a den mother, or a girl-scout leader, and thus encompass other children as well as her own in her activities. Or, at the other extreme, it may be on the level of professional competency as when a member of the League of Women Voters or the Women's Equity Action League or the National Organization for Women does the elaborate research required to arrive at a stand on a controversial issue. It may be traditionally feminine service, as when a member of a church group supplies tender loving care to infants in a hospital or to elderly inmates in a nursing home; or it may be traditionally masculine work, when she writes coldly abstract reports for a citizen's group on impending housing legislation.

Among women of the more affluent classes—once labeled the last leisure class in the United States—sponsorship of art exhibits, symphony orchestras, museums, hospitals, and, in general, other kinds of good works may be the form the effort takes. Such women have no problems with respect to labor-force participation; they are in a position to one-up any professional woman with whom they have contacts. If the woman is not affluent enough to sponsor such expensive community projects, she may sit on boards or contribute in the form of volunteer services in agencies of one kind or another.

Membership in nonprofessional social welfare organizations among women is growing at the rate of 1 percent a year, which is small as compared to a rate of increase of 9.4 percent in membership in sports and recreational groups but large as compared to the losses reported for membership in old-fashioned fraternal, ethnic, and hereditary groups (Ferriss, 1971:173).

For some kinds of volunteer work there is a strong movement to ask for pay for services on the grounds that if they are valuable they ought to be paid for. If women are, in fact, performing at a professional or quasi-professional level, the argument that they should be paid seems legitimate. For them, in fact, this work constitutes a surrogate career.

A considerable amount of consciousness-raising activity is now in process among women in this "other half." They are the women who are in a position to reassess their roles. Many are reevaluating their marriages, their relations with their children, and their position in the community. No longer house bound, no longer responsible for small children, they are beginning to wonder just who they are. Many see themselves as having the worst of both worlds.

Although all of the women in this half have opted to retain their identities as housewives, they do not all define their roles in the same way, nor do they all have the same degree of commitment. Some teeter and may—like some women in the labor force—reverse themselves. Some settle for the "just a housewife" position in a sweetly passive manner. Some with surrogate careers lead lives filled with good-doing and are serenely untroubled. They have no problems with their identity, especially those who have the support of the church behind them. And some, like those who find their privileged status challenged, lash out aggressively in a many-pronged backlash, including lobbying against state confirmation of the Equal Rights Amendment and church-sponsored courses on Fascinating Womanhood, which teach women how to be subservient.

But whichever identity emerges—single or dual—and regardless of the degree of the commitments she makes to it, the woman in middle motherhood remains a mother. And the present-day relationship between a woman in her late thirties and early forties and her teenage son or daughter is one of the most anomalous in human history.

III. Mothers of Adolescents

THE "PROLONGATION OF INFANCY"

All aspects of motherhood are different today from what they were yesterday. But middle motherhood is more different from the past than the others. It is different in two ways: The woman herself is different and the child she confronts is different. A major developmental task of middle motherhood includes the achievement of independence from her children, a task easy for some, difficult for others, desired by some, dreaded by others.

In the past women had had small children in the household until well into their thirties, even forties. In 1890 half of the women with completed fertility had had their last child when they were over 32. Some women, in fact, bore children as long as their bodies held up, so that in effect they never really reached middle motherhood at all, or, if they did, they were already old, and used up. The women who are in middle motherhood today are a relatively new phenomenon. Almost as much as television or computers, they are products of modern technology, products of a medical technology that keeps their bodies youthful and vigorous well into their middle years and even beyond.

The person with whom a woman performs the role of mother is also a new phenomenon. If mothers of adolescents are products of medical technology, their adolescent sons and daughters are products of affluence. Early motherhood has to cope with infants and small children, who are not too different from those of the past. But middle motherhood has to deal with a generational relationship of fairly recent origin.

Philippe Ariès is of the opinion that Wagner's Siegfried was the first typical adolescent of modern times, combining purity, physical strength, naturism, spontaneity, and *joie de vivre*. This conception was to make the adolescent a hero of the century. In France around 1800, Ariès tells us, youth became a matter of concern for moralists and politicians. They wondered what adolescents were thinking. Adolescents seemed to have new values "capable of reviving an aged and sclerosed society" (Ariès, 1962:30). Not until the end of World War I, still according to Ariès, did adolescence expand upward, well into physical adulthood, as well as downward. Marriage did not terminate it. "Henceforth marriage, which had ceased to be a 'settling down' would not put an end to it: the married adolescent was to become one of the most prominent types of our time, dictating its values, its appetites and its customs. Thus our society has passed from a period which was ignorant of adolescence to a period in which adolescence is the favorite age. We now want to come to it early and linger in it as long as possible" (Ibid.). We have now found it necessary for analytic purposes to distinguish these two extensions of the earlier conception, labeling the extension of adolescence as *youth*. But it is the younger adolescent, the one still living in her home, that women confront in middle motherhood.

Although there has thus, according to Ariès, been a literary conception of adolescence for a long time, as a scientific concept it only seriously entered our thinking at the turn of the century. Until that time young people in their teens were young adults and not, as the term *adolescent* implies, in the process of becoming adults. The nineteenth century had played up the concept of "the prolongation of infancy" as an evolutionary adaptation. It was needed because the human infant was born so unprepared genetically for the world it was to live in. It had to have a long time to acquire the know-how that other species were born with.

But if such "prolongation of infancy," that is, of dependency, was originally an evolutionary advantage, its further extension today has become almost a disadvantage. In preliterate societies, and even in Europe until about the fifteenth century, children, especially sons, were sent away from the care of the mother at a fairly early age. In England even today upper-class boys are sent away to school as very young children. Until well into the present century teenagers were no longer viewed as children; most entered the labor force. On the farm they had been contributing substantially ever since they were old enough to take care of themselves. In small towns they had learned useful trades and were well along in their apprenticeships. In mill towns children of 9 and 10 were working at the spinning wheels and looms in factories. In cities young men and women were working in stores and offices.

But as the twentieth century progressed, young people were increasingly excluded from the labor force and required to go to school. They were thus thrown back on their families for support. What work they did was incidental, of the hit-or-miss, odd-job type. It is not unusual today for sons and daughters to remain dependent on their parents through their early twenties, and even beyond. And because of their dependent status, they are, as Ariès reminds us, viewed as children.

But they are not children, except in status. Sociologists have found it inconvenient to have no suitable term for grown sons and daughters. *Children* implies youngness; *offspring* has too biological an implication. The term *sons and daughters,* however awkward, seems the best.

Whatever term is used to refer to them, sons and daughters of women in middle motherhood constitute their major worries. Rebellion against authority, pot smoking, drug taking, long hair, sexual behavior, fighting among siblings, and underachievement were the major anxieties expressed by the women participating in a session sponsored by a county mental health association in a semirural community. They were disturbed by their own anger toward their sons and daughters. They resented the fact that their husbands evaded their responsibilities, dumping all the weight of discipline on their shoulders (Irwin, 1973:27). And they were relieved to find that they were not alone. All the other mothers of teenage sons and daughters were in the same boat.

MOTHERS AND DAUGHTERS IN MIDDLE MOTHERHOOD

The role of mother vis-à-vis an adolescent daughter is rendered especially sensitive because it has been traditionally the mother's obligation to protect a daughter's virginity. The enormous preoccupation with premarital sexual relations in our society has almost an aspect of voyeurism. In the face of almost insuperable forces, mothers are still held responsible for their daughters' virginity. A mother has, therefore, to keep tabs on the daughter's goings and comings. She has to pry. She has to oversee. If there is any talk or scandal around her daughter, she will be held to blame—at least until recently.

Then a change began. All mothers were now asking was that they not be told about such behavior (Decter, 1972, 42–46). For one of the most rapid changes in the script for the role of mother occurred in the late 1960s and early 1970s. Until that time the script called for extreme condemnation for a daughter who lived with a young man without benefit of clergy. Such unofficial liaisons were beyond the pale of respectability. Mothers would be ashamed if behavior of this kind became known. Sanctions in the form of cutting off support would be invoked, if not the nineteenth century order never to darken the parents' door again.

Then, almost overnight, even conservative women were accepting it. All they were now hoping for was that there be no babies born. Even among bastions of moral conservatism, the ethnic enclaves peopled by blue-collar families, "pacesetters . . . dare to countenance guiltless pre-marital relations, casual trial marriages, unapologetic single parenthood, readily secured abortions, considerable sexual experimentation, . . . and other deep-running challenges to conventional morality" (Shostak, 1973:77). In the face of this avalanche of change, what was a mother to do? Tolerance of any unofficial union short of one involving parenthood was gradually incorporated in the maternal script at least for more avant-garde mothers. Others trailed. Some trailed so far behind that they were hardly within hailing distance of their daughters. "My daughter had to write a report on contraception. I think it's horrible" (Irwin, 1973:27). Even sex education was still anathema for some. But it was clear in which direction the winds of change were blowing.

Mother-daughter relations in middle motherhood are complicated because of the biological youthfulness of women even in their forties. A psychologist reminds us of the internal turmoil that may characterize mothers of daughters in middle motherhood. If she had her daughter at the age of 26, a woman is now, let us say, only in her early forties. The old conception of women as bearers of children only and as, therefore, of little real worth still downgrades the postmenopausal woman. "The middle-aged mother . . . is likely to regret, or at least be ambivalent about, her waning, or ended, reproductive capacity. . . . Her forebodings . . . may be intensified by her awareness that her adolescent daughter . . . is, sexually and reproductively, on the upgrade" (Chilman, 1968:306). Further, although the daughter has to rebel, she has to have something to rebel against. And the mother may herself be in the process of rebelling. "Mothers . . . impressed with the need to serve as models to their daughters through the turbulent years, want their daughters to understand their own turbulence and distress . . . but not to understand too much" (Ibid.). The mother of the teenage daughter is in a special bind.

Both halves of the women in middle motherhood—those in the labor force and those not in it—find relations with adolescent sons and daughters trying. For some of those in the labor force, working may be a copout. It excuses them from exerting control over their children. One study found this situation especially characteristic of women with high power motivation. These mothers tended to feel especially inadequate as parents. "An employed woman might feel that she could have controlled her child had she been home. This realization might make her feel guilty about working but less defensive about her lack of influence" (Veroff and Feld, 1970:202). When most parents find it difficult to admit their inability to control their children, "the working mother can freely express her own feelings of inadequacy" (Ibid.).

On such issues as when to date, when to come home, and how often to go out, the daughters of women in the labor force disagree with their mothers more than do daughters of women who are not, and the disagreement is more serious (Propper, 1972:420). What this means is not altogether clear. It may mean that women autonomous enough to take a job have daughters autonomous enough to take them on.

MOTHERS AND SONS IN MIDDLE MOTHERHOOD

In the past, the removal of boys from their mothers' care came at a fairly early age, and meant that motherhood, in effect, was restricted to mother-daughter relations. Boys lived in a male world in which women had little place, and what place they did have was peripheral and usually inferior. In our society today boys live with their mothers long past childhood. They live in daily contact with them. More to the point, the mothers continue to be held responsible for much of their behavior—with, we are told, untoward results.

The necessity to relinquish sons as well as daughters as part of the growing-up process is usually given lip service. A considerable number of literary works deal precisely with this process in the case of fathers and sons who have to fight it out. If the son does not win, both lose. Mother and son have to fight it out, too, but the battle is a different one. The father can use force if need be; the son can return blow for blow. Or the father can withdraw economic support, fairly easily replaced by a son. But the mother can only withhold love or punish with rebukes, and against these weapons sons are usually helpless.

In middle motherhood we have a woman who was withdrawn from the outside world some 15 to 20 years earlier confronting a 15-year-old young man who is entering a world she never knew and which, furthermore, has changed so much that knowledge of it would be all but useless to her now. He is riding the crest of his sexual prowess. Kinsey and his associates reminded us a generation ago of the anomaly of mothers and female teachers face to face with young men.

> As mothers, as school teachers, as voting citizens, women are primarily responsible for the care of these boys; and, to a large degree, they are the ones who control moral codes, schedules for sex education, campaigns for law enforcement, and programs for combating what is called juvenile delinquency. It is obviously impossible for a majority of these women to understand the problem that the boy faces in being constantly aroused and regularly involved with his normal biologic reactions (Kinsey and Associates, 1948:223).

Thus, a woman who has spent her day driving smaller children to and fro or doing volunteer work at the hospital or church, or playing bridge or golf or tennis or what-have-you with other women like herself, sits at the dinner table in the evening with a young man who has seen a best friend brag about his cache of marijuana in the locker room, or been approached by a friend who has just gotten a girl pregnant and has to raise some money to help her, or who was in a friend's car that ran into a guard rail. To her cheerful "what happened in school today?" he replies, "nothing, same old thing," exchanging agonized glances with his sister who, he fears, might give him away. The woman and her son are hardly within hailing distance of one another.

Not until the outside world knocks on her door to tell her that her son is being held on charges of possessing marijuana will the magnitude of the breach between her and her son dawn on her. "But it can't be true! Not our John! He has always been such a good boy!" And then—when she learns that it *is* true, that it *is* their John, that even good boys can land in court— the guilt-wracked "what did we do wrong?"

Probably nothing at all. Nothing, that is, within the framework of their lives. She had been a model mother, performing according to the script. It is the script that is wrong and the stage on which it must be performed.

Although the employment of mothers of adolescents does not show demonstrably harmful effects on boys, there is one shred of evidence that bears scrutiny. In the past when mothers worked and added to the family income, the family could afford to live in neighborhoods that protected children from temptations to delinquency. But in a recent study there did seem to be a relationship between the employment of mothers and delinquency in the case, at least, of middle-class young men. Just why only in the middle class? So far there are few if any research answers, only questions (Hoffman, 1963b:195–196). This study was made before drugs became a serious problem even among middle-class families, so the invasion of drugs into middle-class areas cannot be invoked as explanatory.

Like daughters, the sons of employed mothers were more likely than sons of nonemployed mothers to disagree with their mothers over hair, clothing, and religion, and to disagree more seriously (Propper, 1972:420). The same factors as in the case of daughters might well be involved.

It could be argued that participating in delinquent acts and disagreeing with mothers had a positive import, implying that the boy was breaking loose, achieving autonomy, and that the more conforming behavior of the young men whose mothers were not employed implied too great input from the mother in holding them back.

In any event, middle motherhood is no bed of roses for women. One study found that while children were smaller, mothers could get a sense of achievement from work outside of the home, giving them a positive feeling about motherhood. But work outside the home had a reverse effect when the sons were adolescent (Veroff and Feld, 1970:199). The problems of dealing with potential delinquency may have been involved. At middle motherhood, the role of mother may come to include that of policeman and probation officer as well as nurturer.

THE FLATTENING OF GENERATIONAL TIES

We know, from the witch's brew Freud dredged out of the subconscious of his patients, what the intense and profound relationships of the Victorian family did to people. They produced people who felt strongly about one another whether the feeling was hate, love, fear, or whatever. There was nothing bland or light about them. They took themselves and their feelings seriously. Ties might or might not have been loving, but they were deep. The kind of personality the Victorian family fostered would not suit a mobile, rootless society like ours; it would be reduced to tatters in a world of such transient relationships.

A far more superficial type is called for. People dare not feel too deeply about one another when they are here only today and will be gone tomorrow. Quick intimacy and equally quick forgetting are characteristic. We celebrate reunions of one kind or another—school or family—and find we hardly recognize one another. Still, the more casual style of relations to one another called for in our mobile, rootless age still leave us unsatisfied.

A great cult of physical contact has arisen to supply instant depth to our relationships with even complete strangers. People assemble at prearranged times and places to give one another a chance to experience the emotions our life so inadequately provides us with. But it is ersatz.

A quarter of a century ago, David Riesman first called our attention to the peer-oriented society then emerging. Young people lived in a horizontal peer-group world rather than in a vertical, intergenerational world (Riesman, Glazer, and Denney, 1953). They might reside with their families but they shared a world of their own, a world to which adults were not privy (Esfandeary, 1972). And a report from the 1970 White House Conference on Children commented unfavorably on the segregation of children and adults (1970:5). The woman in middle motherhood could well understand that.

But she knew also that however brittle the ties between her and her sons and daughters might be, they were strong enough to hold her in bondage, if not them.

THE MOTHER'S DECLARATION OF INDEPENDENCE

In the intimidatingly large research and artistic literature on the struggle for independence by sons and daughters we are almost unfailingly on the side of the young people against the clinging mother who refuses to give up her hold on her children. But nowhere, so far as I know, is there a comparable statement of the mother's declaration of independence. Without such an assertion of her independence even after the sons and daughters have long since left home, she remains at their beck and call. There is no recognized "role-exit" for her, no termination date for her responsibilities, as there is in the case of the young, no point at which she can say "enough!"

Thus, for example, there are daily press reports of criminals calling for their mothers or mothers interceding for their criminal sons, or mothers inadvertently involved in criminal activities of sons—drugs, pimping, fencing—all as part of the obligations they feel as mothers to even grown sons.

Or, in a different vein, the daughter of a professional woman asks her mother to meet her plane when she comes home from college for a visit. The mother happens to have a professional obligation at that time and cannot meet the plane but says she will pay for the taxi. The daughter accuses her of not meeting her maternal obligations, of not having her priorities in order. When the mother asks if the father had given the same reason—professional obligations—for not meeting the plane, would the daughter have given the same reply? No, that's different. Or still another young woman who has "deserted" her mother by marrying out of the family's faith and leaving the country calls on her mother to stay with her for several weeks when her baby arrives. The mother replies she would be glad to come for a weekend when she could get off because she did want to see the baby but she cannot leave her job at that particular time. She will, however, be glad to pay for the services of a nurse. The daughter accuses her mother of trying to buy her off.

CASE IN POINT

In her late forties, Mary Stone declared her independence for the third time in her life, this time from bondage to her daughter's needs. She had just bought a Jaguar. Money that for years had been mortgaged for the care of the problem-plagued daughter was now being rechanneled into the new car. Mary is exhilarated but frightened at what she has done. The daughter, who had been a source of family distress for no less than 10 years, had reached the age of 18. She had been in and out of schools and treatment centers and clinics for several years and had left home, ultimately, just a year ago. Now she was pregnant, unmarried, living with a friend, and on welfare. And Mary Stone, a proud and beautiful woman, is able for the first time to finally say, Enough.

She was still not free enough to accept the situation openly. She still sought the shelter of secrecy. She still was unable to muster enough courage to face the world with the situation. She still felt enough guilt to want to keep it from general knowledge. She would still have winced to have it known by her friends and professional peers. Despite years of excruciating anguish, despite years invested in family therapy that might well have been invested in furthering her own professional training, despite bills that ate up incredible amounts of money, she still felt guilt, shame, and certainly humiliation.

Her declaration of independence from her daughter was by far the hardest of all three of her liberations. The first had come at the age of 17 when she had gone to work. This had served notice on her family that she was going to make her own life. It had been brave and courageous but not, after all, traumatic. Nor, she now admitted, complete, for she still felt guilty that she did not do more for her aged mother who lived in a distant city. She ought to visit her more. She should not leave so much of the responsibility to her sister who, though she did not have to take a job, had done so in order to have a good excuse not to chauffeur the mother around.

Nor had there been much of a brouhaha when she continued her professional career after she married. She did not have to make much of a declaration to her husband. They were both members of a generation and a class that took dual-career families in stride.

No, independence from family, from husband, were comparatively simple. Independence from a daughter was the truly traumatic gesture (personal document).

ANOTHER EXTENSION OF MOTHERHOOD-PER-CHILD

In the name of tidiness, middle motherhood ought to end when children leave home—for college, for marriage, for other living arrangements. But with the emergence of youth between adolescence and adulthood, motherhood-per-child is extended as a stage again and middle motherhood along with it. The youth of sons and daughters straddles middle and late motherhood. The sons and daughters may be part of the new youth culture, supported still by subsidies from parents, but insisting on a life style quite at variance with parental, especially maternal, preferences.

As a woman leaves middle motherhood to enter late motherhood today, she is a member of what has been called the "caught generation."

> From the viewpoint of the middle-aged parent, one does, indeed, seem to be caught in the middle of three generational cycles: between the increasingly complex, costly, and disturbing needs of adolescents . . . who are bursting with desire for entrance into the adult world and the increasing problems and needs of the grandparents who, generally, are bursting with desire not to leave their full status in the adult world. The middle-aged adult, who may feel that her own status is threatened somewhat by her own developmental stage, is apt to feel further threatened by the competing, but somewhat similar claims of both the older and younger generations (Chilman, 1968:307).

She is still actively involved in the lives of her sons and daughters, married and unmarried, but she is still also involved in the life of her own mother. She feels responsibilities toward both. The increased longevity, especially of women, means that more and more women are caught in this bind. Baby sitting for her daughter or chauffeuring her mother to the hairdresser may be a perennial choice, neither one of which, as it happens, may appeal to her.

She would probably rather stay home and finish the book due back at the library tomorrow.

THEY CAN'T COME HOME AGAIN! HURRAH!
THEY CAN'T COME HOME AGAIN! ALAS!

Sooner or later, early or late, even youths do leave home, married or single. And the defects in male models of human development show up most glaringly in their ignorance of the crucial importance of living patterns, most especially the sharp break that occurs in parent-child relationships when the children leave the parental roof. Motherhood takes on a wholly different cast. From here on out a mother will see her children on turf of their choosing, and it will not always be on hers. And even when it is, they come as visitors, as guests, more or less uninvolved. They have allies in the outside world. The letters, the telephone calls, the huddles with peers in the recreation room, the bathroom lotions and cosmetics are no longer present to serve as cues to the personal, private life of the son or daughter. Their secrets are better protected. The rewards, punishments, threats, promises have different significance. The separation may be sudden as at marriage, or it may occur in steps, as in going off to college. Sudden or by stages, it is irrevocable. They can't come home again.

The research literature has not adequately explored the change for the mother. A considerable amount has been written about the empty nest. But that is only a part of the picture, even a fading part, and not the most crucial. The long process that precedes the empty nest—"alienation" is too formidable a name for it—has not been studied in enough detail, nor the long process that follows. It would be illuminating to get answers to these questions from women at the end of middle motherhood, when their last child has just left home: "Would you want your children to return to live with you in your home?" And for those whose children were married: "Would you like to live with your son or daughter? Have them live with you?" And for those whose children were married and living in another city: "How long do you like your visits in the home of your sons or daughters to last? Their visits in your home?"

These questions would be designed to explore the parent-child relationship, which might be labeled a "love but . . . " relationship, and which has shown up in all the research for well over a generation. It is a relationship distilled in the expression "I love my children but I wouldn't want to live with them" and "I love my parents but I would not want them to live with us." In the 1930s it referred primarily to adults and their elderly parents. The critical point has now been lowered to the late teens. Increasingly children leave the parental roof beginning at age 18. The separation has profound repercussions on motherhood. Some women are pleased; they draw a sigh of relief. Others are regretful; they draw a sigh of concern. Some are incredulous: "They can't come home again? Who says?" Mom says.

References

Ariès, Philippe. 1962. *Centuries of childhood*. New York: Knopf.

Bell, Carolyn Shaw. 1973. Age, sex, marriage, and jobs. *The Public Interest* 30 (Winter):

Bernard, Jessie. 1956. *Remarriage, A study of marriage*. New York: Dryden. New York: Russell and Russell, 1971.

———. 1964. *Academic women*. University Park: Pennsylvania State University Press. New York: Meridian, 1966, 1974.

———. 1971. *Women and the public interest, An essay on policy and protest*. Chicago: Aldine.

_____ . 1972. *The future of marriage*. New York: World. Bantam, 1973.

_____ . 1974. *The future of motherhood*. New York: Dial. Penguin, 1975.

Birnbaum, Judith Lynn Abelow. 1971. Life patterns, personality style and self esteem of gifted family-oriented and career-committed women. Abstract of Ph.D. dissertation, University of Michigan.

Boulding, Kenneth. 1969. The grants economy. *Michigan Academician* 1 (Winter): 3-11.

Brothers, Joyce. 1972. When your husband's affection cools. *Reader's Digest* (October): 152.

Chilman, Catherine S. 1968. Families in development at mid-stage of the family life cycle. *The Family Coordinator* 17 (October): 306.

Coup, Roger F.; Greene, Shirley; and Gardner, Burleigh B. 1973. A study of working class women in a changing world. Chicago: Social Research.

Decter, Midge. August 1972. Toward the new chastity. *Atlantic Monthly*, 230:42-46.

Dickinson, Jonathan. 1974. Labor supply of family members, in *Five thousand American families—Patterns of economic progress*, vol. 1. Ann Arbor: Institute of Social Research.

Eells, John S., Jr. 1964. Women in honors programs: Winthrop College, in Mitterling, Philip L., ed., Proceedings of the Conference on Talented Women and the American College. Mimeo.

Erikson, Eric H. 1963. *Identity, youth and crisis*. New York: Norton.

Esfandeary, F. M. 1972. A plague on both your tribes. *New York Times*, September 14, 1972.

Ferriss, Abbott L. 1971. *Indicators of trends in the status of American women*. New York: Russell Sage.

M. G. 1972. Should a woman work part-time? in Anne's Reader Exchange. *Washington Post*, October 8, 1972.

Gilman, Charlotte Perkins. 1898. Economic basis of the woman question. *Woman's Journal*, October 1, 1898.

Heilbrun, Carolyn. 1972. Women on women, in American Scholar Forum. *The American Scholar* (Autumn):603ff.

Hellman, Lilian. 1972. Women on women, in American Scholar Forum. *The American Scholar* (Autumn):603ff

Helsen, Ravenna. 1973. The changing image of the career woman. *Journal of Social Issues* 28:33-46.

Hoffman, Lois. 1963a. The decision to work, in Hoffman, Lois, and Nye, Ivan, ed., *The employed mother in America*. Chicago: Rand McNally.

_____ . 1963b. Effects on children: Summary and discussion, in Hoffman, Lois, and Nye, Ivan, ed., *The employed mother in America*. Chicago: Rand McNally.

Holstrom, Lynda Lyttle. 1972. *The two-career family*. Cambridge, Mass.: Schenkman.

Irwin, Theodore. 1973. The power of positive worrying. *Parade*, January 28, 1973.

Kaufman, Frances. 1972. When smugness collapses. *New York Times*, February 7, 1972.

Kinsey, A. C., and Associates. 1948. *Sexual behavior in the human male*. Philadelphia: Saunders.

Lake, Alice. 1973. The revolt of the company wife. *McCall's* (October):22-32.

Lash, Joseph P. 1971. *Eleanor and Frank- lin*. New York: Signet.

Lopata, Helena A. 1972. *Occupation housewife*. New York: Oxford.

Manpower report of the President. 1974. Washington, D.C.: U.S. Government Printing Office.

Matthews, Jay. 1974. The "best"job: Housewife. *Washington Post,* February 21, 1974.

McCarthy, Colman. 1972. Paulo Freire and educating the oppressed. *Washington Post,* July 31, 1972.

Myrdal, Alva, and Klein, Viola. 1962. *Women's two roles.* London: Routledge and Kegan Paul.

National Center for Health Statistics. 1970. *Selected symptoms of psychological distress.* Washington, D.C., U.S. Department of Health, Education, and Welfare.

Propper, Alice Marcella. 1972. The relationship of maternal employment to adolescent roles, activities, and parental relationships. *Journal of Marriage and the Family* 34 (August):417-421.

Rapoport, Rhona, and Rapoport, Robert. 1971. *Dual-career families.* Baltimore: Penguin.

Riesman, David. 1964. Introduction to Bernard, 1964.

Riesman, David; Glazer, Nathan; and Denney, Reuel. 1953. *The lonely crowd.* New York: Doubleday Anchor.

Shostak, Arthur B. 1973. Ethnic revivalism, blue-collarites, and Bunker's last stand. *Sounding* (Spring): 70-77.

Thrope, Elsieliese. 1972. The favored sex. *Reader's Digest* (May):84. Postscripts from "The favored sex," A symposium. *Reader's Digest* (October):106.

Tolmack, Judith. 1972. Crumbling families and the generation factor. *Potomac Magazine,* June 25, 1972.

Veblen, T. B. 1899. *Theory of the leisure class.* New York: Macmillan.

Veroff, Joseph, and Feld, Sheila. 1970. *Marriage and work in America.* New York: Van Nostrand and Rheingold.

Von Mering, Faye Higier. 1955. Professional and nonprofessional woman as mothers. *Journal of Social Issues* 42:21-34.

White House Conference on Children. 1970. Children and parents; Together in the world. Working copy of report of Forum 15.

Women's Bureau. 1969. *1969 Handbook on women workers.* Washington, D.C.: U.S. Government Printing Office.

SEVEN

Late Motherhood

I. What Ever Happened to Mother?

Two laureate poets have paid their respects to Mother. Tennyson wrote:

> No angel, but a dearer being, all dipt
> In angel instinct breaching Paradise,
> Interpreter between the gods and men,
> Who look'd all native to her place, and yet
> On tiptoe seem'd to touch upon a sphere
> Too gross to tread, and all male minds perforce
> Sway'd to her from their orbits as they moved,
> And girdled her with music. Happy he
> With such a mother! faith in womankind
> Beats with his blood, and trust in all things high
> Comes easy to him, and tho' he trip and fall
> He shall not blind his soul with clay.
>   Alfred Lord Tennyson, *The Princess*, VII:301–312.

Well, one man did trip and fall and he did blind his soul with clay, but his mother remained ever-solicitous, as the Nobel laureate in poetry for 1904, Jean Richepin, recounts in a poem, variously translated. Here is one version:

There was a young man loved a maid
Who taunted him. "Are you afraid,"
She asked, "to bring me today
Your mother's head upon a tray?"

He went and slew his mother dead
Tore from her breast her heart so red
Then towards his lady love he raced
But tripped and fell in all his haste.
As the heart rolled on the ground
It gave forth a plaintive sound.
And it spoke, in accents mild:
"Did you hurt yourself, my child?"
    Jean Richepin, "Severed Heart"[1]

The last line has also been translated: "Are you hurt, my child, are you hurt at all?" and "Son of mine, did I hurt you, dear?" This ungrateful son is lost because he did not love his mother. "For one on the ocean of crime long tossed, who loves his mother, is not quite lost." Mothers, unheralded though they be, are the true heroes:

Not for the star-crossed heroes, the men that conquer and slay,
But a song for those that bore them, the mothers braver than they!
With never a blare of trumpets, with never a surge of cheers,
They march to the unseen hazard—pale, patient volunteers.
    Marc Antony de Wolfe Howe, "The Valiant"

And so they go on in poetry and prose, endless accolades for mother, "synonym of all that is good," surrogate of God:

Don't poets know it
Better than others?
God can't be always everywhere: and, so,
Invented Mothers.
    Sir Edwin Arnold, "Mothers," stanza 6

That was the Victorian mother whose image was propagated in song and story well into the present century. Just short of an angel, surrogate of God, she lived in a sphere too gross for ordinary folk to enter. The literary genre glorifying the Victorian model of mother is almost inexhaustible.

Angel to Viper in Half a Century

Less than halfway through the present century this monument of love, sacrifice, tenderness had become a viper. Her caprices now included:

1. Translated by J. Echegaray. The poem has also been translated by Herbert Trench, Arthur Guiterman, and Arthur Stringer.

rage, infantilism, weeping, sentimentality, peculiar appetite, and all the ragged reticule of tricks, wooings, wiles, . . . indulgences, crochets, superstitions, phlegms, debilities, vapors, butterflies-in-the-belly, plaints, connivings, cries, malingerings, deceptions, visions, hallucinations, needlings and wheedlings. . . . (Wylie, 1942:199)

Mother was now "Mom" and it was she who stood behind "this vast aurora of pitiable weakness." The mother who, dipped in angel instincts, once breached Paradise, was now a "thin and enfeebled martyr whose very urine . . . will etch glass" (Ibid.). All her virtues had become vices. She was the cause of all our woe, not, as in the case of Eve, by expanding our horizons and introducing us to knowledge, but by enslaving us, by restricting us, by tying us to her apron strings. Mother Machree had become Mrs. Portnoy.

The midcentury decades were years of almost unmitigated denigration of mothers. How the lofty had fallen! From the angel of the household, mother had become transmogrified into the destroyer of children, especially of sons, a veritable hellion in millions of households across the class structure, across the country. I have not myself researched the literature, but Wolfgang Lederer tells us that "in all mythology and folklore, and in all literature foreign or over a hundred years old, [there is] no precedent [for Mom]. She is . . . truly a new phenomenon" (Lederer, 1968:69).

The fact that Mom became an accepted and well-understood symbol for women in late motherhood who found it impossible to let go of their children attested to the denigrated status of women at this stage of their lives. They were pilloried as a generation of vipers. Momism came to stand for the obsessive attachment sons had for their mothers and mothers for their sons.

Mom was unprepared for the hatred she generated. Mental depression hit her hard. She was among the most vulnerable to suicide. Doctors hated to be bothered by her. Tranquilizing pills were their answer. Why was she so villified? She had played the game strictly according to the rules. She had devoted her life to her family and her home. She knew no other life style. She was prepared for no other. She wanted no other. A life devoted to her home and her family was what she had been prepared for. So what had she done wrong? What had happened? What kind of blight had transformed angelic mothers into harridans? What had produced this strange new creature? What kind of poison had altered maternal genes? *Some*thing must have happened.

The vitriolic attacks on Mom were made by men. I do not know of any made by women. Nor was there anyone to defend this much-abused woman. Not, that is, until later when women researchers came to her defense. Then she was seen as victim rather than as villain (Bart, 1970).

VICTIMS NOT VILLAINS

Mom in the fifties belonged to a generation born at the turn of the century, a generation reared to believe that their place was in the home rearing children. No one could have foretold that active motherhood was going to occupy a smaller and smaller proportion of a woman's increasingly long life, that the span of 20 to 25 years of active motherhood—from the birth of her first child in her early twenties to the marriage of her last child in her late forties—were going to constitute a smaller part of her life than the almost 30 years that followed, that if she achieved the age of 50, her life expectancy would be 25 to 26 more years.

These women had left school at about the age of 14 and the years they had spent in the labor force, if any at all, had come before marriage, and unless they were widowed, certainly before they became mothers. They had learned early the skills needed to operate a household. When they were in their late sixties, Arlie Hochschild recorded their memories of the work they did as small children:

> As Daisy proudly noted about her childhood on an Iowa Farm: "I had to get up on a chair to do the dishes. That's how early I started workin'." As they grew older, they were assigned more tasks about the farmhouse—feeding the rabbits and geese, hanging out clothes on the line or barbed wire, and ironing with an iron heated on the stove. They learned from their mothers to quilt and darn, which they still do. They learned to refill the gas lanterns, to heat bricks to keep the beds warm on winter evenings, to grind coffee, stoke the fire, put up vegetables for winter, and retrieve the pail of milk hung in the well to keep cool. Today they buy their chickens frozen and wear Woolworth's drip-dry dresses (Hochschild, 1973:7).

Another remembered working in the cotton fields as a child, another in a cannery. "They learned early . . . the value of work" (Ibid.:8).

Little by little as they grew older many of their early-acquired skills were rendered obsolete. A host of new equipment lightened the sheer drudgery of running a household. Most of them moved to cities. Among the working classes there remained a considerable amount of work around the house in the form of food preservation, sewing, and "procurement" or careful shopping, all of which raised total family income by a substantial percent, as much as a third in some cases. And these women were not likely to become Moms.

But as housework receded as a major preoccupation, the more affluent devoted more time to their children (Cowan, 1973). The empty nest left many hours to be filled. It was among these women that Mom, like adolescence, emerged as a product of affluence. She could spend "several hundred dollars a year on permanents and transformations, pomades, cleansers, rouges, lipsticks, and the like" (Wylie, 1942:201). And it is in the continuing dedication to her sons that Wolfgang Lederer finds the cause of momism: In most cultures sons escape from the care of their mothers but in our society they are left "at the mercy of mom" (Lederer, 1968:71).

Mom, in brief, was the victim of a series of changes that were coming to restructure all kinds of sex roles including the role of mother as she had been socialized for it.

MOM AS MOTHER-IN-LAW

A great deal of the onus of Momism was borne by mothers-in-law, among the most maligned characters in the popular media. Until recently any stand-up comedian could count on a laugh at the mother-in-law's expense. And here again she illustrated a lag between old role definitions and new life situations.

The perspective from which we view women in late motherhood is often that of the son- or daughter-in-law, especially in the early years of the son's or daughter's marriage when the weight of the woman's loss is felt most keenly. She has invested herself in them so completely that surrendering them to others leaves her vulnerable. Much of the research on this stage in a woman's life has had a Freudian slant. She has been viewed as the focus of her son's Oedipal attachment, and the mother-son relationship appears as having all-but-invulnerable solidity. But one does not need Oedipal concepts to interpret the in-law relationships of women.

The psychological work of women in late motherhood is as arduous as that of any other developmental stage. Part of it is learning to share sons or daughters with spouses, who have a totally different conception of family roles. As the authors of a study of the Jewish wife noted, "the conflicts tend to be greatly exacerbated by the extreme width of the 'generation gap' in Jewish families" (Schwartz and Wyden, 1970:127). Although mother-in-law relations with sons' wives may be more intense among Jews than among non-Jews (Ibid.:142), the pattern described in this study may be characteristic of other groups also:

1. The conflicts tend to be frequent and severe. More often than not, they are clashes between two more or less equally head-strong women, struggling for dominance like two captains trying to gain control of a ship's bridge. . . .
2. There is, nevertheless, much love, warmth and authentic solicitude intermingled in many of these hostilities. . . .
3. Many mother-in-law struggles are caused by attempts to define and redefine the "optimal distance" between the two women—the degree of closeness that allows each to live in maximum comfort with the other. This process *has* to be a tug-of-war, what with Mother trying to keep

close and push closer, and the daughter-in-law trying to pull away—yet
not so far away that her conscience would trouble her too much or that
the family would be too upset. . . . (Ibid.:126).

In view of the amount of attention paid to in-law relationships, it is
surprising to learn that only 10 percent of city wives in one study reported
such relationships as a source of disagreement with their husbands, and
only 6 percent as a major source. Wives with a high-school education
reported in-law trouble more often than those with either a grade-school or
college education. Perhaps the least educated were nearer to the older
women in role conceptions and the most highly educated too distant to
tangle with them (Blood and Wolfe, 1960:241). Expectably, in-law trouble
was reported most often in the honeymoon period (15 percent), for it is at
that time when the mothers of the young people are first coming to grips
with their felt deprivation.

Because kinship relations are controlled by women more than by men
(Adams, 1971:169–170), the young wife rather than the young husband
determines which mother will be closer to the new family, and the chances
are she will decide in favor of her own mother. Husbands are thus likely to
have more contact with their wives' mothers than with their own, and to
accept this modus vivendi. In this case the young wife's mother has in fact
"gained a son" rather than "lost a daughter." Not so the other mother.
Since the wife has less contact with her husband's mother, so also does her
husband. This mother has, then, "lost a son" but not "gained a daughter."
She feels more alienated from her son than from her daughter. It is
understandable, therefore, that the in-law trouble most commonly
reported is between the young wife and her husband's mother (Ibid.:173).

In any event, in-law trouble subsides with time. Evelyn Duvall explains
this decline in terms of the softening effect of becoming a grandmother, of
increased maturity of sons and daughters when they themselves become
parents, the gradual acceptance of the "loss" of sons and daughters with
time, the appreciation sons and daughters feel for the help parents give,
and the decline of the in-law stereotype (Duvall, 1954:70–88). It may also be
due to the fact that more and more wives are entering the labor force, for,
interestingly, employed wives are less likely than nonemployed wives to
report in-law problems (Blood and Wolfe, 1960:246). Apparently a job
keeps a wife from tangling with her husband's mother.

Young women are still being warned against falling in love with men
who live at home as adults, who show too great concern for their mothers,
who find it impossible to face up to them. Popular magazines addressed to
young women chart the signs to look for to avoid marrying such "mama's
boys" (Meade, 1972). But already the whole Mom stereotype has become
anachronistic.

THE DEMISE OF MOM

The story of Mom is now becoming a matter of primarily historical interest. The generation so bitterly punished in the 1940s and 1950s for being caught in a great historical transition, for being left beached on the sand by the tides of time and change is now old and the form its momism takes greatly attenuated. A study of "the good Jewish mother," who was, in effect, a symbol of Mom—for, as the clichè had it, "you don't have to be Jewish to be a good Jewish mother"—states that "the world's most libeled female" was "one generation out of date when its own research was done in the early and mid-1960s and may now be "two or more generations behind the times" (Schwartz and Wyden, 1970:11). The authors tell us that although "30 years ago the caricature that still makes people chuckle today contained more than a kernel of truth, today it is absurdly obsolete" (Ibid.:7).

Young women have been alerted to the hazards of late motherhood. Increasing numbers of them begin to plan early for the years when the children will be gone. One informant comments that she and her friends will run out of conversation "when the kids are grown: then where will I be?" Her husband agrees that she must have a goal "for the future and beyond her role as homemaker" (Ibid.:219). Felicia, eight months pregnant, "had a life-long project in mind," She is preparing to take a job when her child is in first grade (Ibid.:224). Another studies for a license as an insurance agent because she "just wanted something I could fall back on for an outlet" (Ibid.:225). Some had genuinely professional goals: "one was studying to be a psychiatrist; another was going to become an architect. In Forest Hills, the 25-year-old wife of a cab driver was going back to night school for a degree in psychology" (Ibid.).

Nor are these middle-class women alone in preparing early to avoid the hazards of Momism later on. Even working-class women are readying themselves. Women whose children were no longer preschoolers "are now or are planning later on going back to work, taking advanced education or trade school courses, engaging in church, club, or hospital volunteer work" (Coup, Greene, and Gardner, 1973:134). Like middle-class women, "at this stage, thus, Working-Class women are beginning to assert or rediscover that they do not need or want to be perpetual mothers and housewives" (Ibid.). Children are becoming less central in their lives (Ibid.:25). They no longer feel Mom's need to hang on to their children. "They often feel their older children are pressing to be out and away from home most of the time and many are ready to acquiesce in or even encourage this ('Let me alone, already')" (Ibid.:134–135). And a considerable proportion of both black (52 percent) and white (35 percent) widows were reported in another study as complaining that "a big problem with adult children was that they always wanted favors such as baby-sitting, sewing, and the like" (Lopata, 1973a:1016). The oncoming generation is not putting all their eggs in the basket of one role. They do not relish the idea of being left with nothing to justify themselves when the role of mother is over. Especially among young working-class women, "the goal, basically, is to get child-raising, formal homemaking and housekeeping chores, and work and responsibility generally—to get all this nitty-gritty of adulthood—over and done with at a much earlier age and then to anticipate a long, pleasant interlude alone with spouse (or simply alone) in less stressful and crowded circumstances" (Coup, Greene, and Gardner, 1973:136). The "hurrah!" response to the empty nest is increasingly winning over the depressed one. "They can't come home again" is more likely to produce joy than grief. Helena Lopata found at least widowed mothers annoyed at the constant demands made on them by grown sons and daughters.[2]

Not all women, of course, prepare for late motherhood. It is too new a phenomenon in human history to have been assimilated by everyone. Still, fewer and fewer women now arriving at the stage when their children are grown fall into the Momism trap. Fewer and fewer think mournfully of an empty nest. More and more of them are even shouting Hurrah! Mom's daughter or granddaughter has learned that her mother's or grandmother's way of being a mother just doesn't fit this day and age. They are streaming back into the schools and colleges along with younger women, in continuing education programs. They are assuming more and more leadership activities in communities. They are achieving "consciousness." More and more of them are now entering the labor force.

THE "MATURE" WOMAN IN THE LABOR FORCE

As startling as anything else in the recent story of women is the phenomenal increase in the labor-force participation by women whom the tactful researchers label "mature," that is, 45 years of age and over. In the late 1960s almost two-fifths of all women in the labor force were "mature" (Women's Bureau, 1969:20). Between 1940 and 1968 the proportion of women in the labor force who were "mature" almost doubled, rising from 22 percent to 39 percent. Since most of these "mature" women would almost certainly be married and their sons and daughters at least well launched on their own careers, they may be assumed to be in late motherhood.

2. Conversely, however, sons and daughters helped widowed mothers, daughters more than sons. "Only a minority of both samples (32 percent of the whites and 24 percent of the blacks) agreed that sons were more help than daughters" (Lopata, 1973a:247). For further elaboration of the relations of widowed mothers and their sons and daughters see Lopata, 1973b: Chapter 3.

Viewed from the point of the women themselves the trends are just as spectacular. In 1940 only about 24.5 percent of women in the 45 to 54 age bracket were in the labor force (Ibid.:18), the proportion has now more than doubled (*Manpower Report, 1973*: Table 6-2). It is well over half of all women that age, and it is projected to approach three-fifths by 1990 (Ibid.: Table E-2). As many, proportionately, of these "mature" women as of women 20 to 24 were in the labor force.

It is hard to think of them as the harassed, depressed, interfering mothers or mothers-in-law of the stereotype. The chances are almost one in two that the woman we purchased goods from this morning or that the one in three of the women doing clerical work in the offices we enter every day are in late motherhood. They are certainly not the harridans of the media nor the Moms of unsainted memory.

Even among women 55 to 64 years of age the increase in labor-force participation has been phenomenal, rising from 18 percent in 1940 (Women's Bureau, 1969:18), to 42.1 percent in 1972 (*Manpower Report, 1973*: Table 6-2), an increase of almost 140 percent, and projected to almost half (45.8 percent) by 1990 (Ibid.:Table E-2). Again, it is hard to reconcile these women with the stereotype of the devouring, interfering mother-in-law.

As a matter of fact, it is probably the income of this "mature" woman in the labor force that makes it possible for parents to help young couples just starting out. For it is one of the most interesting findings of recent research on kinship ties that such financial help is, in fact, available in many young families (Sussman and Burchinal, 1962; Sussman, 1965). As in so many other instances we have to refocus our lenses to see not the past, but the present, let alone the future.

We do not yet grasp the significance of the emergence of these women as a substantial part of the structure of modern society, analogous to ethnic groups or the "middle class" or other building blocks that social analysts need for interpreting society. For just as the concept of childhood emerged in the fifteenth century, adolescence at the beginning of the twentieth, and youth at midcentury, so, too, has this new stage of "late maturity" appeared on the scene. The daughter or granddaughter of Mom who has not learned how to be a modern mother now sees herself viewed as a luxury for whom her husband ought to be taxed (Preston).

A NEW SEX

These women do not fit any of the old stereotypes. They announce with as much surprise and incredulity as they expect listeners to feel that they are *grandmothers!* Traditionally the image of the grandmother, enshrined in the iconography of Thanksgiving especially, was that of a benign little old lady delightedly serving roast turkey and pumpkin pie to a large family of grandchildren who had arrived on a one-horse open sleigh. It has now become common to speak of "glamorous grandmothers." As, indeed, many of them are, still only in their late forties and fifties. Women in this phase of their lives constitute almost a brand new sex. Here is what these new women are like:

> Something new has been added in recent years. A genuinely new biological subsex has been added to the human stock of sexes. This new kind of woman is the result of cultural forces, technological as well as normative, and of advances in medicine, nutrition, and health care, especially obstetrical. She was not designed and shaped for a specific function, as some other manufactured subsexes were. She was, in fact, an unanticipated consequence of modern science.
>
> In the past when we spoke of "the new woman" we were likely to be thinking of women with new ideas and attitudes, new aspirations and new conceptions of themselves and of their relations to the world. The new women today are new in a quite different way, however. Not in the sense that they are young, for they are not; they may be in their fifties and even, in some rare cases, their sixties. They are new in the sense that women like them have never existed on this planet until now. Their very existence is a brand new human and therefore social phenomenon—as a whole generation, that is; there have always been such individuals.
>
> A demographic revolution has extended sexuality into later years than in the past. The menopause comes later now than it used to. Not only do women live longer than preceding generations did, they also retain their youth and beauty much longer. And those who do not do so naturally can be helped to do so by the new hormonal therapy.
>
> If they were new only in this demographic sense they would not necessarily be new sociologically. They would just be more of the same—old women in larger numbers than before. And in fact, not all of these surviving women really are new. Many still are the same old kind of women as in the past—bitches, moms, Helen Hokinson types. But some are genuinely new (Bernard, 1968:25-26).

These women illustrate what is possible and increasingly probable for more and more women. It is women of this quality who will increasingly face the challenges of late motherhood.

Although the years of late motherhood are, or can be, as good as some of the recent research studies report, it is hard to overcome the old stereotypes. It has been so common to depreciate women in their late forties and fifties that women have come to accept the low self-image. One of the most important tasks the feminists have undertaken is to undo the old patterns of thinking about these women.

CONTINUING DIFFERENCES

The differences among the women themselves are probably greater now than they were earlier, for youth covers differences that experience exaggerates. The difference between the women described above and the ill-nourished or malnourished and worn-out body of the poor woman of the same age is greater than the difference between the affluent adolescent and her less affluent peer. And in the fifties the difference between the more and the less educated is greater than it was in the early twenties.

Some bear their years with aplomb, like Eleanor Roosevelt, or with wit and gaity, like Jean Kerr, and even with chic, like movie stars. At the other extreme are those who are burned out, in a holding operation until they can gratefully, if not gracefully, surrender. The first seem to be gaining over the second.

Some women, in brief, enter the so-called empty-nest stage with zest and excitement; they are delighted at last to be free from the bondage of motherhood. A new and delightful kind of marriage now looms ahead, for they will not become widowed until their early or middle sixties. Others show all the classic symptoms of distress. They act like bereaved women. They have lost their entire raison d'être. They become seriously depressed. Their marriages have become empty shells and offer no haven. The late motherhood syndrome is one of the commonest in folk wisdom, as it is also in the considerable geriatric research literature—much of it well on the way to becoming anachronistic.

II. Family Fissioning

HOUSEHOLD AND FAMILY

The three-generational patriarchal family in which adult sons with their wives remained in the father's household has not been characteristic of our society, except in emergency conditions that call for doubling up, such as the Great Depression. In fact, research by historical demographers has dispelled the idea that the three-generation household was ever widespread.[3] The form in which elderly parents—usually the mother—shared the homes of their adult sons or daughters was not widespread either, but only a relatively transient phenomenon in our history. In the past not enough people lived long enough to make it the common pattern. As more and more people did live long enough to survive until their sons and daughters became parents, the household itself became less and less well adapted to three-generational life-styles. When resources were scarce, however, it was often the only alternative.

In the early years of the century "relative responsibility" as prescribed by law was a big issue. Sons and daughters were legally responsible for their

3. Laslett (1965) was among the first studies to dispel the idea that the three-generation family was ever widespread. Later researchers have corroborated his conclusions.

parents. And if they could not or would not provide for them, there was the county poor farm or poorhouse. Although every effort was made to force sons or daughters to take care of their parents, it became evident as the century wore on that "relative responsibility" was not feasible in an urban society. Sons and daughters during the Great Depression were having as much as they could do to maintain their own families, let alone assume the additional load of parents. All too often forcing dependent old people on adult sons and daughters destroyed whatever affectional bonds there were, for "when actual aid becomes the central fact of the relationships . . . it can weaken the affectional and enjoyable aspects of [the relationship]" (Adams, 1971:170).

In 1935 the coup de grace was delivered to the three-generational household with the old-age and survivors' insurance provision of the Social Security Act. More and more older people could now maintain their own households. Most did. They preferred it that way, and still do.

> There appears to be ample evidence to indicate that, in most instances, neither the old nor the young welcome the prospect of living together. What the older family members want is to maintain their own living quarters and to have frequent and cordial contact with their children. Such contacts, they say, help to assuage their loneliness and provide assurance that help will be forthcoming when needed. (Field, 1972:78)

Close but not too close. Separate but not too separate. Strong ties but not too strong. Together but not too together. That seems to be the ideal. Actually the trend is in the direction of increasing age segregation.

AGE-SEGREGATED COMMUNITIES

In a study of East London less than a quarter of a century ago, an almost idyllic picture was drawn of elderly mothers. Whether living alone or with their husbands, they had sons and daughters living in the immediate environs, sons and daughters who dropped by several times a week, grandchildren who did daily chores for them, and much visiting back and forth among all of them. "Mum"—not to be confused with the American Mom—was an important part of the lives of everyone, especially of daughters; she often took care of their children, as the daughters took care of her. There was enormous stability in the lives of all of them (Townsend, 1968).

There may be pockets of such intimate mother-daughter-grandchild relations in our country today, but it is doubtful that they constitute a typical pattern except, perhaps, in remnants of old ethnic enclaves.[4]

4. Ethnic enclaves are usually composed of working-class families. And, "in general . . . the working classes . . . express a stronger kin orientation, live closer to their

Research does find regular, even frequent, visiting, occasional shopping together perhaps, some sharing of commercial recreation, attending religious services together; it finds different degrees and kinds of financial assistance, of mutual aid, including gifts; telephoning and letter writing; and periodical vacation visits or family holiday celebrations (Field, 1972). But rarely does it uncover the seemingly almost tribal London pattern. There is, rather, a trend toward an increase in the fissioning of families.

A quarter of a century ago David Reisman and his associates (1950) noted that human relationships, especially among the young, were taking on a lateral rather than a vertical direction. Peer groups were encroaching on families as sources of influence. Age segregation was jelling. More recently this process has been commented on among the old population also. They congregate in retirement communities of varying levels of comfort and opulence. The pros and cons of such age segregation continue to engage the attention of those interested in all age-grade levels. But in the meanwhile it continues.

Parents may resist this age segregation. They may cling to the "old house" long after the children have left. But when the husband retires, they frequently do move to smaller quarters, and, more and more, to retirement communities. These so-called retirement communities tend to grow up especially in warm climates. In some cases parents have come to these communities at the suggestion of sons and daughters who are "motivated by a genuine concern . . . for their parents' welfare" (Field, 1972:67). The sons and daughters may even have subsidized the move. There are, however, some parents who have in effect been exiled by their sons or daughters. "By removing the parents a considerable distance from themselves, they at the same time remove themselves from the responsibility of a more intimate involvement. By so doing, they can truthfully say that they cannot visit as frequently as they would like" (Ibid.). The mother, too, can comfortably deceive herself, excusing the infrequent visits by her sons and daughters on the grounds of distance and expense.

Actually, distance does not change much; there was no greater contact even before the move. Thus a study of the relationships between parents-in-the-South and offspring-in-the-North found that "the relationship varies but little from what is found when parent and child live in closer proximity, and that the whole gamut of feelings and relationships can be detected" (Ibid.).

Some of these mothers have sons and daughters who show genuine concern and keep in constant touch, visiting them as often as they can. But others have sons and daughters who admit relief at not being burdened with the day-by-day attention to parents.

kin, and interact with them more regularly than the middle classes. . . . The working classes feel a sense of obligation for more than simple contact, while in the middle classes keeping in touch is enough (Adams, 1971:173–174).

Some of the parents retain feelings of independence, wanting to manage their own affairs in their own way, while others lean heavily on sons and daughters even in the minor exigencies of life. Some are not at all demanding but, indeed, grateful for any evidence of interest. They learn to repress any feelings of resentment:

> I keep a tight grip on my hurt feelings when I do not see any of my children, or hear from them for weeks at a stretch. I try to remember that they are busy with their household, with their families, with the various recreational activities which are to them an essential part of their lives. So, when I do see them, I never reproach them, but tell them how glad I am that they were able to come. (Ibid.:69)[5]

When or if illness strikes, these parental attitudes—plus and minus—become exaggerated.

For the less affluent, not retirement communities but "ghettoes of the elderly" or "senior citizens' hotels" in congested areas of large cities may be where the parents move when they can no longer maintain households of their own. Because of the desolation of these living quarters, sons and daughters find visiting them dispiriting.

THE FISSIONED FAMILY

"The family," as Philippe Ariès has reminded us, is an idea, a concept, rather than a specific entity. Parents and children living together in a common household are real and vivid families. They can be seen and heard and felt and loved and fought with. But once the paths of parents, sons, and daughters diverge, what is left? The "family" is now a number of scattered, dispersed individuals, lost in an amorphous outside world or absorbed in groups and families of their own. It is a mental construct. It exists as an entity primarily only in the mind, in the pictures on the walls, in symbols, in the baby shoes and other mementoes of the past stored—if, in fact, they have even been saved—in dresser drawers, until they are jettisoned for lack of space. The final fission occurs when the mother is widowed.

III. On Her Own

MOTHERS AND DAUGHTERS

Because of the matriarchal emphasis in kinship relations in our society

5. The reviewer of a book on a retirement community noted that relations with the children were not explored. He concluded that the subject must have been too painful (L.J. Davis, reviewing *Rancho Paradiso* by John Deck in *Book World,* August 6, 1972).

(Adams, 1971:169), and because women tend to outlive men,[6] it is mother-daughter relationships that constitute the major relationship component of the older woman's life. Mom was never the ogre, the monster, to daughters that she was to sons. The affectional ties between women and their mothers often grow as the daughters themselves become mothers and old hostilities become mastered. By the age of 40 if not earlier the daughter can be friendly toward her mother. Even in the upper-middle class—where kinship orientation is minimal—many women finally achieve friendship with their mothers. Some even come to like and enjoy one another. Those who do achieve one of the most rewarding experiences their lives have afforded. The daughter has someone to share her "news" with, someone to "brag" to about her possessions or achievements without arousing envy, someone she can trust with secrets. The mother has someone whose life she can share.

But not too intimately. On the average—with all the exceptions the concept of average implies—women become widowed at about the age of 62. Thereafter they tend to live by themselves. In 1972, for example, three-fourths of all noninstitutionalized widowed women 65 years of age and older were heads of their own households, and most (79 percent) were living alone. Most of the remaining fourth were living in families. A few were boarders or roomers or, perhaps, living in foster homes (Bureau of the Census, 1972).[7] Although some may have been self-supporting, most were probably not. They were being supported by Social Security benefits, welfare payments, pensions, inheritances, husbands' insurance policies, sons, daughters, what-have-you.

In many cases daughters are willing, if necessary, to have their mothers come to live with them. And, as a matter of fact, except among professional families of the upper-middle class—who are more likely than families in other classes to be separated from their relatives—most older women live within a hundred miles of their sons and daughters.

Even among these women it is difficult to recognize role changes, to achieve new self-images, new identities. There is psychological work to be done even at this late date. One widow continued to feel the same homemaking responsibility she had felt earlier.

> One of the strangest things that has ever happened to me was the feeling
> I continued to have that since I had four children I had to maintain a

6. There were about four and a half times as many widowed women as widowed men among the noninstitutionalized population 65 years of age and over in 1972 (Bureau of the Census, 1972).

7. Of all those 65 years of age and older, only 7 percent live in institutions (Field, 1972:61). The proportion is, expectedly, higher among those 75 years of age and over (14 percent) than among those 65 to 74 (4 percent). A study in Great Britain found that institutional populations were "recruited" more from those who had no family than among those who did, especially those who had no daughters. "More people in institutions than outside who have children have sons only" (Townsend, 1968:112).

large house for them. My oldest children have long since left home for marriage and college. I had only one child at home and she would be off to college in less than a year. But I still thought of myself as the mother of four children who had to maintain a home for all of them. Not until I was 60 years old and my youngest was a junior in college did it occur to me that I no longer had to maintain a home for her. All she needed a home for was to store her books during the summer when she was off somewhere or other. (Personal document)

The conception she had of herself as "mater familias" was hard to erase. In her case she reconceived herself only when she moved from the large house to an apartment. Living arrangements make a difference.

AN ATTENUATED FORM OF MOMISM

It is difficult to get a good fix on mothers in their later years. The retirement trauma of men has been well researched and the relations of the aging man and his wife have entered the research picture. But the relations of the woman herself with her sons and daughters, now themselves entering middle age, are not well delineated. Old women as mothers have just faded out of the research picture as feeling, acting, individuated human beings. They are present, to be sure, on innumerable questionnaires and they have dutifully answered the interviewers' numerous queries. But for the most part they hardly come through at all. The questionnaires and the interviewers' protocols report how often sons and daughters visit, telephone, or in other ways "keep in touch." But they do not tell us the caliber of these relationships or their significance for the women themselves, though these visits and telephone calls constitute a con- siderable part of the lives of the elderly mothers. Indeed, the sometimes nagging insistence on such visits and telephone calls or letters constitutes a kind of Momism in attenuated form.

One of the hazards of many women now in their late sixties and seventies—the "generation of vipers" of a quarter of a century ago—is that they have lived such a family-bound life that they are almost wholly dependent on family contacts for ties to life. They did not participate extensively in outside activities and are therefore almost exclusively limited to their own sons and daughters for meaningful relationships (Lopata, 1973b:244). They are subject to a social situation that has been labeled *altruistic surrender* (Freud, 1946). This is an exaggerated form of the usual identification with another, or seeing another as an extension of one's self, that characterizes any loving relationship.

Identification is not the same as identity. A recent study of 38 women, all but three of them widowed, found that the identity of these women was as "my daughter's mother" (Hochschild, 1973:97). But identification was more. By seeing her daughter as an extension of herself she could enjoy the younger woman's life without envying it. The new eye-level oven, the new job, the fishing trip could all be appreciated and enjoyed vicariously. "The daughters provided the intimate details of their lives and filled their mothers in on every change of plan and new event, not retrospectively but as they were happening" (Ibid.:103). It was like a continuing soap opera only more vivid. Identification is not, of course, peculiar to old people vis-à-vis the young; it is common among husbands and wives, fans and stars, parents and children of all ages.

Only when the identifier is not in a position to gratify her—in this case—own desires and lives wholly in the life of the identified-with person is the relationship one of altruistic surrender. "A certain degree of identification with another is probably essential to a deep love relationship in that it allows the individual to share the fortunes and misfortunes of the loved one" (Ibid.:105). It is only "when the identification is not reciprocal and when one party substitutes vicarious living for direct living" (Ibid.) that we have altruistic surrender. We see here the importance of the visiting, telephoning, and letters reported in the research literature. They provide the mother the wherewithal to live vicariously through her sons, and, more likely, daughters.

The demands for such life-sharing may become excessive, resented by sons and daughters stretched to the limit by the other demands being made on them. Their resentment in turn generates feelings of guilt. They feel they ought to pay more attention to their mother's needs. Actually such "altruistic surrender" is the form that Momism may take for the generation of women now in their late sixties and seventies. Such "vicarious living, when it becomes a substitute for direct living, is not 'innate' in mothers or old people in their love of others. It is mixed with social deprivation, disguised by the label of 'love'" (Ibid.:110). And, far from being innate, vicarious living is increasingly eroded. For more and more elderly women are being spared the deprivation that leads to altruistic surrender. More and more women are preparing themselves for their later years by beginning to find extrafamily interests earlier, to spare themselves dependence on children. And even for women still unprepared, unexpected communities seem now to be evolving.

AN UNEXPECTED COMMUNITY

One of the most interesting discoveries reported in the recent research literature is the unexpected community that sometimes grows up among widowed women living in proximity to one another. One such "unexpected community" was found in a housing project in the Bay Area of California. These women, in addition to warm relationships with their daughters, had developed peer-group relationships among themselves that performed quite a different function in their lives. For one thing, it gave them activities and interests of their own so that they did not have to live vicariously through their daughters.

> Their society together offers them not just a chance to share their vicarious lives. It offers an alternative to vicarious living—a chance to live directly, in the here and now, in one's given body whatever its disabilities. Among the . . . peers there is seldom the stable patterned relationship of identifier and identified-with as in the case of the daughters. In the . . . peer bond it is not, "You do and I'll watch" but rather, "What did you watch?" "I watched this," and, more important, "I'm doing this, what are you doing?" Thus the bonds with kin and with fellow residents perform different emotional functions, which may account for the fact that, in the lives of the grandmothers, kin ties and peer ties are not interchangeable. (Hochschild, 1973:111).

They shared a "consciousness of kind" which, though it did not have the depth of kinship consciousness nor yet the stimulation of sisterhood, was nevertheless a sustaining one.

THE END OF MOMISM

As long as a woman is running a home, she seems to her sons and daughters to be strong. The power of a mother is so profound—in the literal meaning of that word, that is, deep—that, short of death it is rarely lost. The sons and daughters who have clung to the mother as children, fought with her as adolescents, fled from her as young adults, and merely arrived at a stand-off in early maturity can hardly ever see the woman who is their mother as of merely human size. She has always loomed large in their psychic life. As long as she maintains her own household she remains bigger than life. She may herself sense the waning of her vitality long before the son or daughter notices. For there does, finally, come a time when Momism—even in the form of demands for news that makes it possible to live vicariously—dies out.

To the active, involved daughter, the mother alone in her apartment with only her plants to keep her occupied still looks like a lonely old woman who must be suffering the pangs of exclusion and rejection, for that is how she would feel if she were in the old woman's position. She feels impelled to keep in touch, to visit, to invite, to take out, to keep occupied. In time, to the old woman herself, her "loneliness" looks like solitude and she loves it. A peaceful, quiet life after years of hurly-burly is what she had long dreamed of. *Not* having to keep up contacts with a lot of people is itself a privilege. The insistence of her grown sons and daughters on bringing the grandchildren and inviting her to their homes begins to wear her out. All she really wants is the assurance that if she ever really needs them they will be there, that they are themselves able to carry their own load, that the grandchildren are OK, that none of them has been busted for drugs, that the son's promotion has come through—and otherwise just be left alone. Some students call this "disengagement" (Cummings and Henry, 1961).

REVERSED ROLES

The day finally approaches, early or late, when the two women, mother and daughter, face one another in a harrowing confrontation. The older woman, comfortable and contented in her household, resigned or actively satisfied, finds she must fend off the younger woman's suggestion that she needs more care. She resents the daughter's efforts to control her life. They want to put her away in an old people's home. She won't go. The daughter is torn. Last night as they prepared for bed she confided in her husband. "I'm worried about mother. Yesterday she forgot to unplug the iron and it burned through the ironing board cover. Last week, you remember, she fell asleep with the oven going full blast. I don't think it's safe to leave her alone any longer." Her husband was noncommital or reassuring, but not yet involved. No matter, she knew this problem was hers and hers alone. She discussed it with her sister this morning. Concern, but not consternation. Let's leave well enough alone for the present. Anyway there could never be any question of *her* taking mother to live with her, with her house full of children.

The daughter knows that if her mother were to be taken into anyone's home, it would have to be hers. She has not herself come to terms with that idea; nor she is sure, has her mother. "Honor thy father and thy mother that thy days may be long on the earth" may have made sense once upon a time. It was taken for granted that one would support parents and parents took it for granted that support would be forthcoming. Such dependence was built into the system and could therefore be borne with fortitude if not necessarily with grace. In traditional China a woman looked forward to old age when her burdens would be lightened and her power over daughters-in-law especially enhanced. A far cry indeed to a daughter struggling to solve in her own conscience what to do about her own mother.

Alone she visits homes for the elderly. The most attractive ones are very expensive. Even those that are merely suitable seem far beyond the means available. Those that are within available means are shudderingly inadequate. Perhaps she could go back to work to make up the difference. Mary, the sister, might be able to scrape up money to share the extra burden. Jack's wife might be difficult, but Jack would certainly try.

For the present the decision can be postponed. After all, mother does manage. The daughter visits more often. Between the younger and the older woman the ties are of pity, compassion, guilt, resentment. To the older woman, as deterioration progresses, the younger woman seems increasingly like a stranger. The world they once shared is hardly even a memory any longer. Love in the sense of joy and tenderness vanished some time ago. To the younger woman there is a kind of aching horror to see the woman who once loomed so large in her mind's eye so shrunken, so stubborn, so resistant.

Daughter: You would be so much better taken care of at the Stacy Home. It's really lovely.

Mother: I can take good enough care of myself right here.

Daughter: But I can't come every day to check. There's always something I have to do.

Mother: You don't *have* to come every day. I wish you wouldn't.

The same dialogue goes on for varying periods of time, perhaps a few months, perhaps even a few years. The older woman wants nothing but to be left alone. Her mind has long since melted into a vague blur. But she feels safe here surrounded by familiar effects. She has long since forgotten whose pictures are on the walls, all those grandchildren, sons-in-law, daughters-in-law. But they are reassuring. True, she is incontinent from time to time. But she can keep herself clean. . . .

THE BURDEN OF GUILT

The burden of guilt among sons and daughters of parents who are placed in nursing homes or other kinds of institutions is so great that one physician has inaugurated rap sessions to help them work through their emotions:

> "Half of our problems in the nursing home field are psychological and are related to the children, not the parents." Dr. Lichtman . . . refers to the informal gatherings at DeWitt as rap sessions and at a recent one he sat facing the people whom he calls children but who are mostly middle-aged men and women.
>
> They had just come from visiting a relative who, in most cases, had been in the nursing home only a short time, and what Dr. Lichtman wanted was for them to air whatever doubts and feelings of guilt they might have. . . .
>
> Mrs. Melvin Brod started the discussion by saying, "I've thought of what you've said about the umbilical cord, Doctor, and I suppose it's true of me and my mother—the cord has never really been cut. I come here seven days a week to see her but I had guilt when I brought her in here and I still have guilt."
>
> Mrs. Brod, who is a painter, went on to say that her 82-year-old mother had been living alone in a small apartment and that she had accidents. "She had blackouts and once she fell and cut her head so

badly that she needed 13 stitches; maybe I should have taken her into my home," said Kathy Brod.

Then she added, "But I couldn't. She gets into mischief and must be looked after constantly. I simply couldn't stay with her 24 hours a day, and if I had her at home I know she wouldn't get the care she gets here. She's eating well and while she missed her apartment terribly at first, she now calls her room here her apartment. Yet I have guilt." . . .

Dr. Lichtman said, "We have to fight dehumanizing here. The activities group is trying to make the elderly feel that they are important persons. And there are other little ways to do that. The hairdresser, just having her here, means something and, when a woman no longer cares to have her hair done, it means she's no longer interested in herself as a person."

"I wish I didn't have a guilty conscience," said Mrs. Brod. . . . "I'm the youngest in the family and maybe that's why I feel the way I do. . . . My mother always spoiled me and now I feel I should be spoiling her. Even while I'm sitting here I know my mother is waiting for me to take her out into the garden. . . . (Warren, 1972).

Kathy Brod's anguish has its counterpart in her mother's insistence to others in the nursing home on Kathy's concern. Mothers in institutions tend to protect themselves from feelings of rejection and seek to impress others with their daughters' concern; they deny rejection, they emphasize closeness of family ties, they play up any attention they receive from their families, they point to the evident concern shown by them for her welfare and happiness (Field, 1972:84).

There are differing opinions on the pros and cons of nursing homes. Some argue for making more nursing care available by the community to the old person in her own home. "Meals on wheels" and help with routine household chores are among the ideas advocated. Such "community services must no longer be thought of simply as replacing the services of the family or substituting for them. . . . They must also be increasingly thought of as supplementing or complementing the services of the family" (Townsend, 1968:113).

Others still argue for care in the homes of sons and daughters. In families that "feel they can incorporate an aged parent into their household without trouble" and "are willing to attempt it," such an arrangement can work (Adams, 1971:170). But "when obligation to help becomes the dominant element in the relation, so that friendship yields to dependency, . . . the relationship is weakened" (Ibid.). Much of the success or failure of such an arrangement depends on "the feelings carried over from earlier years—the unresolved frustrations and stresses experienced by the children in the past, or the persisting authoritarian attitudes of the parent. In addition, the older person's reaction to sharing the children's home is colored by the implied need to give up his [her][8] independence. One study found that the morale of

8. When a parent is taken into a child's home it is more likely to be the mother than the father (Field, 1972:60), and more likely to be a daughter's home (Adams, 1971).

the elderly was lowest among those who were living with a child" (Field, 1972:75). And at least one leader in the field of geriatric psychiatry agrees. He demolishes the romanticized, nostalgic notion of the three-generation family.

There is, he points out, far more brain damage than is commonly recognized: 5 percent among those over 65, but 20 to 25 percent among 75-year-olds and 40 percent among those over 85. "We have confused issues of actual physical care and affectionate and protective feelings. We talk as though the best way to take care of a person in pain is to hug and kiss him rather than to take him to a place (an institution) where he [she] can get the physical and psychological care he [she] needs" (Skerly, 1972). So far from being callous and uncaring, sons and daughters "tend to maintain their parents at home much past the point when they can give them adequate care" (Ibid.). He disagrees strongly with doctors who "Feel these people shouldn't be admitted to institutions, that the daughter should stay at home and take care of the individual. But the family can't provide that kind of care in the home" (Ibid.). And it is not best for the parent.

Such reassurance from specialists in geriatric psychiatry is designed to reassure daughters like Mrs. Brod and the thousands of other daughters like her. It may help; it may assuage their guilt. It cannot eradicate it. Only the death of the mother can probably do that.

PRESENT PROLOGUE TO FUTURE?

This is the end of motherhood today for women born around the turn of the century. It will be different for women born in the middle or latter half of the century. All the research to date deals with the way things are today and they reflect the way they were yesterday. At this particular moment of history, the relationship between women in late motherhood is complicated by certain peculiar, extrinsic, and fortuitous historical factors. In some cases, for example, the mother is of an immigrant generation, her sons and daughters are native-born and there is a built-in"generation gap." Or the mother has a rural background and the sons and daughters an urban background. The mother belongs to a time of simpler technologies, especially of transportation. There is little public transportation so she is more dependent than in former times for getting around. New ways of thinking have evolved since her own patterns were established more than half a century ago. Margaret Mead has concluded, in fact, that the difference between preatomic and postatomic generations is greater than that between any others in human history.

But as the escalators of time bring new generations of women to late motherhood, they will be better educated, they will have more relevant skills, their bodies will have had better care. Fewer of them will be poor. They will have had fewer children. Better services will be available for them in their own homes. The gap between them and their daughters will be narrower. Altruistic surrender will be increasingly postponed.

References

Adams, Bert N. 1971. Isolation, function, and beyond: American kinship in the 1960s, in Broderick, Carlfred B., ed., *A decade of family research and action*. Minneapolis: National Council on Family Relations.

Bart, Pauline. 1970. Mother Portnoy's complaint. *Trans-Action* 8 (November-December):69–74.

Bernard, Jessie. 1968. *The sex game, Communication between the sexes*. Englewood Cliffs: Prentice-Hall. New York: Atheneum, 1972.

Blood, Robert O., and Wolfe, Donald M. 1960. *Husbands and wives: The dynamics of married living*. New York: Free Press.

Bureau of the Census. March, 1972. *Current Population Reports*, Series P-20, no. 242 (November).

Coup, Roger F.; Greene, Shirley; and Gardner, Burleigh B. 1973. *A study of working-class women in a changing world*. Chicago: Social Research.

Cowan, Ruth Schwartz. 1973. A case study of technology and social change. Paper presented at Berkshire Conference on Women Historians, March, Rutgers University.

Cummings, Elaine, and Henry, W. 1961. *Growing old: The process of disengagement*. New York: Basic Books.

Freud, Anna. 1946. *The ego and the mechanisms of defense*. Trans. Cecil Baines. New York: International Universities Press.

Hochschild, Arlie Russell. 1973. *The unexpected community*. Englewood Cliffs: Prentice-Hall.

Duvall, Evelyn Millis. 1954. *In-laws: Pro and con*. New York: Association Press.

Field, Minna. 1972. *The aged, the family, and the community*. New York: Columbia University Press.

Laslett, Peter. 1965. *The world we have lost*. New York: University Paperbacks.

Lederer, Wolfgang. 1968. *The fear of women*. New York: Harcourt Brace Jovanovich.

Lopata, Helena Z. 1973a. Social relations of black and white widowed women in a northern metropolis. *American Journal of Sociology*. 78 (January): 1003–1010.

———. 1973b. *Widowhood in an American city*. Cambridge, Mass.: Schenkman.

Manpower Report of the President. 1973. Washington, D.C.: U.S. Government Printing Office.

Meade, Walter. 1972. Mothers and sons. *Cosmopolitan* (December):210ff.

Preston, Samuel. 1962. Female employment policy and fertility. Report of the President's Commission on Population Growth and the American future. Reproduced.

Riesman, David; Glazer, Nathan; and Denney, Reuel. 1950. *The lonely crowd*. New York: Doubleday-Anchor

Townsend, Peter. 1968. The structure of the family, in Shanas, Ethel, et. al., eds., *Old people in three industrial societies*. New York: Atheneum.

Schmiedeler, Edgar J. 1955. *The mother the heart of the home*. St. Minard, Ind.: Grail.

Schwarts, Gwen Gibson, and Wyden, Barbara. 1970. *The Jewish wife*. New York: Wyden.

Skerly, Nada. 1972. New view urged for aged care. *Washington Post,* October 8, 1972.

Sussman, Marvin B. 1965. Relationships of adult children with their parents in the United States, in Shanas, Ethel, and Streib, Gordon F., eds., *Social structure and the family: Generational relations.* Englewood Cliffs: Prentice-Hall.

Sussman, Marvin B., and Burchinal, Lee. 1962. Parental aid to married children: Implications for family functioning, *Marriage and Family Living* 24 (November): 320–332.

Warren, Virginia Lee. 1972. With a parent in a nursing home, offspring need to express their emotions. *New York Times,* September 4, 1972.

Women's Bureau. 1969. *1969 Handbook on women workers.* Washington, D.C.: U.S. Government Printing Office.

Wylie, Philip. 1942. *Generation of vipers.* New York: Rinehart.

PART IV

AGE, CLASS, RACE

THE PAPERS IN PART IV examine three major variables—age, class-ethnicity, and race—as they impinge on feminist issues. Although only age and race are biological variables, all three are fundamentally sociological in their impact.

Age, for example, is one thing among an educated population, another among an uneducated, not only biologically but also attitudinally. Education, as the first paper suggests, makes people "think young." And educated people, other things held equal, tend to be more sympathetic with the feminist movement. Closer scrutiny of the female population, however, reveals complex undercurrents that tend to blur the impact of age per se. Cohorts of women reflect the historical period in which they were born and reared. Thus we have "depression babies," "wartime babies," "cold-war babies" and so on. Age becomes complicated in its impact by these generational differences.

Because the context for which the paper on age was prepared did not seem to warrant it, no attention was paid to a special kind of "ageism" peculiar to women which has become a feminist issue. It has to do with "the double standard" with respect to age among men and women. Despite the fact that any objective, disinterested comparison of men and women in the years beyond 40 shows the women at least as attractive as the men, if not more so, they "must endure the specter of aging much sooner than men.

. . . This cultural definition of aging gives men a decided psychological, sexual and economic advantage over women" (Bell, 1970:75).[1]

The second paper attempts first to clarify the position of the feminist movement with respect to class and then to show the impact the feminist movement is having on working-class women today. Alice Rossi has perceptively analyzed the complex history of feminist positions on class. The nineteenth-century feminists spoke as though they were interested in the welfare of working-class women but they were, in fact, interested only in their own kind of women—middle-class like themselves. When the chips were down, Rossi reminds us, the women in the suffrage movement were anti-immigration. But twentieth century feminists—many of them, including both the earlier ones as well as those who sparked the recrudescence of the movement in the 1960s—were socialists in orientation. Rossi reminds us also of Florence Kelley, Sophonisba Breckenridge, Edith Abbott, Jane Addams, Emma Goldberg, and Margaret Sanger, all of whom were fundamentally concerned with working-class women (Rossi, 1973). The charge, therefore, that the feminist movement is primarily a middle-class movement in behalf of middle-class women cannot be accepted as valid.

Nor can the stereotyped position that working-class women reject the feminist movement any longer be accepted. Working-class women and middle-class women share a common life as mothers: "the concept that husband and children are their main responsibility and the activity area from which they derive the most satisfaction is repeated over and over by Working-Class women" (Coup, Greene, and Gardner, 1973:133). But so is it by middle-class women. The period when children are small is "a life stage in which Working-Class women have traditionally 'stayed put,' emotionally bogged down in the ruts of drudgery such as cleaning, cooking, shopping, driving children to their various appointments, etc., etc. In this situation, the women are apt to be overly busy and tired, demanding and complaining, and feeling that their husbands may be losing interest in them" (Ibid.). The same scenario could be written about middle-class mothers. "But the winds of social change and stirrings of 'liberation' appear to be effecting the decline or demise of this Working-Class tradition" (Ibid.:134). Ditto for the middle-class tradition.

Class, it may be noted in passing, as it has been researched by men is not a very suitable concept for understanding women. The formidable tools social theorists have developed for the analysis of the male world do not fit the task. Income, education, and occupation, three master variables used to

---

1. For example, "a man's wrinkles will not define him as sexually undesirable until he reaches his late fifties," but a woman's, long before. Advertisements for jobs addressed to women "use physical descriptions almost entirely lacking in men's ads. 'Attractive' . . . is typical." Hugh Hefner fires his bunnies when they reach 30; air line companies would like to do the same to their stewardesses. The life of a female sex object ends at 30.

operationalize class, do not operate the same way among women as among men. Nor do the Marxist conceptions of class in terms of the ownership of the means of production. Women are presumed to take the class position of their husbands, but there are enough inconsistencies to blur the picture. As more and more women enter the labor market, many wives of blue-collar men are in white-collar occupations; whose work determines the family's "class"?[2] In a great many cases it is the working wife who pulls the family up into the middle class, or out of the slough of poverty (Bell, 1973).

An enormous area calling for research cultivation has to do with the relationships between and among women of different occupational, ethnic, racial, and class backgrounds. For some purposes, Judy O'Grady and the Colonel's lady are, indeed, sisters under the skin; for others they may be antagonists. We ought to know a great deal more about these relationships.

The third paper deals with the relative impact of sexism and racism especially in the case of black women who feel the effects of both. I always apologize when I express the enormous admiration I feel for black women. I do not want to sound patronizing, for that is the farthest possible position from my own attitude toward them. In 1966 I dedicated a book to them:

> With a minimum of preparation, against all but insuperable odds, these women have borne the major burden of pulling up the Negro population by its bootstraps. They have been spirited and independent, as well as self-sacrificing. As wives, they have not taken advantage of their—"unnatural"—superiority; as mothers, they have worn out countless washboards, earning money to educate their children. They deserve a place alongside the women who pioneered another frontier— one fraught with no less danger than the West, against odds no less formidable, and, it is hoped, with equal, if delayed, success. (Bernard, 1966:x)

The paper shows that their success has continued up to the present. Still fighting the odds, they are making it.

A common misapprehension should, finally, be corrected. It is sometimes assumed that black women work more and earn more than black men. Not so. Black men have lower unemployment rates than black women and earn more. The power of black women does not depend entirely on an economic base.

---

2. In 1967, almost three-fifths (57.1 percent) of husbands who were craftsmen, foremen, or kindred workers were married to women who were professionals, technical workers, managers, officials, proprietors, clerical workers, or sales workers (Women's Bureau, 1969: Table 15, pp. 38–39). For husbands who were operatives and kindred workers, the figure was 41.1 percent. Even for husbands who were service workers, it was 43.6 percent.

References

Bell, Carolyn Shaw. 1973. Age, sex, marriage, and jobs. *The Public Interest* 30 (winter):80–82.

Bell, Inge Powell. 1970. The double standard. *Trans-Action* 8 (November-December): 75-81.

Bernard, Jessie. 1966. *Marriage and family among Negroes*. Englewood Cliffs: Prentice-Hall.

Coup, Roger F.; Greene, Shirley; and Gardner, Burleigh B. 1973. *A study of working-class women in a changing world*. Chicago: Social Research.

Rossi, Alice. 1973. Feminism and class politics, in Rossi, Alice, ed., *The feminist papers from Adams to de Beauvoir*. New York: Bantam.

Women's Bureau. 1969. *1969 Handbook of women workers*. Washington, D.C.: U.S. Goverment Printing Office.

EIGHT

Age and Attitudes on
Feminist Issues

I. Age, Aging, and Education

Two major distinctions related to age as a variable must be made, one between age and aging and one between age and education.

AGE AND AGING

Because cross-sectional studies, usually in the form of surveys or polls, show older respondents of both sexes almost uniformly more conservative than younger ones, it is generally implicitly assumed that individuals become more conservative with age or that aging per se has a conservative effect. Actually, only longitudinal or before-and-after studies could tell us about the effect of aging per se on the attitudes and opinions of individuals. And we have few if any such studies.

An interesting surrogate for such a study compared the present attitudes of a sample of 89 fathers averaging 50 years of age with their attitudes as they remembered them some 30 years earlier, and suggested that these men did not become more conservative with time (Claven and Robak, 1973). To be sure, as compared with their sons, who averaged 20 years of age, these men were in fact more conservative, suggesting that aging had slowed change down but had not inhibited it. On all but 4 of 17 items on a questionnaire, the men were more permissive now than they remembered themselves as being in their youth.[1] On 3 of the remaining 13 items they had become more like their sons than they had been as they remembered themselves at their sons' age.[2] On the other 10 items the fathers, even when they had changed, remained nearer to themselves in their youth than to their sons.[3] They had not become more conservative than they had been in their remembered youth—except in the items referred to above—but they were nevertheless more conservative than their sons were. The effect of aging as—however inadequately—measured here was not, in brief, to reverse attitudes or to prevent change but only to slow it down. Exposed to the same influences as their sons, they had not become as permissive as their sons were, but more permissive—with the noted exceptions—than they had been in their youth.

Another surrogate-type study is the replicated Harris Poll of women in 1972 as compared to the original poll in 1971. The two polls show that older women tended to approach the position of the younger women even over such a brief span of time as a single year. Thus, for example, if one compares the replies of women to a question on attitudes toward efforts to strengthen or change women's status in society, one finds that in 1972, 41 percent of the women 50 years of age and over were catching up to the 46 percent of the women 18 to 29 years of age in 1971; so, also, had 42 percent of the women in their forties. Women in their thirties had overtaken the 1971 18-to-29-year-olds; but by that time, the younger women had outdistanced all the others (Harris and Associates, 1972:2).[4] Again, then, although in cross-section the older women were uniformly more conservative than the younger, they had changed, and in a modern rather than in a traditional direction. In the absence, therefore, of convincing longitudinal data on the effect of aging per se on attitudes, no assumptions are made here that such an effect can be expected.

1. The four items had to do with premarital sexual behavior among girls. More now than when they were young would think less of a girl if she is agreeable to petting on a date, initiates necking and petting, agrees to sexual relations, and initiates sexual relations.

2. The three items had to do with helping wives with housekeeping and child care: help with cooking; help with feeding, bathing, and diapering children; and help with taking care of children when wife is away.

3. Or, as on four items, they had come about halfway between their position in their youth and their sons' current position. One of these halfway items had to do with accepting the right of a girl to call to arrange a meeting; the other three had to do with the acceptance of financial responsibilities by women, that is, they would not think less of a girl if she agrees to a dutch treat, they would expect a wife to work before children were born, they would expect their wives to earn part of the regular family income.

4. In 1972, among the young women, over half (56 percent) favored efforts to strengthen women's status. In addition, there was also a slight tendency for the proportion of respondents giving a "not sure" response to decline. The same trend for older age-groups to "catch up" with younger age-groups was found by William Ronco in a study of polls since 1930. For example, people in their thirties in 1945 tended to disapprove of women working; when they were in their sixties, most tended to approve. "The aging process may close some minds, but it must open more; the figures change in the direction of approval" (Roundup of Current Research, 1974:12). See also Bernard, 1974: Introduction.

AGE AND EDUCATION

The fact that more older than younger respondents in most surveys and polls tend to be conservative may be related more to their lower level of education than to age itself. The Daniel Yankelovich polling agency told us several years ago, in fact, that the really important "gap" was not so much the widely publicized "generation gap" as the less publicized "education gap." There were, by and large, as many differences between young college and noncollege youth as between youth and their parents (Yankelovich, 1969). For, in general, less-educated persons tend to be somewhat older as well as more conservative than the better-educated[5] and, conversely, older persons tend to be less well educated than younger.[6] Thus any comparison of older with younger women involves comparing quite different populations. Any cross-section comparison of women of different ages tells us as much about their schooling as it does about their age, if not more. Since the trend is in the direction of increased years of schooling for women,[7] it is, inferentially, in the direction of greater acceptance by them of feminist views.

II. Sex Differences
   on Feminist Issues
   by Age

The significance of age differences, whatever they are due to, takes on salience when sex is also taken into account, for interesting differences

---

5. Among male eighth-grade graduates, two-thirds (66.9 percent) were 35 years of age or over in 1972, among females, 70.1 percent; among high-school graduates, the proportions 35 and over were, respectively, 53.3 and 56.2 percent (Current Population Reports, 1972:45).

6. In 1972, only a little over half (52.7 percent) of all women 35 years of age and over had completed high school, almost three-fourths (73.2 percent) of women 30 to 34 had. Only about two-thirds as many women 35 and over as women 30 to 34 had had any years of college. The contrasts were, of course, even more marked between women 35 years of age and over and women under 30. More than twice as many 25-year-old women as women 35 and over had had some college (Ibid.). Since the present paper was written, Daniel Yankelovich has released some findings of a new study showing that between 1969 and 1972 the education gap was closing, especially on work-related items on a survey questionnaire. Non-college youth in 1972 were approaching the position of college youth of 1968. Among women, however, although non-college women were showing change, there was still a wide gap between them and college women. Thus almost half of the non-college women (47 percent) rejected the woman's-place-is-in-the-home ideology, but among women entering college in 1972, almost three-fourths (74.4 percent) did. The Yankelovich data are from an interview reported by Stephen D. Isaacs, "A Rapid Change from Counter to Culture," *Washington Post*, May 22, 1974. The data on entering college women are from the American Council on Education.

7. Thus, for example, whereas 5.8 percent of young (white) women 25 to 29 in 1972 had had only an eighth-grade education or less, 17.8 percent of women 45 to 54 had. Conversely, whereas 4.6 percent of the younger (white) women had at least one year of college, only 2.8 percent of the older women had.

Table 8.1

Proportion of Men and Women Who Favor Efforts to Strengthen Women's Status in Society, by Age

AGE	1971		1972	
	MEN	WOMEN	MEN	WOMEN
18-29	53	46	61	56
30-39	37	40	47	49
40-49	52	39	50	42
50+	38	35	44	41

SOURCE: Harris and Associates, 1972:2.

show up with respect to feminist issues that involve political action.[8] And here an unexpected, at least unanticipated, finding is that more men than women tend to be sympathetic with the feminist movement.[9]

The 1972 Harris poll, for example, asked respondents about sympathy with efforts of women's liberation groups and found overall that 42 percent of the men replied in the affirmative compared to 39 percent of the women.[10] Another poll conducted in 1973 reported essentially the same thing. Almost half (46 percent) of the men compared to two-fifths (41 percent) of the women concurred in the statement that "while I might not agree with all their tactics, in general I agree with the goals of the Women's Liberation Movement" (Sorensen, 1973: 10).[11] Both sexes had gained in sympathy for the liberation movement, but men more than women.

More interesting than these overall differences was the difference between men and women by age, both with respect to strengthening women's status in society (Table 8.1) and sympathy with the efforts of women's liberation groups (Table 8.2). Among the respondents in the 1972 Harris poll who were 50 years of age and over, the men were more favorable

8. Among nonpolitical sex-role issues are such issues as men helping with the housework, sexual freedom, whether men or women have an easier life, and the like.

9. The generally positive male attitude toward women seems to be of fairly recent origin. Hazel Erskine has assembled the results of a series of polls from 1937 to 1969 on willingness to vote for a woman as president. Until 1955 more women than men replied affirmatively. From 1963 on, more men than women did. By 1969, 58 percent of the male respondents would be willing to vote for a woman as president; only 49 percent of the women would (Erskine, 1971:281). It may not be in voting and in legislation that women's rights suffer as a result of sex differences in political participation, but in the implementation of the laws and decisions and administrative rulings that result. It is here that age may make a difference. Although there is not yet available so far as I know any research on the bureaucrats and commissioners charged with executing the laws and rulings dealing with women, the expectation would be not unreasonable that the older male administrators would be less vigorous than younger ones in scrupulously applying them.

10. Exceptions occurred among divorced and separated men, young men, low-income men, and city men; but even among these exceptions the differences from other men were minimal.

11. This poll was conducted by Daniel Starch and Staff, Inc.

Table 8.2

Proportion of Men and Women Who Are Sympathetic with the Efforts of Women's Liberation Groups, by Age

AGE	MEN	WOMEN
18-29	46	49
30-39	41	39
40-49	40	34
50 +	42	34

SOURCE: Harris and Associates, 1972:4.

than the women; the difference was less among the respondents in their thirties and forties. But among those in their twenties, the attitudes of the sexes had reversed themselves. Among them more women than men favored efforts to strengthen women's status in society and were sympathetic with the efforts of women's liberation groups.[12]

III. The Significance of Sex Differences for Feminist Issues

The significance of sex differences in attitudes on feminist issues lies in the impact they may have by way of participation in the political process. Overall, participation increases with years of schooling (Table 8.3) and this is favorable toward feminist issues since increased education is related to profeminist positions (Tables 8.4 and 8.5), and the general trend in our society is in the direction of more years of schooling for both sexes.

The pattern of political participation by sex also favors feminist issues both in the present and in the future. Until now more men than women have tended to participate at all ages (Table 8.6). Thus even though women outnumber men to a rather substantial extent in the politically most active years,[13] this advantage in numbers has been cancelled by a lower rate of

12. Of special interest is the position of the sexes on the abortion issue: men are more lenient than women. Judith Blake (1971:544) has summarized a series of polls on the subject from 1962 to 1969; in all of them there were more women than men who disapproved. Only in 1969 among those 45 years of age and over was the proportion of women who disapproved equal to that of men. In the *Parade* poll of 1973, considerably more men (57 percent) than women (50 percent) believed there should be no laws against abortion. Here as with other issues there has been an interesting shift, in this case a reversal of the sexes in attitude with age. Thus in the 1973 poll far more women (68 percent) than men (52 percent) in the youngest age bracket (18 to 24) favored abortion; in the 40 to 59 age bracket there was rough agreement (54 and 53 percent); and only in the over-60 bracket did the old pattern remain, more men (62 percent) than women (35 percent) showing leniency (Thomas C. Sorenson, p.10).

13. The sex ratio at conception has been estimated at roughly 150 males to 100 females. The greater fragility of the male fetus reduces this ratio to about 104 or 105 at birth. The continuing inferior male viability further reduces the sex ratio so that by the early twenties it has declined

Table 8.3

Voting·History of Women by Years of Schooling

VOTING HISTORY	YEARS OF SCHOOLING			
	EIGHTH GRADE	HIGH SCHOOL	COLLEGE	BEYOND COLLEGE
Registered to vote (year unspecified)	63	70	82	
Voted in 1970 Congressional election	41	53	62	
Voted in 1968 Presidential election	55	65	76	
Registered to vote in 1972 election	65.2	74.6	87.6	89.2
Voted in 1972 Presidential election	51.5	66.2	83.2	85.5

SOURCE: Data on 1968 and 1970 elections, Harris and Associates, 1972:23. Data on 1972 election, Bureau of the Census, 1973, Table 7.

participation. The result has been a plus for feminist issues because of the more favorable attitudes of men than of women (Table 8.1 and 8.7).

But changes seem to be in process. In the elections of 1968 and 1970, for example, although overall more men than women participated, the exceptions were all in the younger age brackets. By 1972 there were more exceptions and, again, they were all in the younger age brackets. In all three elections (one Congressional and two Presidential) young women were voting more than young men and, since young women favor feminine issues more than young men, this fact is a plus for feminist issues in the future. If women voted as a bloc, they could—for good[14] or for evil[15]—

to rough equality. Thereafter it continues to decline so that when the age bracket 65 to 74 has been reached, there are only 78 men left for every 100 women, and by the age of 75 and over, only 64. Thus in the ages when political participation is greatest for both sexes, there are potentially more women than men voters.

14. During the early years of the suffrage movement it was argued that, given the vote, women would introduce a salutary force into the whole political process. The success of the Eighteenth Amendment was, in fact, attributed to the "woman's vote." A lingering belief that women would raise the level of political life remained until fairly recently. A Gallup poll in 1952, for example, found 59 percent of the women and 51 percent of the men believing that greater participation by women would reduce graft and corruption; 31 percent of the men and 47 percent of the women in the same poll believed that greater participation by women in government would mean better government. (When satisfaction was expressed by some feminists that not a single woman was involved in the Watergate scandals, the cynical reply of others was that this was only an index of their lack of participation in positions of power. See Joseph, 1973.) By 1969, there had been a letdown. Now only 26 percent of the women and 20 percent of the men believed we would be governed better if women had more to say in politics. (These polls are summarized in Erskine, 1973:282.) As voters, women do show greater concern for humane values; they are "more responsive to issues with moral overtones" (Cosentini and Craik, 1972:218).

15. This aspect of the "conventional wisdom" with respect to the female electorate was stated by Maurice Duverger in 1955 as follows: "women . . . have the mentality of minors in many fields, and, particularly in politics, they will accept paternalism on the part of men. The man—husband, fiance, lover, or myth—is the mediator between them and the political world" (quoted by Cosentini and Craik, 1972:218). This, Cosentini and Craik note, "highlights what has become a virtual truism regarding women and politics." It undoubtedly has a modicum of validity for traditionalist women.

Table 8.4

Proportion of Men and Women Who Are Sympathetic with the Efforts of Women's Liberation Groups by Education

EDUCATION	MEN	WOMEN
Eighth grade	45	37
High school	36	36
College	49	46

SOURCE: Harris and Associates, 1972:4.

Table 8.5

Proportion of Men and Women Who Favor Efforts to Strengthen Women's Status in Society, by Education

EDUCATION	1971		1972	
	MEN	WOMEN	MEN	WOMEN
Eighth grade	40	36	38	42
High school	43	38	45	43
College	49	44[a]	62	57[a]

SOURCE: Harris and Associates, 1972:2.
[a]Includes postgraduate work

prevail and vote their convictions into practice. It is not likely, however, that women, any more than men, will ever vote as a bloc for, although they do differ from men on issues, they also differ among themselves as well.

IV. Differences among Women On Feminist Issues by Age

Since sexism pervades our entire society from cradle to grave there are feminist issues for all ages,[16] and women as well as men take sides on all of them.

At the youngest age levels girls today are protesting the inequality of monies spent for boys and girls by boards of education for athletic

16. Women differ by age on other than feminist issues also. The 1972 Harris poll found, for example, that "young women tend to be more troubled by the war, the economy, racial problems, the environment, and poverty, while older women are disturbed more by drugs, crime, unemployment, and taxes" (Harris and Associates, 1972:69). Interestingly, the set of issues of concern to young women paralleled that of the more affluent; thus more women among those with incomes of $15,000 and over than among low-income women also showed concern "about the war, the economy, racial problems, the environment, welfare, and foreign relations." In general, on most issues young women more than older women tended to be in favor of change. More were in favor of gun control, were willing to pay to eliminate smog and pollution health hazards, did not feel blacks were moving too fast, felt blacks were justified in their demands, approved of busing school children to achieve integration, approved of more money for cities, favored welfare over defense expenditures, and viewed themselves as "liberal" (Ibid.:79ff.).

Table 8.6
Political Participation of Men and Women by Age

AGE	REGISTERED				VOTED					
	1968, 1970		1972		1968 CONGRESSIONAL ELECTION		1968 PRESIDENTIAL ELECTION		1972 PRESIDENTIAL ELECTION	
	MEN	WOMEN	MEN	WOMEN	MEN	WOMEN	MEN	WOMEN	MEN	WOMEN
18-29	57	55			37	38	27	29		
30-39	84	76			75	77	64	59		
40-49	84	81			83	81	74	70		
50+	85	84			86	80	79	66		
18-20			57.9	58.3					47.7	48.8
21-24			58.6	60.3					49.7	51.7
25-29			66.0	66.2					57.6	58.0
30-34			71.6	70.8					62.1	61.7
35-44			74.4	75.1					65.9	66.7
45-54			79.9	78.9					72.0	69.9
55-64			81.1	79.4					72.4	69.2
65-74			82.9	75.1					73.2	64.3
75+			80.0	64.9					65.9	49.1

SOURCE: Data for 1968 and 1970, Harris and Associates, 1972:23. Data for 1972, Bureau of the Census, 1973; Table 7.

equipment, training, coaching, sports, team uniforms; at the oldest age levels, "Gray Panthers" protest inequities in Social Security and pension rights. In the age brackets between these extremes, issues also vary. Among the younger women they take the form of concern about abortion, contraception, rape, child care, sexual mores, and the like. Older women in the middle-age range find divorce, child support and equal economic and professional opportunity more immediately pressing. These differences in major interest may be schematized as in Table 8.7. This table controverts the age-related allegation sometimes made against the feminist movement, that it neglects old women. It states that "women . . . sixty-five years of age and older . . . are being ignored by the women's liberation movement" and asks "why is a socially sensitive movement like women's liberation neglecting its older sisters, leaving them to find for themselves?" (Lewis and Butler, 1972:223). The answer given is in terms of "ageism," a process "of systematic stereotyping of and discrimination against people because

Table 8.7
Issues of Major Concern to Women by Age

GROUP	AGE OF LEADERS	ISSUES OF MAJOR CONCERN
Women's Equity Action League	Range: 29-67[a] Median: 47[a]	". . . dedicated to improving the status and lives of *all* women. Our goal is equal participation in society with all the rights and responsibilities of full citizenship. WEAL works primarily in the field of education, legislation to achieve these ends. We seek to promote the economic well-being of women whether they work in the home, outside the home, or both" (WEAL flyer. Emphasis in original).
National Organization for Women	Range: 26-55[a] Median: 38[a]	The total spectrum of human issues, including, among others: poverty, minimum wage, child development programs, welfare, full employment, social security, equal opportunity, prostitution, needs of minority persons, sexuality and lesbianism, volunteerism, older women, rape, sports, marriage and divorce laws, the male mystique, etc. (NOW, 1973:26).
Radical feminist (liberation) groups	Late twenties-early thirties[b]	The conceptualization of sex roles.
Antifeminist groups	Roughly[c] same as NOW[a]	The conceptualization of sex roles.

[a]Carden, 1974:185.
[b]Personal estimate. Actually, consciousness-raising groups do not have "leaders."
[c]Personal estimate.

they are old, just as racism and sexism accomplish this with skin color and gender" (Ibid.).

The answer to this allegation is two-fold. First, the feminist movement does not ignore older women. Resolution 147 of the February, 1973 NOW convention reads:

> Be it resolved that NOW establish a Task Force on Older Women, the functions of which shall include:
>
> (1) to investigate how women can document cases of age discrimination
>
> (2) to give attention to a "supportive community" for older women: e.g. alternate life styles
>
> (3) to promote affirmative action legislation to insure that employers have proportionate percentages of older women to develop a policy regarding the issue of equitable Social Security benefits for all women, including housewives, and
>
> Be it further resolved that the Sixth Conference recommend that NOW Legal Defense and Education fund support test cases on discrimination against women on the basis of age, and
>
> Be it further resolved that the Sixth National Conference of NOW go on record attacking the cult of youth which applies mostly to women (NOW, 1973:10).[17]

A year later the NOW monthly newsletter of March, 1974, reported a strong response. "Older women's committees and task forces are forming in many chapters. The excellent response to the kit prepared by the Task Force on Older Women reflects interest in this new area for feminist attention." Women tend to become more aggressive with age (Arlie Hochschild wonders where all that aggression was in their youth) and men more dependent. All they had needed was leadership. There is considerable agitation to correct the inequities for older women in the Social Security benefits system (see for example, Bell, 1973); there are NOW members in the Gray Panthers (Gresham, 1973:16); and poverty, the bane of old age, is a major concern in the NOW agenda.[18]

The second answer is subtler. In the very oldest age brackets, specifically feminist issues tend to fade out. Sex roles have lost their saliency. The consciousness-raising techniques do not operate very well among the truly old women (Gresham, 1973). It is, as the statement quoted above points out,

17. In connection with the cult of youth, see Bell, 1970.
18. See NOW resolution on poverty in the following paper, "Class and Feminist Issues."

ageism rather than sexism per se that is salient in their lives, as it is in the lives of old men.

Ageism is, indeed, a worthy cause, as racism is, and exploitation of all kinds. And it is part of the sexist ideology that women should come to the rescue of all ill-used people, cooperate in all worthy humanitarian causes. In the past they have, indeed, tended to conform to this expectation, putting every other group's interests ahead of their own. There is a persisting temptation among feminists to continue in this admirable tradition. But now they try to do it their way. This means a self-help way— in this context, a Gray Panthers way. And when people are beyond self-help, they are a charge on the whole community. The feminist movement keeps us alert to this responsibility.

V. Sex-Role Definition as a Feminist Issue

Although sex-role definitions may have ultimate political implications, especially as symbolized in the Equal Rights Amendment, they differ from more practical issues in that they are more profoundly personal and moral than political in nature. And here the relationship with age is equivocal, for it is not always the oldest women who are most likely to be traditionalists, as might be expected from the discussion so far, but women in their forties. Education can explain some of the relationships reported, but generational factors may also be involved.

Three indexes of traditionalism in role definition are selected here: preference for a status of dependency, feeling that life under the traditional sex-role definitions is easier for women than for men, and lack of sympathy for efforts of women's liberation groups (Harris and Associates, 1972:4, 8).[19] In all three, women in their forties tend to differ from both younger and older women (Table 8.8). In the absence of other data available for explanatory purposes, only two possibilities are commented on here, one having to do with education and one with the peculiar circumstances under which this generation of women were reared.

Education seemed to be related to these indexes of traditionalism in a way similar to the way age was related to it. Young women and college-educated women resembled one another, as did also women in their forties and high-school graduates (Table 8.9). On the basis of the data here available it is not possible to tease out the relative impact of these two variables—age, and education—on traditionalism. But sooner or later the

19. In the case of many of the other possible items available in this poll to serve as indexes, education seemed to be roughly adequate to explain differences. On 6 of the 10 items dealing with "certain feelings"—related to sex-role attitudes—women in their forties were out of line, differing from women both older and younger than they were.

Table 8.8

Traditionalism in Role Conception of Women, by Age

	18-29	30-39	40-49	50+
Want husband to take care of me: agree				
frequently	50	57	61	59
occasionally	21	19	18	13
hardly ever	26	21	17	23
not sure	4	3	4	5
Women have easier life than men: agree				
frequently	21	29	37[a]	29
occasionally	23	27	22	19
hardly ever	54	42	39	49
not sure	2	2	2	3
Attitude toward efforts of women's liberation groups:				
sympathetic	49	39	34	34
not sympathetic	41	50	53	51
not sure	10	11	13	15

SOURCE: Same as Table 8.3.

[a]In a 1973 poll, far more women 40 to 59 (58 percent) than women 18 to 24 (37 percent) agreed that "in America, women mostly have an easier life than men" (Sorensen, 1973:10). The responses for women 25 to 39 are not reported in this poll.

technical researchers will apply their high-power machinery to the problem and we will learn precisely, to the last decimal, how much each one contributes to traditionalism. For the present we evade the issue by concluding simply that education tends to make women "think young," which in the present context means "thinking free."[20]

Years of schooling is only one differentiating characteristic of generations. It is at least a quasi-continuous variable and can therefore be dealt with as though it were a quantitative one. But there are other differentiating characteristics that are harder to quantify, or even to label. We speak of the "depression generation" or the "wartime babies" or the "postwar babies," suggesting that the situation prevailing during the years

20. Karen Mason and Larry L. Bumpass, (1973) in a study on women's sex-role attitudes in the United States in 1970 based on data gathered in the Ryder-Westoff 1970 National Fertility study, found education to be the most significant factor in sex-role attitudes. But they found no differences in sex-role attitudes between women under 30 and those 30 and over. They concluded that whatever changes may have occurred have affected women over 30 as well as women under 30. "The age control . . . provided in an attempt to discern whether more recent cohorts are more egalitarian in outlook . . . provided no evidence of such intercohort difference, nor of possible aging effects." Their measure of the age variable—under 30 and 30 and over—may have been too gross to ferret out nonlinear relationships.

Table 8.9

Traditionalism in Role Conception of Women by Age and Education

	18-29	COLLEGE	40-49	HIGH SCHOOL
Want husband to take care of me: agree				
frequently	50	49	61	63
occasionally	21	19	18	17
hardly ever	26	29	17	17
not sure	3	3	3	3
Women have easier life than men: agree				
frequently	21	24	37	32
occasionally	23	25	22	22
hardly ever	54	50	39	44
not sure	2	1	2	2
Attitude toward efforts of women's liberation groups:				
sympathetic	49	46	34	36
not sympathetic	41	47	53	50
not sure	10	7	13	14

SOURCE: Same as Table 8.3.

of their early socialization leaves a mark on them. Fortunately there is a longitudinal study (Elder, 1974) that traces one such "generation" and its findings are here invoked to help understand the women who were in their forties in 1972. It found that among women who lived in deprived households during the Depression of the 1930s, familism has been especially strong.

Glen Elder summarizes the findings of this study as related to traditionalism in women:

> Our data suggest that receptivity to traditional roles is concentrated among women who grew up in deprived households that depended heavily upon the involvement of female members. From adolescence and the late 30s to middle age, a domestic life style in values and action is more characteristic of these women than of women from non-deprived homes. They were more involved in household chores, expressed greater interest in domestic activities, and, in the middle class, were more likely to marry at an early age. . . . The daughters of deprived families were most likely to stop working at marriage or when they gave birth to their first child; and (if from the middle class) to enjoy the common tasks of home-making. The meaning of family preference centered first on the value of children and secondarily on the interpersonal benefits of marriage (Ibid.: Chapter 8).[21]

21. Quotation from manuscript.

The women who were in their forties in 1972 were born between 1923 and 1932 and hence their earliest socialization occurred during the Depression when many families were likely to have suffered deprivation. If Elder's analyses of his sample are valid for other women, this generational factor may help explain the traditionalism shown in Table 8.8.

It is, of course, possible that findings reported in the Harris poll result from sampling errors. But a combination of educational and childhood-deprivation factors may, conceivably, have produced them.

Traditionalists, whatever their age, range from those who merely accept the sex-role status quo to those who are passionately and actively defensive of it. Not only are they not feminists, they are strongly antifeminist. At one end of the scale are some top-level professional women—Tiger Ladies or Queen Bees—who have made it in a man's world and want to pull the ladder up after them. They do not welcome their sisters as competitors or want to change the rules in any way. "I made it, why can't you?" is their response to the arguments of the liberation movement for change.[22] They are vocal and articulate and do not call for comment here. At the other end are the sheltered housewives who are terrified at the threat to their security which they see in the liberation movement. These antifeminists have not been subjected to as much research attention as have the feminists; there is therefore relatively little firm data to report on them and "equal time" is not called for. But some attention to them is warranted.

VI. Antifeminists and Age

On the basis of a purely cursory examination of mainly journalistic reports, antifeminist leaders seem to come from Glen Elder's "children of the Depression." They are in their late forties and early fifties, with a range including the late thirties. The followers seem to be somewhat younger, corresponding in age to the women who participate in local consciousness-raising groups, late twenties and thirties. The leaders of three organizations—the Pussycat League, Happiness of Women (HOW), and Fascinating Womanhood—may serve as samples.

The most trivial and least significant is The Pussycat League, which was organized by Lucianne Goldberg "to answer militant feminism." Her book, *Purr, Baby Purr: The Case Against Women's Liberation* stated its position: "the general thrust was that the kind of equality women's lib is talking about is a step down to any woman who enjoys being a female. You can be in a man's world and be a female. . . . You can get more flies with

22. For a perceptive analysis of the Queen Bee syndrome see Staines, Jayaratne, and Tavris, 1974.

honey."[23] Neither the author nor the book had any significant impact. Although the thesis of the book was vintage antifeminism, its facetiousness discounted the message it conveyed.

Both HOW and Fascinating Womanhood have strong biblical underpinnings. The HOW pamphlet, for example, states that "man was divinely ordained to be the head of the family." God commanded Eve, "thy desire shall be to thy husband and he shall rule over thee." Still, in actual practice its leaders may be more symbolically than actually opposed to feminism. In a public debate, for example, Ms Barbara Harris, a leader in HOW,

> turned out to be an attractive young woman, who announced . . . that she was the mother of two children ("Its a sacred trust!"). . . . Her position was that "women should be respected as the bearers of children," the family is sacred, the equal-rights amendment would erase "over 160" Federal laws from the statute book, and "over 200 state laws protecting women would be wiped off in Arizona alone." . . . "I don't see any reason not to have laws protect women from having to pick up loads that weigh more than 30 pounds—extended to men too. Look at the number of them that have bad backs and hernias at the age of 40. . . . We want more and better protection, for men and for women " (Korda, 1973:17).

Precisely the feminist position. When asked if her husband made the final decision in her family, Ms Harris replied certainly not. Although a man was head of the family, "I think you have to make decisions together, in the interests of the whole family. After all, we both work. What I'm against is something like the ERA, because it would simply make us all men, or second-rate men, instead of being equal *as women*" (Ibid.). A woman who has a job, two children, and shares decision-making with her husband can hardly be viewed as a traditionalist in her conception of roles.

Helen B. Andelin, 51 and mother of eight, is the founder of a movement known as Fascinating Womanhood. Her book with that title, which tells women how to please men by being feminine,[24] sold 250,000 copies. Its success led to the establishment of the Andelin Foundation, which her

23. Quoted by Witcover, 1973. Ms Goldberg was later engaged by Republicans as a spy during the McGovern campaign. The comments of her male fellow-journalists were not supportive. She was ignored, and "regarded as a pest." Apparently the "click" never occurred to her.

24. The tenets of Fascinating Womanhood are those that define traditional sex-role conceptions: make your husband feel like a man; he must be number one; though marriage is a democracy, the man must be president; the ideal woman must be feminine, have a lovely character, find happiness in being a good homemaker and mother; retain a certain amount of childlikeness. Combined with complete understanding of her husband, these rules will help her find complete love. She fascinates, amuses, enchants him, and arouses in him a desire to shelter and protect her. Both the meek and the overbearing husband undergo complete change under the influence of her new subservient behavior. No longer threatened, he becomes more tolerant and understanding himself. More love is needed in the world today and this is not to be achieved by creating jobs for women or by Supreme Court decisions.

husband, a dentist, left his own profession to run. It sells franchises (at $10.00 each) for the privilege of offering an 8-week course based on the book.[25]

The followers of the antifeminist leaders seem to be the mirror-image of the young women in consciousness-raising groups. But instead of fighting against the sex-role status quo, they fight to come to terms with it, to learn not only to live with it but to glory in it. One such group, consisting of 14 women in a Fascinating Womanhood course, ranged in age from 25 to 52; 8 of them were in the 28 to 38 age range. In response to essay questions, such antifeminist themes as the following showed up: the feminist movement is against Biblical teaching, against the will of God; it is run by women seeking attention rather than beneficial results; it offers no effective solutions for happiness; "I am opposed to the movement in general and give it little attention"; it has gone too far beyond equal pay, the rest of its ideas are nonsense; "I am for equal pay"; the movement is based on confusion and is uninformed, uncertain, and therefore ripe for propaganda; the members have lost sight of what it *really* means to be a woman; "I cannot relate to women's liberation, I have never cared to enter a man's world"; the women in the movement are out for revenge because they are unhappy in marriage or if single because they have never had pleasant experiences with a man; the movement is a reaction against superficial aspects of women emphasized in the papers and the beauty and do-good organizations; the movement is part of an overall scheme to destroy or eradicate American values, that is marriage and the family.

On the more positive side, the salvaging nature of the teachings of Fascinating Womanhood show up on the statement by a 29-year-old mother, a high-school graduate, married at the age of 17. After years of struggle she surrendered: she is now a happy (read "reconciled") housewife:

> Fascinating Womanhood has meant a whole new life for me. I realise that women have suppressed men to the point of making them very unmasculine. I also realize that I enjoy living with a man that rules our home instead of me ruling him. For many years I have tried to put myself on the same level as my husband. The results were drastic. To the point of ruination of marriage, personality, heart and soul. Since my husband regained leadership, we are all so much more happy and content. I have no desire to work, study, or anything. My work is here at home and there are areas in my home that I can use my talents. My fulfillment in life is happy well-adjusted children and a happy husband. My husband takes pride in being the sole moneymaker. He

25. To receive a franchise a woman must be convinced of the principles of Fascinating Womanhood, experience them successfully in her own life so that she has a happy marriage, have a good appearance (not be grossly overweight), use proper language, be a good housekeeper, not smoke, and qualify as a teacher.

also likes the new submissive me. He does not demand anything from me unfairly.

I am for equal pay. I am not for women working and pawning their children off on someone else to raise. The unmarried girl is one thing, the married girl is another. The will of God is that married women stay home and take care of their families. If all women live and act under the will of the Lord they will be blessed with happiness unlimited. I have yet to see a happy working woman. They are irritable, tired and bossy. Their kids are unruly brats or mental cases. I am a servant and comforter to my husband and in return I have received a love from him that is so deep he cannot put it into words. . . . The most important thing in my life is my family and I care for nothing else except the will of God in our lives.

A glance at Table 8.2 suggests that the women in their thirties—as the women in this particular group were—constitute a sort of rear guard. They tend to resemble the older women—40 and over—more than they do the younger (18 to 29). On all three items in Table 8.8 the break appears between those under 30 and those 30 and over.[26] On two of the items the nontraditional point of view has gained acceptance by about half of the young women. The trend seems thus to be in the direction of attenuation of the traditional role definition.

Basically, opposition to the feminist movement is opposition to the twenty-first century. It is a last-ditch stand against the demands of the modern world for a restructuring of sex roles. It is supported by women reared in a particular historic context who wish to remain protected and sheltered in the home, who want to invest their lives in their families. They feel threatened by the feminist movement.[27] They ignore it when they can and turn to women who can fight it for them. Whether their position is theologically, naturally, or scientifically the best, they seem to be fighting a losing battle. They do not even have the total backing of men.

26. But see footnote 20 above.

27. In the May, 1972, issue of the *Reader's Digest*, there appeared an article that revealed the feeling of threat many housewives were experiencing. "Women's libbers" were rocking a very comfortable boat. If they did not stop, men would catch on to the fact that women really were the favored sex and would cease to pamper them.

References

Bell, Carolyn Shaw. 1973. Age, sex, marriage, and jobs. *The Public Interest* 30 (winter):76–87.

Bell, Inge Powell. 1970. The double standard. *Trans-Action* 8 (November-December):75–80.

Bernard, Jessie. 1974. *The future of motherhood.* New York: Dial. Penguin, 1975.

Blake, Judith. 1971. Abortion and public opinion: The 1960–1970 decade. *Science* 171 (February):544.

Carden, Maren Lockwood. 1974. *The New Feminist Movement.* New York: Russell Sage.

Clavan, Sylvia, and Robak, Nicholas. 1973. Perception of masculinity: Fathers and sons. Paper presented at the meetings of the Society for the Study of Social Problems, New York.

Cosantini, Edmond, and Craik, H. Kenneth 1972. Women as politicians. *Journal of Social Issues* 28:217–236.

Current Population Reports. 1972. *Educational attainment: March 1972.* Series P-20, no. 243 (November). Washington, D.C., U.S. Government Printing Office.

Elder, Glen. 1974. *Children of the Great Depression.* Chicago: University of Chicago Press.

Erskine, Hazel. 1971. The polls: Woman's role. *Public Opinion Quarterly* 35 (Summer):pp. 217–236.

Gresham, Martha. 1973. Report on a Gray Panthers conference, October, 1973. *The Vocal Majority* 4 (November):16.

Harris, Louis, and Associates. 1972. *The 1972 Virginia Slims American Women's Opinion Poll.* New York: Published by the Authors.

Joseph, Geri. 1973. Women: Still on the sidelines of politics. *Washington Post,* August 5, 1973.

Korda, Michael. 1973. Liberation, U.S.A. *Newsweek,* July 16, 1973.

Lewis, Myrna I., and Butler, Robert N. 1972. Why is women's lib ignoring old women? *Aging and Human Development* 3:223–231.

Mason, Karen, and Bumpass, Larry L. 1973. *Women's Sex Role Attitudes in the United States, 1970.* Paper presented at meetings of the American Sociological Association, New York.

NOW. 1973. *NOW Acts.* Proceedings of the Sixth National Conference of NOW.

Roundup of current research. 1974. *Society* 11 (March-April):12.

Sorensen, Thomas C. 1973. What does a woman want? *Parade,* April 15, 1973.

Staines, Graham; Jayaratne, Toby Epstein; and Tavris, Carol. 1974. The Queen Bee syndrome. *Psychology Today* 7 (January):55–60.

Witcover, Jules. 1973. McGovern's Mata Hari: Suspected once, ignored often. *Washington Post,* August 21, 1973.

Yankelovich, Daniel. 1969. *Generations apart.* New York: Columbia Broadcasting company.

NINE

Class and Feminist Issues

The Charge of Middle-Class Bias

A common allegation made against the women's liberation movement is that it is a white, middle-class movement concerned only with professional and career women, with no concern for so-called "working-class" women.

> Women's liberation concentrates on middle-class women. It doesn't have much to do with lower-economic groups. The goal of most middle-class women is to get enough money to hire someone to clean her [sic] house. So middle-class women's emancipation from home is predicated on the notion that they can have a domestic to come in, and when you talk to them about emancipation of the domestic worker you are striking at their self-interest. (Ferman, 1973)

The first comment to make is that whatever the goal of "most middle-class women" may be, the goal of the woman who is a member of the women's liberation movement is not "to get enough money to hire someone to clean her house." Quite the reverse. The literature on the women's liberation movement is filled with moral scruples and concern about the practice of hiring other women to do their menial work for them; strong objection has been expressed to the idea, especially among the younger women. One of the outstanding leaders of the movement,

Roxanne Dunbar, has spent her life organizing women, especially in the South. The movement to organize domestic workers to improve pay and working conditions has had support from NOW. Women have made a strong case for defining poverty as a woman's issue, since most of those suffering from poverty are in fact women household heads and their children. Women have been more insistent than men that the contribution of the housewife be recognized both in status and in pecuniary reward. Indeed, all one has to do is examine the issues that NOW is concerned with to see how erroneous is the conception of the feminist movement as class-biased in its goals.

At the February, 1973, NOW conference, for example, one of the first resolutions to pass (No. 136) had to do with poverty as a woman's issue:

> Therefore be it resolved that the National Conference designate 1973 as NOW's Action Year against Poverty, during which all NOW chapters, task forces (national and local), and members are strongly urged to focus their activities on strategies and actions to dramatize the problems of women in poverty and effect meaningful changes in the economic status of all women, and Be it further resolved that the national Task Force on Women in Poverty be designated as the coordinating group for NOW's Action Year against Poverty, and Be it further resolved that the top four legislative priorities for NOW in 1973 be
>
> a) Revision of the Fair Labor Standards Act and similar state laws to provide for a minimum wage of at least $2.50 per hour, and extension of coverage under FLSA to include all workers, including domestics. (Note: This extension would incorporate these newly covered workers under the Equal Pay Act Provisions.)
> b) Passage of a comprehensive child development program, at least as good as the one vetoed by President Nixon last year (including health, nutritional and educational components and providing for free services to low-income parents and a sliding scale for others).
> c) A complete overhaul of the welfare program to provide for federalization of welfare in order to eliminate variations in requirements and payments, assurances that no custodial guardian or parent of preschool or school age children will be required to work outside of the home and provision of supportive services including realistic job training . . . . (NOW, 1973:7).

It is admittedly true that working-class women—like old women, though for different reasons—sometimes find it difficult to work in the middle-class style of the organized feminist groups. Many feminists, especially the more radical ones, are well aware of this hurdle and make a determined effort to overcome it. Some even study in detail the specific behavioral differences that have an alienating effect on working-class women in order to have their own consciousness raised and hence be themselves better prepared to overcome the class-bound hurdles.[1]Their efforts to overcome class bias remind us that the most radical feminists had their intellectual and ideological roots in the New Left. And Pamela Roby, interviewing working women across the country, was impressed with "the strong feeling of sisterhood" and also with "the efforts of professional and middle-class women to reach out to low-paid women workers and to homemakers and to include them in the movement for equal opportunity" (Austin, 1974).

Even in that bastion of status and rank, the military, women exposed to the feminist ideology break class-bound barriers, as in the case of Fran, wife of a submarine commander. Says the president of the local NOW chapter:

> Many Navy wives are very aware of status. Fran isn't. She writes the newsletter for NOW and runs consciousness-raising sessions that include enlisted men's wives. They feel they can say anything to her and drop by to talk over their problems. She doesn't come on like a commander's wife at all. (Ashby, 1973:86)

Sisterhood is not only powerful. It is also a great equalizer.

Misconceptions about the feminist movement's goals arise from the lack of understanding of its total scope. A fragment here, a fragment there is snatched upon and taken for the whole. "The women's liberation movement is . . .". "The leaders of the movement are . . .". No such grab-bag approach does justice to it. The feminist movement is a great, amorphous, variegated, lumbering, capacious, evolving entity or organism. Any more precise definition would be too limiting to express the nonspecificity of its many-faceted concerns. It finds and fights for feminist issues in all classes. It embraces quarreling, bickering, differing persons who have in common a consciousness-of-kind that has to be experienced or empathized to be fully understood. They have also in common a conviction that human beings must be dealt with as individuals on their own merits and not ascribed a status on the basis of preconceptions. All the statistics and polls and surveys are useless as sources of insight unless the critical "click" is heard. (The "click" is the term used to refer to a phenomenon many women experience when, for the first time, they suddenly recognize from something said or done in their environment its sexist nature. It was first described in the first issue of Ms.)

Actually the real exclusionary women in the middle class are not the feminists but the housewives. A study of women union members "disputes still another stereotype in which the blue-collar worker (male or female) is pictured as 'disinterested,' 'apathetic,' and even 'incompetent' or 'unable'

1. Especially noteworthy was a series of articles in the first volume of a feminist journal, *The Furies*. Among them were Myron, 1972; Berson, 1972; and Bunche and Read, 1972.

to comprehend community issues. The fault for this stereotype may lie squarely in the lap of the middle class, in this case middle-class women. It has been known for a long time that middle- and upper-class women tend to exclude working-class women from meaningful participation and leadership in community organizations" (Raphael, 1971).[2]

Working Women or Housewives? Class or Occupation?

In a thicket as complex and dense as the current feminist scene a number of distinctions have to be made, and contradictions, inconsistencies, and paradoxes have to be expected. Workingmen's wives and middle-class housewives have similar reactions to the feminist movement; working-class employed women and middle-class employed women have much in common vis-à-vis the feminist movement. Occupation in these cases— "housewife" versus labor-force participant—is more differentiating than class.

As a matter of fact, "class" has not been a suitable concept for interpreting the world women have traditionally inhabited.[3] The formidable tool-kit of concepts and paradigms developed by social scientists to understand the achievement-oriented macho world—power, mobility, stratification, status—do not apply in the ascribed-status world most women have lived in. The usual variables used to operationalize social class—income, occupation, education—do not behave the same in the case of women as in that of men, even in the male occupational world. Duncan and Blau, for example, have made clear that education is a prime factor in upward mobility (Duncan and Blau, 1967). Yet we have incontrovertible

2. Actually, the most serious rift was not between the middle-class feminists and working women nor between housewives and working women but between poor working women and women on welfare, for at the same time that more and more nonpoverty level women—often members of ethnic groups—entered the labor force, fewer of those at the lowest level did. "As women in the nonpoverty segment of society are found more and more in the labor force . . . the labor-force participation of low income women is dropping. The result is a growing rift between the poor and nonpoor. As the latter increase their labor-force participation, the former go on welfare and reduce theirs. A comparison of the income distribution of female-headed families with children in 1967 to those in 1970 shows that between 1967 and 1970, while the total number of female-headed families with children increased by 16 percent, the number of female-headed families with children with no income other than Public Assistance increased by 39 percent over twice as fast. Furthermore, those with income [presumably wages] other than Public Assistance . . . actually declined" (Ross, 1973). Because there have been allegedly racist overtones to this rift it is important to note that a new coalition of urban ethnic working-class women and black women was being organized under the leadership of the National Center for Urban Ethnic Affairs (Seifer, 1973:61). The National Project on Ethnic America is a "Depolarization Program" of the American Jewish Committee's Institute of Human Relations.

3. For a brief statement on the inadequacy of current approaches to class as related to women, see Acker, 1973.

evidence that although the educated woman may climb higher than the uneducated woman, she does not climb higher than less educated men. In 1972, for example, the woman with five or more years of college had a lower median income ($8580) than the male high-school graduate ($12,502) (Bureau of the Census, 1973: Table 51).[4]

A distinction has also to be made between the political and economic issues that feminists deal with and the quite distinct, though related, issues of sex-role redefinition. The first have more relevance for the employed woman, whatever her class; the second have more immediate relevance for the housewife and mother. "Equal pay for equal work"resonates one way for the female schoolteacher who earns $7200 when she sees her male fellow-teachers earning $10,000. It resonates quite differently for the wife of the workingman with five children who sees an unmarried woman receiving as much pay as her husband.

Political and economic issues on one side and sex-role redefinitions on the other are by no means wholly disparate. Even the matter of legislative protection for working women is, basically, a sex-role issue, for the way a role is defined affects identification with it; it specifies rights and obligations so that any issue that modifies rights and obligations ipso facto redefines roles. Equal opportunity may mean that jobs formerly forbidden to women are now open to them. To this extent their role has been redefined. Sex equality, in fact, redefines a wide gamut of sex-role patterns.

Still, such economic and political issues and role definitions are not identical. Role definitions include also more personal aspects of relationships, especially in the case of those between the sexes. Class has had a different effect on attitudes toward economic and political issues than it has had on role—especially sex-role—definitions. Working-class women have been more receptive to the feminist position on economic issues than to the feminist position on sex-role redefinitions. But they have been greatly influenced by both.

The Political and Economic Issues

A study of working-class women, practically all of them housewives, in eight cities in the fall of 1972, found that "as a declaration of women's rights, three main goals seem important and necessary to Women's Lib: economic equality, open participation, and self-determination. These three goals, gaining across-the-board approval and support from most women of all walks of life, identify Women's Lib as an important, basic, progressive movement" (Coup, Greene, and Gardner, 1973:108). Of these

4. For a discussion of the reasons for the differences in income between the sexes, see Suter and Miller, 1973.

three goals, "economic equality is the most widely espoused of all. 'Equal pay for equal work,' and 'equal work with equal skills' are banners carried by nearly all women—even those who hope to remain at home and never be a part of the work force" (Ibid.). It has, of course, been pointed out on numerous occasions that "equal pay for equal work"—who could be against it as a principle—is quite meaningless if women are not permitted to achieve the training called for in many occupations or, if they do, to get the jobs, or if they get the jobs, to escape hazing and/or impediments.

The second of the three goals, "open participation," refers to "the opening up of opportunities in areas outside the home for women who need or want them. These are, especially, the areas of employment, political action, involvement in government and other major organizations, and the pursuit of advanced education and training" (Ibid.:109). Here there is agreement with employed working-class women. In March, 1974, the first national conference of labor-union women was held in Chicago. Their goals "were to work as women and as union members for equal pay, equal rights, and equal opportunity and to make plans for organizing the unorganized women workers and involving more women in union structures and policy-making decisions" (*Ms*, 1974:19). The working-class woman may use a different vocabulary but she is sending the same message as the middle-class working woman. Feminist issues may be formulated in a different manner, the style is different, but the contents are the same.

The original objection of many working-class employed women to the feminist movement was related to the fear that women workers would lose the protection of labor legislation, ostensibly passed in their favor, if equality were achieved. The Civil Rights Act of 1964 forbade special protective legislation for women as the Equal Pay Act of 1963 forbade unequal pay. Although there were some episodes in which hostile employers did use the Civil Rights Act of 1964 to exploit women, the general effect has not been to deprive women of protection. The position of the feminist movement has become increasingly clear: we want to extend protection to men, not withdraw it from women. Equality means upgrading the position of men, not degrading the position of women. In any event, women are learning to organize for self-protection, as men have learned to do, in unions.

A study comparing union members with nonunion members found that the union member "calls into question the stereotypes about the blue-collar wife and worker . . . as a person with very limited abilities or interests outside of her home and family . . . . In fact, through her political activities the blue-collar-sewing-machine-operator-labor union member perhaps takes as lively or even a more lively interest in community affairs than the middle-class home-maker" (Raphael, 1971).

Political and economic issues are one thing: role redefinition is something quite different. It is easier for working-class women to accept the feminist position in the outside world than it is in the world of the family. It is easier to be for equal pay than for equality vis-à-vis husbands.

Sex-Role Redefinitions as an Issue

The working-class housewives interviewed in the eight-city study referred to above made a distinction between the principles of the feminist movement, with which they agreed, and sex-role definitions as exemplified by the leaders of the movement, whom they saw as radical, excitable, idiosyncratic, biased, extremist, formidable, strong, domineering, authoritarian (Coup, Greene, and Gardner, 1973:103).[5] They rejected the definition of feminine roles which, it seemed to them, the leaders were trying to foist on them as women, as wives, as mothers. Even women who were "liberation-oriented" where economic and political issues were concerned were "offended by what they saw as an attempt by Lib leaders to tell other women what they ought to do, feel, be proud of or ashamed about" as women, wives, or mothers. It seemed to these women that the leaders were trying "to do what they have accused men of doing" (Ibid.), namely telling them what to do, think, or feel.

The most publicized and most criticized tactics used by the early leaders of the feminist movement practically all had, one way or another, to do with standards of what was appropriate feminine behavior for women, namely: "bra-burning, the no-bra campaign, the comparison of the lot of women to the lot of Blacks, the marching and picketing and similar forms of protest, the use of rough-tough language, the objections to the use of women as 'sex symbols,' the 'Ms.' appellation for single and married women, the campaign against special legal 'protection' for women, and the presumed downgrading of the male sex" (Ibid.:106). Many working-class women saw the economic and political issues as pluses, but the loss of "femininity," "safekeeping," "courtesy," and "long-established feminine prerogatives" as negatives. In brief, although "overall Women's Lib enjoys a wide appeal as helping to establish new rights for women . . . it is meeting with some uncertainty or downright hostility as helping to

5. I feel it incumbent upon myself to come to the defense of the much maligned early leaders of the women's liberation movement. Now that they have made it possible for the rest of us to behave like ladies it is de rigueur to patronize or denigrate them as uncouth bra-burners (no bra was ever burned). I think we owe those brash young women an enormous debt of gratitude. They communicated. I would myself never had been able to do the things they had to do in order to be heard—snatch microphones from speakers, take over editorial offices, invade men-only bars, face down television talk-show celebrities—but I am grateful that there were some women who were able to do so. I prefer the company of well-mannered women who never act bitchy no matter what the provocation, but I'm not sure they are always good for me—or for men or anyone else either.

undermine certain privileges women have grown used to or dependent on" (Ibid.:108). They wanted "to remain 'sexual objects' in the eyes of men" (Ibid.:114).

It may be noted parenthetically that although the tactics listed above were severely criticized, "on the whole, the extremist image is no great detriment to the movement" (Ibid.:103). The tactics were viewed "as only indirectly relevant to and, on the whole, beneath the dignity of a well-advanced movement which is pursuing more important goals" (Ibid.:106).

These working-class women were offended also by behavior that violated their conception of the role of wife. Dependent as most of them were on their husbands, they rejected what looked to them like the downgrading of men. Thus, among the negatives of the liberation movement they counted "the fear of usurpation of long-established male prerogatives" such as women taking over men's jobs, undermining men's pride in earning capacity, physical prowess, family leadership, and services to wife and family.

> Central here is the potential for making the man feel unworthy and impotent in the eyes of his loved ones. Older, religiously oriented, and/or Working-Class women are the most likely types to manifest an intrinsic need to believe that men are somehow better, stronger, wiser, more courageous, more stable and unemotional than women, and to insist that men already carry enough burdens to excuse them from the demands of housekeeping and child care (Ibid.:114).[6]

But most sensitive of all was the denigration of the role of mother that seemed implicit in the attitudes of some of the leaders, as we shall note presently. First however, a word on ethnicity and feminist issues.

Ethnicity and Feminist Issues

We get a similar picture of the working-class woman when we view her through the lens of ethnicity. As a matter of fact, class and ethnic characteristics are closely related. Ethnicity has to do with the survival into the second, third, and even fourth generation of old-world, often rural, sex-role patterns in ethnic urban enclaves.

> In the early years of the century the lower classes in cities were often immigrants . . . . The emphasis in thinking was therefore on their ethnicity more than on their class . . . [With time, however,] the old immigrant component in the community became greatly attenuated.

6. Even successful professional women seem to have the same need to think their husbands are superior to them. See Bernard, 1974:Chapter 9.

The children might still live in ethnic areas but they looked and acted like everyone else. They became, in research and in theory, blue-collar workers, the working class or the lower-middle class rather than immigrants or ethnics. The fading—though not the disappearance—of ethnicity as such thus left the class rather than the ethnic characteristics of this generation highlighted (Bernard, 1973:55).

It is expectable, therefore, that research on working-class women in terms of their ethnic backgrounds gives results very much like those of the survey just reported.

One study reviewing the "new ethnicity" found major changes in the sex-role definitions of working-class women in process. On the basis of admittedly uneven data, Arthur Shostak reported some of them. As a member of the labor force, the working-class wife expects more emotional support and physical help from her husband at home. The Old World ethnic patterns that defined sex roles have become watered down:

> Such women are less ethnocentric and far less insulated than at any other time before in blue-collar history. The nunnery-like walls of the blue-collar neighborhood as an ethnic enclave have collapsed for them. They go out to meet and explore a dynamic world that their tradition-bound mothers and grandmothers feared, despised, and shunned (Shostak, 1971).

And, it may be added, as these tradition-bound women still do. They are among those who find the feminist movement "harmful, ridiculous, incredible—or a combination of all three. Many . . . vociferously repudiate the movement and see it as an abomination which threatens their security and way of life" (Coup, Greene, and Gardner, 1973:11). They react by becoming even more dependent and passive. "This is the traditional Working-Class woman we have studied in the past" (Ibid.).

But even these women, even women who remain in the home have not been able to escape the forces making for change. "For the past 20 years the most powerful cultural equalizer we have ever known has been coming into their world to 'work its thing' on blue-collar family members. TV afternoon soap opeas, evening situation comedies, late-hour talk shows, and nightly feature movies . . . all stir new role expectations" (Shostak, 1971) for both sexes, for the husband as well as for the wife. One of the most perceptive studies of working-class women, conducted by the director of Community Relations for the National Project on Ethnic America, Nancy Seifer, gives an insightful picture of what is actually happening to working-class women. Although the author recognizes that "in many ways, change is perhaps more threatening to working class women than to either middle class or poorer women," still "working-class women— absent from the majority and still sorely underrepresented in the ranks of the [women's] movement, may well become its cutting edge" (Seifer, 1973:2–3).

Ms Seifer notes that in the 1960s "a fluctuating economy forced many who had never held a job at all, or had not worked since their youth, to find employment" (Ibid.:15). Threats to their neighborhoods led an increasing number to participate in community action, even public protest. These trends "brought many working class mothers into head-on collision with age-old beliefs, values and traditions" (Ibid.:16), and especially with those involved in sex-role definitions:

> New threats to neighborhood safety and stability in the 1960s also served to drive many working class women out of their homes and into community activism. Perhaps as women and mothers, they sensed a greater urgency than their husbands; perhaps they had more time (if they were housewives); or perhaps, not having the false pride of manhood at stake, they were more willing to fight and risk defeat at the hands of government officials or politicians. For whatever reasons, it was the women who became the troops of the new white ethnic organizations that began to take shape at the end of the 1960s in . . . many cities. (Ibid.:18)

Confronting public officials, testing themselves out against them, they were surprised to learn their own strengths. And this new sense of their own value had its effect on their relationships at home also:

> When a wife comes home after testifying at a City Council hearing, from a meeting of the local school or hospital board, or from helping to out-maneuver a local politician or win a vote for day care in her union, she is changing the balance of power in her marriage in the most fundamental way, often without realizing it. (Ibid.:45)
>
> In the same way, having a job of her own with her own paycheck also modifies sex-role definitions. "When she becomes a breadwinner too, she chips away at his [her husband's] small sense of self worth" (Ibid.:44). Activism in the community to protect their neighborhoods was powerful schooling for the working-class housewife; activism in the union movement was an equally powerful school for the working-class woman in the labor force. Long neglected by most labor unions, women are now beginning to organize in their own behalf.

> "Over the past few years, women unionists have made significant strides. A number of women's caucuses and departments have sprouted up recently within existing unions to promote concerns of special interest to women workers, such as equal pay, advancement, and training opportunities; day care, family health care, and legal services; maternity leaves and benefits; voluntary overtime and equality in pension and seniority systems. (Ibid.:34–35)

They speak even of unionizing housewives (Ibid.:40)!

Thus, despite the lingering rejection of the "bra-burners," despite the charge still made that the feminist movement is a middle-class movement for middle-class women, working-class women have become as feminist as anyone else.

> The impact of the movement upon working class women is undeniable. Despite the still pervasive feeling that the movement "doesn't speak for us," the evidence of that impact lies in such developments as the recent surge of activism among women trade unions, the protests and organizing efforts of women office workers, the community activism, the increasing independence of many housewives, and obviously the formation of consciousness-raising groups (generally called by other names). (Ibid.:59–60)

So what's in a name? A rose by any other name . . . .Whatever it is called— the women's movement, feminism, community activism, union organization—it reflects the same idea.

Motherhood: Class or Feminist Issue?

At the end of the eighteenth century, motherhood became an economic, political, and class issue all at the same time. The working classes, it seemed to some observers, were not exercising enough restraint; they were indulging in reproduction to an excessive extent. The effect was, according to the iron law of wages, to keep their pay at a subsistence level. If wages were increased they would only breed even more freely and thus reduce themselves once more to a subsistence level. A generous dole had the same effect on the poor. Providing for them simply encouraged them in their reproductive profligacy. They had only themselves to blame; certainly not the comfortably secure affluent strata of society. So there it was, motherhood as an economic, political, and class issue all at once. But it was not a feminist issue.

It remained an economic, political, and class issue throughout the nineteenth century. Some special interests wanted to increase the birth rate, others to decrease it. Generals wanted lots of babies for what reluctant women came to call cannon fodder; industrialists wanted lots of babies for cheap hands in the mills, mines, and factories. Ambitious nationalistic rulers wanted lots of babies in order to outbreed the competition. Believers in the Malthusian principles wanted a moderated birth rate to prevent the negative checks Malthus specified as the inevitable consequence of too many babies, including famine and plague. Whether the arguments were militaristic, industrial, or nationalistic, the issue was always implicitly a class issue, for it was always women in the lower classes who were having most of the babies. Among all the differentials in the birth rate that the demographers have reported, the class differential has always been salient. There are, in fact, some theorists who, despite the lessening of this differential, think "there is reason to believe, on theoretical grounds, that some differential [class] fertility is an ingrained characteristic of industrialized and urban society and will persist" (Duncan and Blau, 1967:427).

In one form or another the issue has remained an economic, political, and class issue to this very day. We see the old story reenacted in congressional debates even now, complicated, elaborated, and extended in our time by the unexpected rise of female-headed families (Ross and MacIntosh, 1973). It is also reflected in popular discussions of the right to contraception and abortion. But now motherhood has, in addition, become a feminist issue also.

Middle-class women had had access to contraception knowledge and equipment and to abortion even in the nineteenth century, and they were among the leaders in the movement to extend the privilege of birth control to poor women also. Margaret Sanger (1928) wrote about mothers in bondage and crusaded to liberate them from unwanted motherhood. Voluntary motherhood was not a plank in the suffrage movement nor were its advocates all feminists. But it was a woman's issue.

Women were becoming aware of all the forces operating on them to become mothers, the subtle as well as the more blatant. It was easy to see the more obvious ploys—medals, ribbons, accolades of one kind or another— but it was not so easy to see the subtler pressures to make women want to have babies. Picking up a trace laid down half a century earlier (Hollingworth, 1916), the feminists of the late 1960s began to reject the pressures operating on all women to become mothers. They rejected the idea that the lives of women were limited to *Kinder, Kuche,* and *Kirche.* They rejected the "barefoot and pregnant" stereotype for poor women. There was, in fact, a strong association between rejection of the definition of motherhood as intrinsic to the feminine role and acceptance of the women's liberation movement. A study of university students, for example, documented the fact that "a significant number of the most forceful spokeswomen for liberation have essentially very little use for children. When spoken of at all, the tendency is to do so coldly and unsympathetically, and to project the view that children are nuisances and a major barrier to one's path toward fulfillment in the larger world outside one's home" (Lott, 1973:373). The author cites the work of Ti-Grace Atkinson, Shulamith Firestone, Laurel Limpus, Kate Millet, Betty Rollins, Beverly Jones, Una Stannard, and Germaine Greer to make her point.[7] She goes

7. Lott does not charge that such antinatalism is characteristic only of women in the liberation movement. She sees them, in fact, as merely reflecting an antichild bias in our

even further. On the basis of a research instrument she administered to her own students, she reports proliberation views stronger among women who are not much interested in rearing children than among those who are so interested.

Among older working-class women, for whom the role of mother has been especially salient, any denigration of that role is anathema. The study of working-class women cited above found the traditional motherhood theme more prevalent in the working class, especially the lower working class, than in the middle class. "Their thought and interests tend to center inward on their immediate families and the need to serve and satisfy them. Children are especially important in this scheme of things, and their triumphs are vicariously enjoyed by the mothers . . . . As might be expected, they tend to be in opposition to 'Women's Lib' " (Coup, Greene, and Gardner, 1973:55).

It would be a mistake, however, to conceptualize the issue as one of middle-class feminists versus working-class mothers. Not all feminists underplay the role of mother. What many object to is the insistence that *all* women must become mothers, that motherhood is *every* woman's destiny, that *only* through bearing children can women find fulfillment. What they are for is not only voluntary motherhood but voluntary desire for motherhood, an uncoerced desire. Betty Friedan tells us she observed a great sense of relief among women when she spelled out to them her own reconciliation of the feminist and the maternal horns of the dilemma. "The assumption of your own identity, equality, and even political power does not mean you stop . . . caring for your kids" (Friedan, 1973:37). One could, as a feminist, be in favor of maternity benefits, paternity leave, child-care centers, free access to contraception, abortion on demand, and at the same time fight to protect the right of poor, especially black, women to have as many children as they pleased, oppose legislation or administrative rulings that put pressure on women on welfare rolls to limit family size or to accept sterilization or to accept "workfare" instead of payment to take care of their own children at home. Feminists were *for* mothers of all classes, and *for* women of all classes who did not want to be mothers.

Winds of Change

The older working-class women may reject new role definitions of women, wives, and mothers, but change is certainly in process among the younger ones. For some the winds of change bring only confusion and uncertainty.

---

whole society today. By espousing an antinatalist stance they are, she believes, playing into the hands of sexist forces.

A reader of *True Love*, whose readership is presumably made up of working-class women, reflects this mood:

> Today's woman thinks and knows she has a right to her own thoughts. She knows she has a right to her own pursuits and endeavors. She knows she has a right to self-realize. She knows motherhood is not all bliss, and that to be a better mother she needs to be a well-rounded person . . . She does not feel guilty for wanting to enjoy life, to enjoy sex, to enjoy the pursuit of womanhood toward personhood . . . She's confused about her level of aspiration . . . Motherhood's not always as clean and sweet as the ads show . . . Her husband doesn't know what she's talking about. She can get a job, return to school, (avoid the issue), and/or begin to self-fulfill. No matter what she chooses, it'll mean changes. She's not prepared for the real world. But then the real world is unprepared for her reality . . . She has trouble making decisions on her own authority and following through on them with security . . . She's reacting the way anyone does when *he* realizes how much *he's* let *himself* be had . . . She would have a great cultural weight lifted from her shoulders if some qualified "male-business-habituated" female authority would come along to tell her that all the subtle truths she feels about being a woman, and subtly denies herself, are really true. (Anonymous, 1972)

Others, Arthur Shostak tells us, are "heady with their new-found freedom from conception fears and challenged by the gossip of still-better-lives-yet that they pick up at work or from the TV" (Shostak, 1973:75).

> [They] bitterly denounce their homey prototype "Edith Bunker" when I ask about this popular TV heroine in my research. They especially disown her Old Country passivity, naivete, and doltishness. Working outside their homes and ethnic neighborhoods, as many do, these free-wheeling women are often aggressive, sophisticated, and mentally adroit. Long accustomed . . . to manipulating the men folk (of all ages), modern blue-collar women more often resemble (and seem to identify with) Gloria than Edith in the Bunker household. (Ibid.:73-74).

Although as yet admittedly a minority,

> their marriages are variously characterized by an animated companionship, a challenging notion of the ideal, and a substantial reservoir of happiness and love . . . . Such families are presently a very distinct minority among all blue-collar units. But they exist, persist, attract ever more curious and envious attention from blue-collar neighbors and co-workers, and may even quietly be earning cautious emulation that not even the "modernites" themselves are aware of. (Shostak, 1971).

Directly or by way of friends and neighbors, these working-class women, in their own way, are redefining their family as well as their work roles.

Then there are those, neither confused nor "heady" with new-found freedoms, who know what they want and are on their way. They are planning for full-time employment, long-term careers, and small families. More and more are going on to college. Among them the future will be quite different from the present. A study of more than a thousand first-year college women in an urban university, most of them with working-class backgrounds, reported that only a quarter of them saw themselves 15 years hence as "housewives with one or more children" (Epstein and Bronzaft, 1972). Almost half, on the other hand, saw themselves as "married career women with children." They will settle for neither full-time motherhood nor full-time career; they want both. These "younger women will be able to exercise a degree of control over their own lives that their mothers never had." Call it liberation, call it control over their lives—the significance is much the same.

For all these young women, confused, "heady," or on their way, the third goal listed earlier—"the right to self-determination"—is as important as the first two, "economic equality" and "open participation." This right

> has basically to do with a woman's sense of her inherent worth and individuality, a release from thinking of herself as menial, subservient, and incompetent in any role other than that of mother and homemaker. It has to do with a woman's right to make up her own mind about what she wants or does not want to do, to speak out when she has an opinion, to share in important family and money management decisions, and to have her own friends, interests, activities, and right to privacy. (Coup, Greene, and Gardner, 1973:109).

These rights have not traditionally been in the female role script, certainly not among the women of the working class. Their inclusion now represents an enormous change. The women themselves may not see the change as related to the feminist movement, but it is hard to imagine it without such a movement.

It may be, as one study of working-class women states, that they have "been the least successful, overall, in adapting to the stresses of recent social change" (Ibid.:53). The older women may complain that they are tired of hearing so much about the Women's Lib movement. Not so the young ones. But even the older ones cannot escape it. "Almost all the homemakers in our study are aware of and feel touched by the Women's Lib movement . . . . [It] is seen as on the move, in the air, on the airways, in the halls of legislatures, on the pages of newspapers and magazines" (Ibid.:101). Even those who wish it would go away and leave them alone recognize that it is not a fad or passing phase, that it is here to stay (Ibid.).

They may not themselves come to terms with it, but their daughters surely
will.

References

Acker, Joan. 1973. Women and social stratification: A case of intellectual sexism.
American Journal of Sociology 73 (January):174–183.

Anonymous. 1972. When you think you're God, you can go to the devil in style, a
True Love mini story. *True Love* (October).

Ashby, Babette. 1973. A submarine commander joins women's lib. *Family Circle*
(November).

Austin, Dorothy. 1974. Social ills foil low paid women. *Milwaukee Sentinel,*
January 16, 1974.

Bernard, Jessie. 1973. *The sociology of community.* Glenview: Scott, Foresman.
————— . 1974. *The future of motherhood.* New York: Dial.

Berson, Ginny. 1972. Slumming it and the middle class. *Furies* 1, (March-April):3.

Bunche, Charlotte, and Read, Coletta. 1972. Revolution begins at home. *Furies* 1,
(May):4.

Bureau of the Census. 1973. *Money income of 1972 of families and persons in the
United States.* Series P-60, no. 60 (December).

Coup, Roger F.; Greene, Shirley; and Gardner, Burleigh B. 1973. *A study of
working-class women in a changing world.* Chicago: Social Research.

Duncan, Otis Dudley, and Blau, Peter M. 1967. *The American occupational
structure.* New York: Wiley.

Epstein, Gilda F., and Bronzaft, Arline L. 1972. Female freshmen view their roles as
women. *Journal of Marriage and the Family* 34 (November):671–672.

Ferman, Louis. 1973. Quoted in Chapman, William. Over 40: "No-woman's land"
for jobs. *Washington Post,* September 16, 1973.

Friedan, Betty. 1973. Up from the kitchen floor. *New York Times Magazine,* March
4, 1973.

Hollingworth, Leta S. 1916. Social devices for impelling women to bear and rear
children. *American Journal of Sociology* 22 (July):19–29.

Lott, Bernice E. 1973. Who wants the children? *American Psychologist* 28 (July):
573-582.

Ms. 1974 Vol. 2 (March).

Myron, Nancy. 1972. Class beginnings. *Furies* 1, (March–April):3.

NOW. 1973. *NOW acts.* Proceedings of the Sixth National Conference of NOW,
Washington, D.C.

Raphael, Edna E. 1971. From sewing machines to politics: The woman union
member in the community. Paper presented at meetings of the Society for the
Study of Social Problems, August.

Ross, Heather L. 1973. *Poverty: Women and children last.* Washington, D.C.:
Urban Institute. Working paper 971-08-02 (December 5).

Ross, Heather, L., and MacIntosh, Anita. 1973.*The emergence of households
headed by women.* Washington, D.C.: Urban Institute. Working paper 776-01
(June 1).

Sanger, Margaret. 1928. *Motherhood in bondage.* New York: Brentano.

Seifer, Nancy. 1973. Absent from the majority: Working class women in America.
National Project on Ethnic Research.

Shostak, Arthur B. 1971. Working class Americans at home: Changing expectations
of manhood. Paper prepared for Conference on Problems, Programs, and

Prospects of the American Working Class in the 1970s, October, Rutgers University.

———— . 1973. Ethnic revivalism, blue-collarites, and Bunker's last stand. *Sounding* (Spring):68-82.

Suter, Larry E., and Miller, Herman P. 1973. Income differences between men and career women. *American Journal of Sociology* 73 (January):200–212.

TEN

The Impact of Sexism and Racism on Employment Status and Earnings

The Problem

Of the four sex-race categories of workers—black and white men and women—white men are subject to neither racism nor sexism. They may, therefore, be taken as the standard when neither of these factors is present. Black men are subject to racism but not to sexism and white women to sexism but not to racism. The status of black men vis-à-vis white men may thus be taken as an index of racism uncomplicated by sexism, and that of white women as an index of sexism uncomplicated by racism. Only black women have both sexism and racism to contend with; they are therefore pivotal in comparing the relative impact of both. Their disadvantaged position is reflected in both their employment status and their earnings as compared with the other three categories.

Caught in this two-way bind, leaders among black women have been struggling with a major dilemma: where should they invest themselves to best advantage, in the struggle against racism or in the struggle against sexism? If this were a purely economic question it would be amenable to an objective research solution. We know, of course, that it is far more than that. A great deal of emotion is involved. Further, the research data justify their uncertainty. The data presented here show that so far as earnings are concerned, black women are more handicapped by sexism than they are by racism; as related to employment status, on the other hand, the reverse is the

Table 10.1

Employment Status and Earnings, 1972, for Specified Categories of Workers

CATEGORY OF WORKER	UNEMPLOY-MENT RATE[a]	"PART-TIME" UNEM-PLOYMENT RATE (LESS THAN 14 WEEKS OF PART-TIME EMPLOYMENT)	YEAR-ROUND (50-52 WEEKS) EMPLOYMENT RATE	
			FULL-TIME	PART-TIME
EMPLOYMENT STATUS				
White	5.00	5.5	67.7	6.5
Nonwhite or black	10.00	6.4	53.9	6.2
Men	—	3.6	66.0	4.4
Women	—	8.2	42.2	9.6
White men	3.6	3.4	66.8	4.4
Nonwhite and/or black men	6.8	5.5	60.6	3.8
White women	4.9	8.4	41.6	9.7
Nonwhite and/or black women	8.8	7.4	46.9	9.0
MEDIAN EARNINGS				
White	—	—	$5,757[b]	—
Black	—	—	4,306[b]	—
Men	—	$341	10,202	$1,751
Women	—	306	5,903	1,976
White men	—	346	10,593	1,774
Black men	—	307	7,301	1,371
White women	—	306	5,998	2,036
Black women	—	301	5,147	1,562

SOURCE: Data on unemployment, Bureau of the Census, 1973, Table 27. The data are for "Negro and Other Races." Other data from Bureau of the Census, 1973, Table 54. Data are for "Negroes."

[a]These figures are for adults. Including young people they were higher for 1971. Seasonally adjusted for October, 1971, they were: black males, 8.9; black females, 8.4; white females, 4.9; and white males, 4.0 (Bureau of Labor Statistics press release).

[b]Wage or salary income, employment status not specified (Bureau of the Census: Table 65). *Money Income in 1972 of Families*, etc.

case. Although they have been racing fast in the last third of a century, even when their earnings have caught up with those of white women, they still have not caught up with those of black men. But even when their unemployment rate approaches that of black men, it is still considerably greater than that of white women. There is good reason for the perplexity black women feel.

The relative position of the four categories of workers in 1972 with respect to employment status and earnings is shown in Table 10.1. The situation shown here is familiar and widely known; it results from a wide variety of structural (economic, political, sociological) and psychological factors. The present paper deals with only one, namely the part played by sexism and racism.

The Institutional Nature of Sexism and Racism

Racism refers to discrimination built into the institutional structures of our society. The term only entered the dictionaries in the late 1960s. Until that time race prejudice seemed an adequate conceptual tool for sociological analysis (Bernard, 1970). But when it was found that discrimination on the basis of race persisted even among those who felt no prejudice and who even tried to lean over backward to avoid discrimination, it became clear that even in the absence of prejudice, institutional structures carried discriminatory consequences.

A similar but more complex situation has called for the concept of sexism also, a term that will, presumably, now enter the dictionaries to refer to the institutional frameworks that have discriminatory consequences for women. In the context of the discussion of workers here, the term would include such customary items as sex-typing of jobs, the differential wages paid for such jobs, the differential opportunity to train for and enter jobs, the effects on aspirations and motivation of such differentials, the power to influence the pay of jobs, access to full-time rather than part-time employment or year-round rather than intermittent employment, as well as all the other forms discrimination may take that ultimately contribute to earnings. In addition to these familiar forms, the term is increasingly coming to include a much wider gamut of practices. That is, the consequences of a growing number of institutional practices are now being interpreted by law, guidelines, administrative orders, and court decisions as having discriminatory consequences for women workers. A mother who wants to work, for example, may not be denied employment only because she has small children if a father is not also denied employment for this reason. A seaman who bears an out-of-wedlock baby may not be discharged since a man who fathered an out-of-wedlock baby would not be; an Air Force captain may not be deprived of her son's presence when she is transferred to the Philippines since a man would not be so deprived of his dependents in a similar situation. Almost all practices that take the present sexual allocation of functions—except reproduction—as given are being tested for discriminatory consequences for women workers.

In addition to these time-honored and newly emerging practices is the fact that the work men do is everywhere accorded more prestige than the work women do. A large component of the difference in earnings of men and women can thus be accounted for by the higher monetary value placed

Table 10.2

The Effects of Sexism and Racism on Employment Status as Measured by Ratio of Rates for Women to Rates for Men and of Rates for Nonwhites or Blacks to Whites, 1972

	UNEMPLOY- MENT	"PART-TIME" UNEMPLOYMENT[a]	YEAR-ROUND (50-52 WEEKS) EMPLOYMENT	
			FULL-TIME	PART-TIME
SEXISM[a]				
A. Overall (women/men)	—	2.27	.64	2.18
B. Black women/black men	1.29	1.35	.77	2.37
C. White women/white men	1.36	2.47	.62	2.20
RACISM[b]				
D. Black/white	2.00	1.16	.80	.95
E. Black women/white women	1.80	.88	1.13	.93
F. Black men/white men	1.88	1.62	.91	.86
BOTH SEXISM AND RACISM				
G. Black women/white men	2.44	2.18	.70	2.04
NEITHER SEXISM NOR RACISM				
H. White men/white men	1.00	1.00	1.00	1.00

SOURCE: Same as Table 10.1. Data on unemployment for nonwhites; on other employment statuses, for blacks.
[a]Less than 14 weeks of part-time employment.
[b]The higher the ratio, the greater the effect of sexism.
[c]The higher the ratio, the greater the effect of racism.

on the kinds of work men do (janitorial, for example) as compared to the kinds of work women do (like teaching). The sexism in such cases inheres not so much in an imposed sex-typing of work as in the differential pay accorded to the two sexes, even when the work itself is a consequence of preference rather than discrimination. Such differential pay is itself a consequence of discrimination resulting from differential power.

We are not, therefore, discussing the personal attitudes or prejudices of whites or of men as manifested in discrimination against blacks or women, but rather the system that produces and reinforces it.

The discussion here is limited to workers. Sexism and racism are therefore operationalized on the basis of two work-related kinds of indexes, namely employment status and earnings. The first includes four "degrees" of employment: (1) unemployment, (2) "part-time" unemployment, referring to part-time employment for less than 14 weeks during the year,[1]

1. Since part-time employment for less than 14 weeks means a considerable amount of unemployment, this employment status is conceived of as more related to unemployment

(3) part-time employment for 50 to 52 weeks; and (4) full-time employment for 50 to 52 weeks. When not otherwise specified, the second index refers to year-round full-time earnings.

Assessment of the Relative Impact of Sexism and Racism

In both types of indexes, racism is measured by comparing black men and women with white men and women, and sexism by comparing black and white women with black and white men. In the first type of comparison, sex is "held constant" and race varied; in the second race is "held constant" and sex varied. A ratio of 1.0 (Table 10.2) or a percentage of 100.0 (Tables 10.3, 10.4, and 10.5) means equality. The nearer a ratio or percentage between the indexes of any two categories approaches 1.0 or 100.0, the less the effect of sexism or racism is assumed to be. For negative indexes such as unemployment or part-time unemployment, a ratio above 1.0 indicates discrimination, the higher the more serious. For positive indexes such as earnings, percentages below 100.0 indicate discrimination, the lower the more serious.

If, for example, black women are more like white women (row E) than black men are like white men (row F), that is, if black women approach equality with white women more nearly than black men do with white men, racism is assumed to be more important for black men than for black women. Or if black women approach more nearly to equality with black men (row B) than white women with white men (row C), sexism is held to be greater for white than for black women. Or if black women approach equality with white men (row E) more nearly than with black men (row B), sexism is taken to be greater than racism. (The cognate analysis—white women compared with black men—while interesting, did not appear to warrant the additional complexity it would introduce.)

RESULTS

With respect to unemployment, racism seemed to be more important for black women than sexism (Table 10.2). Their rate of unemployment was nearer to that of black men (1.29) than to that of white women (1.80). The black woman's race seemed to have more to do with her securing employment than her sex. Put another way, eliminating sexism would

than to employment. It is, incidentally a great equalizer. The lowest earnings ($301) for those in this employment status were only 13 percent lower than the highest ($346). In the case of part-time year-round employment, the lowest earnings were about a third lower than the highest, and, in the case of full-time employment, they were only about half as great as the highest (Table 10.1).

Table 10.3

The Effects of Sexism and Racism on Median Earnings as Measured by Women's as Proportion of Men's and of Blacks' as Proportion of Whites', by Employment Status, 1972

	"PART-TIME" UNEMPLOYMENT[a]	YEAR-ROUND (50-52 WEEKS) EMPLOYMENT	
SEXISM[b]		FULL-TIME	PART-TIME
A. Overall (women/men)	89.7	57.8	113.6
B. Black women/black men	98.0	70.4	113.9
C. White women/white men	88.4	56.6	133.0
RACISM[c]			
D. Overall (blacks/whites)	—	—	—
E. Black women/white women	98.4	85.9	66.2
F. Black men/white men	88.7	69.0	77.3
BOTH SEXISM AND RACISM			
G. Black women/white men	87.0	48.6	113.9
NEITHER SEXISM NOR RACISM			
H. White men/white men	100.0	100.0	100.0

SOURCE: Bureau of the Census, 1973; Table 54, and Table 65.
[a]Less than 14 weeks of part-time employment.
[b]The higher the ratio, the greater the effect of sexism.
[c]The higher the ratio, the greater the effect of racism.

reduce her unemployment rate by 22.7 percent, but getting rid of racism would decrease it by twice that amount, 44.3 percent (Table 10.7). But, having said this, it must be pointed out that with this exception, sexism was more important than racism.

So far as earnings are concerned, the results shown in Tables 10.3, 10.4, and 10.5 may be summarized briefly as follows: (1) racism tends to be more serious for black men (row F) than for black women (row E); (2) sexism tends to be more serious for white women (row C) than for black or nonwhite women (row B); and (3) while both racism and sexism handicap black women, sexism is more serious than racism (row B, row E).[2]

2. It is interesting to note in connection with the discrepancy in earnings between black women and black men that the average IQ of black females is, reportedly, higher than that of black males (Sowell, 1974). The discrepancy in earnings is especially relevant in the case of families headed by women. A University of Michigan five-year panel study found that "if women who headed families in economic need had been paid wages equal to the wages paid men of comparable skills and experience, 55 percent would have been nonpoor" (Ross, 1973:13).

Data were not available to examine the effect of age, but both years of schooling and occupation showed the same general relationships as those summarized above. Racism in the case of women declined so markedly with years of schooling that the differential in earnings between black and white women had all but disappeared at the college level (Table 10.4, row E).[3] Nor was there a great amount of racism evident in the white-collar occupations. The earnings of black professional women were approaching those of white professional women, and in the case of clerical workers they were just about the same. Most striking in both Tables 10.4 and 10.5 is the far greater sexism among white than among black workers. At all levels of schooling and in all occupations, black women were more nearly like black men in earnings than white women were like white men.

Year-round part-time employment clearly favored women of both races, both in incidence and in earnings. More than three times as many black women as black men and almost three times as many white women as white men had year-round part-time jobs. The anomalous nature of this employment status for men in a society where industry is organized as it is in ours shows up in the higher earnings of women than of men with year-round part-time jobs. For those who view part-time jobs as just a step beyond unemployment itself—more probably men than women—a high rate of part-time employment will be taken as a negative index; but for those—more probably women than men—who see it as a valid and desirable compromise between un- or nonemployment and full-time employment, it will be taken as a favorable index. The current reappraisal of the potential benefits of part-time employment as an option for both men and women further clouds the picture. The advocacy of more part-time employment for women as an accommodation to their family responsibilities finds increasing support.[4] At least so far as women, if not as yet men, are concerned, the situation shown in year-round part-time work seems to deny the existence of discrimination. But feminists point out that it is precisely the allocation of family responsibilities so exclusively to women that necessitates the accommodation of their work to these responsibilities. It is the institutional structure that produces the discriminatory consequences for which "reverse sexism" is merely a palliative.

3. If black and white women are compared on the basis not of year-round full-time earnings but on the basis simply of "total money income" the superiority of black women over white women at the higher education levels is striking. Among those with high-school education, the total money income of black women was 103.4 percent of that of white women, at the high-school graduation level, 102.2 percent, and at the college level, 118.7 percent (Bureau of the Census, 1972: Table 51). It may be that the pressure in large cities which has called for so many public welfare workers, nurses, teachers, mental health aides, and clerical workers in metropolitan corporations makes being black especially relevant.

4. There is research support for the positive effects of part-time employment on the marriages of working wives and on the children of working mothers.

Table 10.4
Median Earnings of Persons 25 to 34 Years Old in Experienced Labor Force Who Worked 50 to 52 Weeks in 1969, by Years of Schooling: 1970

	8 OR LESS	YEARS OF SCHOOLING				
		9-11	12	13-15	16	17+
SEXISM[a]						
A. Overall (women/men)	—	—	—	—	—	—
B. Black women/black men	61.9	63.9	67.6	72.0	80.0	79.9
C. White women/white men	60.1	54.1	58.5	62.3	64.3	68.8
RACISM[b]						
D. Overall (black/white)	—	—	—	—	—	—
E. Black women/white women	73.7	85.8	91.2	96.9	96.7	97.9
F. Black men/white men	71.7	72.7	78.8	83.8	77.7	84.3
BOTH SEXISM AND RACISM						
G. Black women/white men	44.3	46.4	53.3	60.3	62.2	67.4
NEITHER SEXISM NOR RACISM						
H. White men/white men	100.0	100.0	100.0	100.0	100.0	100.0

SOURCE: Bureau of the Census, 1973, Table 15.
[a]The higher the ratio, the greater the effect of sexism.
[b]The higher the ratio, the greater the effect of racism.

TRENDS

Some idea of what the trends have been in the last generation can be gleaned from Table 7. A comparison of the median wage or salary income for year-round full-time employment in 1939 with that in 1972 showed a decline in racism for both nonwhite men and women, spectacularly so in the case of nonwhite women (Figure 10.1). In 1939 the median wage or salary income for nonwhite men ($639) was less than half (45.0 percent) that of white men ($1419); in 1972 it ($7548) was almost three-fourths (70.0 percent) that of white men ($10,766). In the same period, the corresponding figures for nonwhite women were 37.9 and 86.8 percent respectively. The median wage or salary income of nonwhite women had increased more than twice as fast as that of white women, from $327 in 1939 to $5320 in 1972, as compared with $863 to $6131 for white women. Racism had declined far faster than sexism (Figure 10.2).

Sexism has declined also during the same period in the case of nonwhite women, but not at all in the case of white women (Figure 10.3). If anything, it had increased. Nonwhite women were catching up to nonwhite men, but white women were falling farther behind white men.

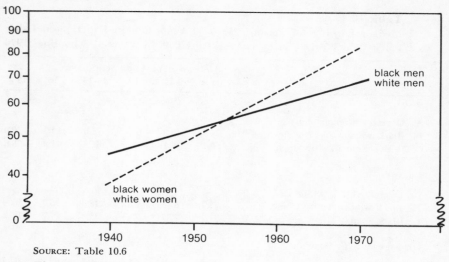

SOURCE: Table 10.6

Figure 10.1

Median Wage or Salary of Black Men and Women as Percent of Median Wage or Salary of White Men and Women.

Discussion

No attention has been paid here to alternative or supplementary interpretations of the data in Table 10.1. There are some who argue that race and sex explain them better than racism and sexism do.

In the current revival of interest in race differences, the concept of "heritability," developed in connection with the IQ, has been extended to explain stratification (Herrnstein, 1971). Aside from the fact that the "heritability" factor for blacks is not known, the short period of time covered by the research precludes sweeping application to stratification. If the decline in differences shown in rows E and F of Table 10.6 can be so great in only 33 years, an increase to equality—100.0 percent—in the next half century is certainly not improbable.

There are others who, while recognizing the discriminatory consequences of societal structures in the case of women, nevertheless conclude that they are intrinsic and hence inevitable. No matter what the institutional structure of an industrialized society may be, the reproductive function of women has discriminatory consequences for them in the work world, if not elsewhere. So long as child rearing is also assigned exclusively to women, this is true. Still, as noted earlier, there are some now arguing that such an assignment of child rearing to women exclusively is a structural, not an intrinsic imperative (Bernard, 1971: Part 5). Or that, if it is, structural correctives are possible. However one views the situation, it is clear that eliminating sexism calls for far more drastic reorientation of our

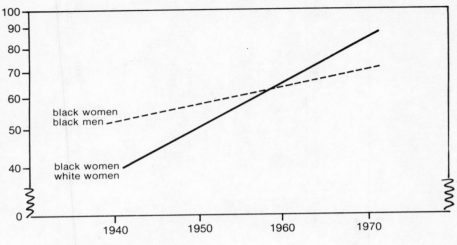

SOURCE: Table 10.6

Figure 10.2
Median Wage or Salary of Black Women as Percent of Median Wage or Salary of White Women and of Black Men.

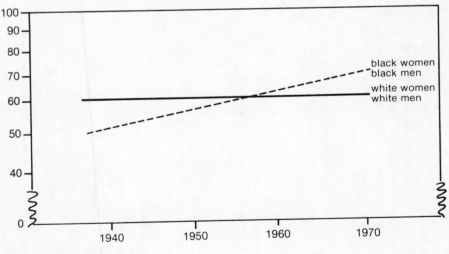

SOURCE: Table 10.6

Figure 10.3
Median Wage or Salary of Women as Percent of Median Wage or Salary of Men.

Table 10.5.

The Effects of Sexism and Racism on Median Earnings for Year-round Full-time Employment as Measured by Women's as Proportion of Men's and Blacks' as Proportion of Whites', by Occupation, 1972

	PROFESSIONAL, KINDRED	MANAGERS AND PROPRIETORS	CLERICAL	SALES	CRAFTSMEN	OPERATIVES	SERVICE	LABORERS
SEXISM[a]								
A. Overall (women/men)	64.6	52.1	62.3	38.3	53.3	57.2	58.8	62.0
B. Black women/black men	84.5	—	72.8	—	—	66.3	73.3	—
C. White women/white men	63.9	51.2	61.0	38.3	52.5	56.2	55.5	59.3
RACISM[b]								
D. Overall (black/white)	—	—	—	—	—	—	—	—
E. Black women/white women	91.2	—	98.4	—	—	92.5	101.5	—
F. Black men/white men	69.0	73.2	82.5	—	80.4	78.5	77.0	75.6
BOTH RACISM AND SEXISM								
G. Black women/white men	43.7	—	60.0	—	—	52.0	56.4	—
NEITHER SEXISM NOR RACISM								
H. White men/white men	100.0	100.0	100.0	100.0	100.0	100.0	100.0	100.0

OCCUPATION

SOURCE: Bureau of the Census, 1972, Table 58.
[a]The higher the ratio, the greater the effect of sexism.
[b]The higher the ratio, the greater the effect of racism.

Table 10.6

Trends in Effects of Sexism and Racism as Measured by Women's Median Wage or Salary for Year-round Full-time Employment as Proportion of Men's and Nonwhites' as Proportion of Whites, 1939 and 1972

	1939	1972
SEXISM[a]		
A. Overall (women/men)	57.9	57.9
B. Nonwhite women/nonwhite men	51.2	70.5
C. White women/white men	60.8	56.8
RACISM[b]		
D. Nonwhites/whites	—	—
E. Nonwhite women/white women	37.9	86.8
F. Nonwhite men/white men	45.0	70.0
BOTH SEXISM AND RACISM		
G. Nonwhite women/white men	23.0	49.3
NEITHER SEXISM NOR RACISM		
H. White men/white men	100.0	100.0

SOURCE: Bureau of the Census, 1972, Table 61.
[a]The higher the ratio, the greater the effect of sexism.
[b]The higher the ratio, the greater the effect of racism.

Table 10.7

Effect of Eliminating Racism and Sexism on Earnings and Unemployment

	BLACK WOMEN	BLACK MEN	WHITE WOMEN	WOMEN	BLACKS
EFFECT ON EARNINGS					
Eliminating racism[a]	+16.5	+42.3	—	—	+33.8
Eliminating sexism[b]	+41.8	—	+76.6	+74.5	—
Eliminating both[c]	+105.8	—	—	—	—
EFFECT ON UNEMPLOYMENT					
Eliminating racism[a]	−44.3	−47.1	—	—	−50.0
Eliminating sexism[b]	−22.7	—	−26.6	—	—
Eliminating both[c]	−59.1	—	—	—	—

SOURCE: Table 10.1.
[a]By bringing earnings of black women up to those of white women and of black men up to those of white men.
[b]By bringing earnings of black women up to those of black men and of white women up to those of white men.
[c]By bringing earnings of black women up to those of white men.

211

thinking than does the elimination of racism. The dimensions of this reorientation are only now becoming visible.

There is no room in a research paper to explore policy implications in any depth. Still, there is no reason to reject a primitive kind of "simulation." Thus in Table 10.7, the results for earnings and unemployment expectable if racism and sexism were eliminated are shown. It corroborates the three generalizations. If racism were eliminated the earnings of black men would be increased by 42.3 percent and their rate of unemployment decreased by 47.1 percent; of black women, 16.5 and 44.3 percent. If sexism were gotten rid of, the earnings of white women would be increased by 76.6 percent and their unemployment rate decreased by 26.6 percent; of black women, 41.8 and 22.7 percent. If both were removed, the earnings of black women would go up 105.8 percent and their unemployment rate down 59.1 percent.

References

Bernard, Jessie. 1970. Sexism and discrimination. *American Sociologist* 5 (November):374–375.

———— . 1971. *Women and the public interest: An essay on policy and protest.* Chicago: Aldine.

Bureau of the Census. 1973. *Money income in 1972 of families and persons in the United States.* Series P-60, no. 90 (December).

———— . 1973. The social and economic status of the Black Population in the United States. Series P-23, no. 46 (July).

Herrnstein, Richard J. 1971. I.Q. *Atlantic Monthly* (September):43–64.

Ross, Heather L. 1973. *Poverty: Women and children last.* Washington, D.C.: Urban Institute. Working paper 971-08-02 (December 5).

Sowell, Thomas. 1974. Black excellence: The case of Dunbar High School. *The Public Interest* (Spring).

PART V

THE WIDER SCENE

THE PAPERS IN PART V assume a somewhat different perspective from that of preceding papers, for the "values and options" in the subtitle of this book are relevant with respect not only to women themselves but also to our society as a whole. As a society we have to make choices, and these choices will be determined at least in part by our values. What kind of family do we want? What are we willing to pay for it? Or do we, as a matter of cold fact, really have choices? If we do, what are the limits within which we must choose among them? Is it true, as Talcott Parsons has noted (1959:273), that "if the United States is to remain and develop further as a democratic, urbanized, industrial society, with a large measure of equality of opportunity, the range of possible family structures which are compatible with its type of society is very narrow"? These kinds of questions have sociological, economic, and political aspects. The sociological have to do with the functions that have to be performed, whether by the unit we call the family or some other; the economic questions have to do with the division of labor between the sexes in the production, distribution, and consumption of goods and services; the political questions have to do with what is possible given the pluralistic structure of our society and the nature of the human nature it produces.

The first paper is a condensation of two papers. The first part deals with mothers, the second part with fathers. Because much of the material originally included in the first part is dealt with, one way or another, in

213

other papers in this collection, the first part was further condensed. Only enough is included to support the major thesis, namely that the extreme sex-role specialization characteristic of our society, however adaptive it may once have been, has now become maladaptive, bad for mothers, bad for fathers, bad for their marriage, bad for their children, and therefore bad for the social order. It is, further, apparently contrary to the apparent trends in economic development. This paper admittedly "maximizes the variables"—that is, the "pathogenic mother" and the "work-intoxicated father—in order to highlight these points. Their importance seems to warrant this procedure.

The second paper scans the dusty answers that policy-relevant research offers the policy maker. Decisions with respect to motherhood present the policy maker with options quite unique and peculiar. Ordinary considerations do not apply. True, we do not always know just where sanctions imposed with any policy will finally be felt, but in the case of the family we know that sanctions leveled against adults will ultimately be felt by children. Thus the usual instruments at the disposal of the policy maker are blunted. He cannot escape a built-in dilemma: anything that brings sanctions to bear against mothers is paid for by children, and it is intolerable that children should be punished for the errors of their parents. Few would argue that it is just for the "sins" of the mothers or fathers to be visited on their children.

Two paradigms guide research with respect to motherhood. One has to do with the nuclear family as articulated especially by Talcott Parsons, and one has to do with demographic trends. If the policy maker follows the recommendations that flow from research based on the Parsonian statement of the nuclear family paradigm he will support one kind of policy, a kind that shores up the nuclear family as it operates today. If he follows the recommendations that flow from research based on the demographic paradigm, he will support a policy that encourages women to soft-pedal the maternal role and emphasize nonfamily roles. If he selects a policy that helps mothers bear the load, if it is one that shares the costs of motherhood, if it is designed to make it easier, there is a danger that women will elect to have many babies, an outcome not called for at this point. If he makes motherhood too hard, the children may suffer. So the policy maker must steer a careful course.

Not all policy-relevant research is designed in advance for policy decisions.[1] All kinds of research may be seized upon by the policy maker. A

1. Examples of research designed specifically for policy makers are: *Economic Problems of Women*, three volumes of Hearings before the Joint Economic Committee, Congress of the United States (Washington, D.C.: U.S. Government Printing Office, 1973); *Work in America*, Report of a Special Task Force to the Secretary of Health, Education, and Welfare, Subcommittee on Employment, Manpower, and Poverty (Washington, D.C.: U.S. Government Printing Office, 1973); *Studies in Public Welfare*, Paper No. 12, The Family, Poverty, and Welfare Programs; Household Patterns and Government Policies; Paper No. 13, How

considerable amount of the research that looks so antiseptically free of applied use is of a kind that ultimately finds its way into government white papers, Supreme Court briefs, and congressional hearings. It is relevant to note therefore that the choice of research questions, the statement of research problems, of funding of research, and the uses to which findings can be put are all, willy-nilly, whether we recognize it or not, basically political phenomena.

The conference for which the final paper was prepared addressed itself to "changes in women's behavior" and "changes in society with respect to women" vis-à-vis higher education, the occupations, the media, government and politics, and new social structures. We were invited to think in new ways, "to project what . . . events have to tell us about the social challenges of the future," "to explore the many new potentialities open to women," "to go beyond a restatement of old ills to specification of new goals." I was asked "What new societal forms might develop?" "What changes in social institutions should we seek?" The paper discusses who the American woman will be and some of the new structural forms beginning to appear. The answers proposed were, in essence, that the American woman is going increasingly, at least until the end of the century, to be both a mother and a labor-force participant, and that the new societal forms we are going to need will therefore be those that spread to all both the monetary and the nonmonetary costs of these two roles. As one way to achieve this end, the system Gösta Rehm calls one of "generalized drawing rights" is proposed.

Reference

Parsons, Talcott, 1959. The social structure of the family, in Anshen, Ruth Nanda, ed., *The family: Its function and destiny*. New York: Harper.

Income Supplements Can Affect Work Behavior (Washington, D.C.: U.S. Government Printing Office, 1974); Isabel Sawhill, Heather L. Ross, and Anita MacIntosh, *The Family in Transition* (Washington, D.C.: Urban Institute, 1973); Heather L. Ross, *Poverty: Women and Children Last* (Washington, D.C.: Urban Institute, 1973); Heather L. Ross and Anita MacIntosh, *The Emergence of Households Headed by Women* (Washington, D.C.: Urban Institute, 1973).

ELEVEN

The Bitter Fruits of Extreme Sex-Role Specialization

I. The Pathogenic Mother

CHERCHEZ LA MÈRE

With an animus hard for me to understand, almost every conceivable human woe—autism, schizophrenia, psychosomatic illness, psychopathologies of all kinds, you name it—is laid at mother's feet. It's all her fault. No matter what it is, if it is serious and disturbing enough, *cherchez la mère*. She is, according to one psychiatrist, "pathogenic." She literally breeds pathologies. Anyone, including fathers, would be better for the care of children than mothers. "Even if men performed the caretaking duties of the mothering person," Joseph Rheingold tells us, "it is doubtful that they would exert comparable harmful influence, because very few men have the destructive drive toward children common to mothers. What appears from observation and from the memories of patients is that the father is often the tender parent, inverting the myth of the stern father and the succoring mothers" (Rheingold, 1967:107). Psychiatrists report in fathers only death wishes toward their children, but mothers have fantasies of destruction (Ibid:108). The fathers only passively wish the children would disappear, the mothers actively want to destroy them (Pollack, 1950:20-23, 84-88).

The evidence adduced to support these charges is, admittedly, not all that hard. Rheingold finds it in "consensual insight" (I wonder whose?), in

217

"common experience," and in "professional opinion derived from direct observation of mothers and children," in retrospective accounts of patients, and in experimental studies. He finds it also in the "collective contribution of creative writers and of workers in different scientific disciplines in various parts of the world" (Rheingold, 1967:104). Wolfgang Lederer supplies some of the research of the 1950s as reported by Reichard and Tillman, Spitz, Despert, Gerard, Mahler, Sperling, Starr, Moss, Johnson, Bateson, Karon and Rosberg, and Searls (Lederer, 1968:6–7). Even so, Lederer tells us, the list is incomplete, almost random. Complete or not—I am not personally familiar with the literature—it is enough to illustrate "the psychiatric mood of suspicion toward mothers" (Ibid.:7).

Nor is the pathogenicity of mothers limited to clinical cases, to psychiatric patients. It is, Rheingold tells us, universal, "unexceptional." No one escapes. We all recognize the pathogenicity of maternal brutality, harsh discipline, rejection, neglect, and persecutory attitudes. And more and more of us are coming also to recognize the pathogenicity of the possessive, overprotective, perfectionist mother.

> What is not fully envisaged, however, is that the more overt manifestations spring from certain impulses, usually repressed, and that these impulses have deleterious effects even in the presence of a conscious benign disposition toward the child. . . . Not observable behavior but the mother's unconscious propensity is the crux of the matter. (Rheingold, 1967:105)

Rheingold explains why we refuse to accept the idea of maternal pathogenicity: We do not want to believe in its existence.

Doesn't it seem strange that if mothers are indeed such pathogenic characters we still insist—no one more strongly than psychiatrists themselves—on assigning to them the almost exclusive care of children? And on making such care their exclusive activity? If mothers are really so dangerous for children why do we insist on forcing the care of children on them at all? Wouldn't one think all sensible people would be shrieking for child development centers to rescue the children from such pathogenic women?

Quite the reverse, inconsistently enough. Along with the horrendous charges of maternal pathogenicity can also be found a movement to tie mothers ever more closely to the crib (Bowlby, 1951, 1969). Among the most frequently heard objections to all forms of child care by surrogate mothers is the so-called separation argument, which attributes pathogenic results for children to lack of sufficient contact with their mothers. It would be helpful if all the psychiatrists would get together and make up their mind. Which is it? Pathogenicity or indispensability?

Although Rheingold believes in the universal, "unexceptional" existence of maternal pathogenicity, he does not necessarily believe in its inevitability. "If," he assures us, "we could make all mothers nurturant (or just eliminated the unconscious aggressive impulses) and observed the result after a generation or two, not much mental (and social) disorganization would remain" (Rheingold, 1967:106). Cure mother, cure the social order. St. Augustine said about the same thing. It is a great idea, a beguiling prescription—but, of course, far easier said than done.

MORE CONVINCING EVIDENCE

The evidence produced by the psychiatrists is not too convincing. But when young mothers themselves come to us with a similar charge I begin to take it more seriously. They are among the first to corroborate the clinical data, to proclaim the existence of hostile attitudes and behavior, "propensities" no longer all that unconscious. For the first time that I know of, women themselves are crying out that although they love their children, they do not like motherhood (Radl, 1973)! It drives them up the wall! It drives them crazy! In some cases, it leads to serious abuse, even, in extreme cases, to infanticide. The facts adduced to support the concept of the pathogenic mother are not what is hard to take, but the psychoanalytic explanations offered for it.

If we wish to change the situation we have to know why mothers are pathogenic when they are. Where do we look for explanations? To instinct? To intrinsic family relationships? To the inbred nature of the female human being? Actually, quite matter-of-fact explanations seem quite enough: to the extent that mothers are pathogenic it is an almost inevitable consequence of the way the maternal role is institutionalized in our society today, to the extreme specialization of women in the maternal role.

THE INSTITUTIONALIZATION OF MOTHERHOOD TODAY

We all want mothers to be loving and nurturant, not pathogenic. We want to make it possible for them to be that way. And, as it turns out, it is not impossible to do so. It takes no stupendous change in human nature, as we learn from anthropologists who have studied the matter. In one such study of mothers in six cultures around the world, Lambert found that the more help women had with child care the more nurturant they tended to be. The help might come from older siblings, from fathers, from old men, from sisters, whoever. Just so there was help, relief (Minturn, Lambert, and Associates, 1964:56, 66, 97, 290–291). Round-the-clock care of small children is enough to fray anyone's nerves. No matter how much one loves the child, its constant care will get on one's nerves in time.

So also will the weight of exclusive responsibility we assign to mothers for the care of children in our society. The mother gave birth to the child, didn't she? She nurses it, doesn't she? She is, obviously, we conclude, solely responsible for it. Even when she can get help, time off, reprieve, relief for several hours during the day, the responsibility remains hers. During any absence she remains on call. At the theater, at work, at the party, her ear is always half-cocked for the telephone message to come: the child is ill. If anything happens to the child it is she, not the father, who will be held responsible.

The role of mother as we define it is almost unique. Motherhood as we institutionalize it is a product of affluence. Few if any societies have ever been able to spare adult, able-bodied women from the work force and specialize them so exclusively for the care of a small brood of children for almost a lifetime. Women were too badly needed in field or garden. Not only is our system unique, it is good for neither mother nor—as the pathogenicity concept shows—for child (Bernard, 1974:Chapter 5). Nor, for that matter, even fathers. For we have specialized the role of men as providers to the same degree as we have the role of women as mothers, and with about equally, though different, untoward results. And the way we institutionalize fatherhood is just as relevant as the way we institutionalize motherhood.

II. The Work-Intoxicated Father

A LOT OF EGGS FOR ONE BASKET

"Virtually the only way to be a real man in our society is to have an adequate job and earn a living" (Parsons, 1959:271). A man validates his maleness by his success as a provider. "Deviant," unsuccessful, underachieving men have generally been despised in American culture, divorced by their dissatisfied wives, or at least eternally nagged and blamed for their failure, and considered "less of a man" (Brenton, 1966:194). We have, in fact, specialized the father almost out of the family in any but the provider role. We have defined his role almost exclusively as that of provider, and nearly everything else about him as a human being depends on how well he performs that one function. If he does well in that role he can get away with almost anything else in the bosom of his family. He can sit uncommunicatively in front of the TV set drinking beer or even leave and go to the local tavern to drink his beer with the boys; no one will hold it against him so long as he is a good provider. But let him cease to be a good provider and no other virtue will compensate for this failure. Everything else collapses, including his manhood. No wonder success in the provider role assumes so much importance for men. All their eggs are in that one basket.

COME HOME, FATHER!

A nineteenth century prototype of what would today be a gold-seal record was a song called "Come Home, Father." It was about a little girl who went to a saloon every night to plead with her father to come home.

> Father, dear father, come home with me now.
> The clock in the steeple strikes one.
> You said you were coming right home from the shop
> As soon as your day's work was done.

Every hour on the hour she returned. The clock struck two and little Willie was sick and calling for him. The clock struck three and little Willie was worse, coughing and crying. The clock struck four, five, six. The fire went out; the house got cold; mother was waiting. When the clock struck ten in the morning father finally went home. Too late. Willie was dead.

It was a tear-jerker if ever there was one. In those days it was alcohol that intoxicated fathers. Today it is almost as likely to be work. We sometimes speak of golf widows and, more recently, of women widowed by television football broadcasts. And now we have work- or career-widows, from the wife of the top-level executive who devotes more time to his work than to his children, to the wife of the moonlighting blue-collar worker—5 percent of all workers have two jobs (Zigler, 1973:68)—who feels that he is doing the best thing for his family by supplying them with more income through a second job than by devoting more time and attention to them. Robert Coles (1973:111) quotes the factory worker who complains of overwork: "work . . . is my whole life. I work my regular shift, then I work overtime . . . . It means that I practically never get to see the kids, except on Sunday, and then I'm so tired I can barely do anything but sleep and eat and get ready for the next week." Urie Bronfenbrenner notes that even after the rats are gone—referring to poverty—the rat race remains.

> The demands of a job, or often two jobs, that claim mealtimes, evenings, and weekends as well as days; the trips and moves necessary to get ahead or simply hold one's own; the ever increasing time spent in commuting . . . produce a situation in which a child often spends more time with a passive babysitter than a participating parent. (Bronfenbrenner, 1973:151)

He then documents his charge with a study showing that although middle-class fathers thought they averaged 15 to 20 minutes a day playing with their year-old infants (Ibid.), actually the average number of interactions per day was only 2.7 and the average duration of the interactions, less than a minute—37.7 seconds (Ibid.). As a result, says Robert Coles, "during crucial stages of growing up, the fathers of these children are too occupied with career matters to take an active or significant role in their upbringing" (Coles, 1973:111).

The situation is equally grim for the mother. Ann Landers's readers fill us in on the picture as it looks to them. "Another Victim of the Money Bug" writes:

> Dear Ann Landers,
> You let the families of "work-aholics" down when you said hard work never killed anybody, that if a man enjoys what he's doing, let him alone . . . My husband works 10 or 12 hours a day six days a week. On Sunday, he sleeps round the clock. He gets up only to eat. There is no time or energy left for his family. My children are growing up without a father. Just because a man enjoys his work is no excuse to give himself completely to the job and ignore his wife and children. . . . Certainly we enjoy the fruits of his labors, but we'd settle for a lot less if he'd pay some attention to us. (*Washington Post*, March 4, 1974)

And less than three weeks later, still another:

> Dear Ann Landers,
> I'd like to delve further into your response: "hard work never killed anybody." Maybe hard work never killed anybody, but it sure has destroyed a lot of marriages. The man who is obsessed with his job is just as hooked as the alcoholic, the junkie, or the compulsive gambler. The big difference is that the "work freak" is admired by society, considered a "go-getter." The other guys are considered "sick" or "bums." . . .
> More and more marriages are breaking up because husbands are spending all their time and energy piling up money. The final battle cry of the driven loon is, "Look how hard I work to provide my family with something better! All I get is criticism." What he DIDN'T provide his family with was his presence when they needed him. (*Washington Post*, March 21, 1974)

Ann Landers replies:

> The man who puts in so many hours at his job that his family gets no time or attention is short-changing them AND himself. Those dynamos pay a big price for their so-called success. Often they end up with a large net worth, a bleeding ulcer, and no relationship with a wife or child. (Ibid.)

The evidence for the maladaptive effect of such extreme role specialization does not depend solely on Ann Landers's correspondents. Jan Dizard, following up on marriages studied originally in the 1950s, found 20 years later that those in which role specialization had been most marked were more likely than others to have deteriorated into "empty shell marriages."

He found that "decreasing husband-wife happiness and permanence is disproportionately common in those marriages which move toward a greater degree of role differentiation" (Dizard, 1968:73), especially on the part of the husband. "The primary source of increasing husband-wife role differentiation . . . is to be found in the occupational demands made upon the husband and his reaction to these demands. With increasing success in occupational endeavors (as measured by the degree to which the husband's income increased), we found increasing role differentiation and loss of gratification" (Ibid.:76).

A study in Great Britain showed similar results. It was based on the responses of some 200 women who had been graduated from the university in 1960, and the responses of their husbands. It contrasted the conventional pattern of marriage with the coordinated pattern, the first being the most differentiated and the second the least differentiated. Anything that tended to exaggerate differentiation in conventional marriages—such as many children or husband's satisfaction in his work—lowered the level of happiness. "Common interest seems particularly important for the success of a pattern based on rather strict differentiation of roles" (Bailyn, 1939:105). The level of happiness in marriages of the coordinate pattern depended more on the amount of sharing there was in the responsibility of child care and homemaking (Ibid.:106–107).

Erik Grönseth (1971), a Norwegian sociologist, has been one of the severest critics of the specialization of the husband in the provider role, which he finds has dysfunctional consequences throughout society.

The somewhat facetious tone of the sketches of women as pathogenic mothers and men as work-intoxicated fathers is not intended to suggest that they are meant to be discounted as amusing exaggerations. They are, in my opinion, to be taken seriously as examples of the maladaptive nature of sex-role specialization carried to the extreme we carry it to in our society today. What is sometimes defended as an adaptive pattern is becoming a threat rather than a contribution to survival. It is a reductio ad absurdum, absurd not in the sense of silly or ridiculous but in the sense of illogical, opposed to reason.

It may be true that role differentiation is a basic condition of all group life. And it may also be true that certain roles—"instrumental" and "expressive"—are inevitable in any task-oriented group (Bales, 1950). It is even true that there is a modicum of logic in specializing women, the "lactating sex," for the infant-nurturing role. One could grant these conclusions with the usual provision for exceptions and modifications. But surely the practice of sex-role specialization has now reached unrealistic proportions. Talcott Parsons told us some time ago, in fact, that "in certain respects the differentiation between the roles of the parents becomes more rather than less significant for the socialization process under modern American conditions" (Parsons, 1955:24). More significant and, as the pathogenic mother and the work-intoxicated father suggest, more maladaptive. When productive work and child care and rearing took place on the same site, the two functions might still be differentiated by sex but they were not segregated. It was only as the work of the father was removed from the home that the maladaptive consequences of the role specialization began to reveal themselves. It proves to be good for neither mothers nor fathers nor for their marriage nor for their children.[1]

PROVIDERS AND NURTURERS

Malinowski (1930) tells us that in all preliterate societies the father performs the provider role, but when we actually look at the research reports we find that women have done a very considerable amount of the providing, certainly of food. (Both Ceres and Artemis were females.) They have been gatherers, gardeners, fishers, poultry raisers, milk processors, and farm workers, supplying much if not most of human food from the beginning, with the possible exception of meat. (And I would not be surprised if we learned that they were the first to scavenge the carcasses left by the predatory animals, thus introducing human beings to the taste of meat.) Only since provisions have had to be purchased with cash in a market have men become so exclusively specialized in the provider role; they were the members of the family who had the money with which to purchase provisions. Even this is changing, for women are now demonstrating that they can be providers in this sense also. In fact, they are showing that they can be both nurturers and providers. Many are mothers

1. The dysfunctionality of sex-role specialization is not peculiar to our country; it is found in Soviet Russia as well. I am indebted to Vladimir de Lissovoy for the translation of a paper by Professor Igor S. Kon of the National University of Pedagogical Faculty, Leningrad, called "Why are Fathers Necessary?" Professor Kon reports his own research on attitudes of schoolchildren toward their parents and notes that "the traditional position for the men in the family has become problematical. Prevented from being the sole 'breadwinner,' man has lost his former power; all his human weaknesses are now exposed and no one sees him as 'husband and sovereign' any more. Productive labor, which has been and still is the main sphere of self-assertion for a man, today is physically separated from family life. In the overwhelming majority of cases, a child does not see how his father works. This is happening somewhere behind the scene. Even in conversations, the working activity of the parents is reflected incompletely. Only that man who is really happy with his work brings home the joy of creation and accomplishment. Irritation or disappointment, inevitable in any work, is spilled out on everybody at home in full measure. This suggests the necessity of reorientation of family roles and the search for some new, supplementary basis of father's authority." The author defends the perpetuation of sex-role differentiation. He would not think of restricting Soviet women to the narrow world of traditional family relations, still "complete equality of rights for women, their involvement in social and productive activity, and the advancement of women in the family, not in an expected role, but in a role based on moral and psychological values (of love, mutual respect, etc.), undermine the traditional structure of sex roles." He does not "mean to suggest that the cleaning of apartments and upbringing of the children 'is not man's business'." It is incorrect to say men care less about the family. They just do not know what to do. In a Conference of Fathers two years ago, "it turned out that the men themselves keenly felt the inadequacy of their relationships with their children. They were concerned, but they did not know what to do about it."

as well as participants in the labor force. True, the load is heavy. But then we expect women to carry heavy loads.

Malinowski alerts us also to the equivocal nature of the nurturing role. Referring to fathers in what he calls savage societies, he tells us that the father might in some cases conform to the stereotype of the nonamiable stern patriarch; but in other societies he might be "a drudge within the household, the assistant nurse of his children, the weaker and fonder of the two parents, and later on the most faithful and often the most intimate friend of his sons and daughters" (1930:118). The role of father—as distinguished from the role of progenitor—is a cultural creation. It varies over time and place (Malinowski, 1930).

To anyone, whatever his or her culture, the sex-role structure it provides seems natural. "Nature" dictates just what men will do, just what women will do. It is understandable that "Nature dictates" that women will be the people who gestate and bear children. But she (interesting gender) is not all that dictatorial. She is quite permissive beyond that, as the archetypes of the providing mother and the nurturant father referred to by Malinowski suggest.

Some go beyond the concept of a dictatorial Nature and insist that she is always right, that the natural is the correct, even the best, way to do anything. But there is no consensus on this point. There are some who, like the sociologist, L. F. Ward, insist that the artificial or cultural is better than the natural and that, in fact, it is the function of the cultural to improve on the natural. And, further, there has been a long-standing contrast between Nature seen as benign and harmonious and Nature viewed as red in tooth and claw, the contrast between the garden and the weed patch, the noble savage and the brutish hunter. All of this may have only tangential relevance when the "natural"—reproduction—is quite distinct from the cultural—parenthood. There is certainly an imposed specialization by sex in the reproductive function; but there are limits on Nature's dictatorial powers beyond that.

Would the sharing of child-rearing chores desex men, downgrade them, rob them of their masculinity? The men performing the father role are as varied as the roles. Whatever the prescribed behavior for fathers may be, some are hateful, some loving, some bored, irritated, indulgent, harshly disciplinary, amused, annoyed—the whole gamut from querulous Lears and compassionate Prosperos to Abrahams sacrificing sons, Lots offering daughters to the angry mob, and traditional Chinese fathers selling daughters into bondage. Personal differences as well as the institutional structures that define their role affect the way fathers behave, and if some have felt it beneath their dignity to share in the care of children, others welcome it.[2]

2. For examples of nurturing attitudes in men, see Bernard, 1974: Chapter 18. In a St. Louis suburb, as in other places, it has been found that some schoolboys, given the opportunity to be

BEYOND ROLE

The discussion in this paper centers largely on the concept of role and a great deal of it implies that roles and role modifications tell the whole story. But there is more. "Nature" and culture play out their duet within individuals as well as within societies. For a certain, as yet indeterminate, proportion of work addicts it is not role requirements that make them run but a built-in dynamo. They work because they have to. They prefer their work to their families, as they candidly admit (Talbot, 1952:109). Although they can be found in the arts, in the sciences, in academia (Bernard, 1964:317–318), in any field whatever, they have been most intensively studied in industry where they are at a premium.

There is a considerable research literature dealing with these work-addicted men as great industrial leaders or tycoons. Most of it is approving; in fact, much of it is a kind of how-to-do-it genre. Here is what these men are like:

> One central characteristic of business leaders is their enormous concentration on their careers. All of these mobile men show up in the interviews to be devoting almost all of their energies to the forwarding of their business careers, the company they are with, and their position in the company. . . . This driving concentration on the career is necessary to mobility. [And, of course, mobility is essential for maleness.] The task of moving through the business hierarchy is a hard, demanding one, and requires the intense focusing of great interests and energies and skills. We have seen that this is a characteristic of these men, the ability to focus their energies in this fashion on the tasks they set themselves. Without this capacity they would not have moved as they have. . . . Most of these men . . . share many basic attitudes. First, the wife must accept and work toward the goals set by the mobile man. She above all must learn to tolerate and even encourage the long hours, many business trips, and frequent moves dictated by the nature of his time or of his interest. Manifest by the kind of job concentration these men reveal, even their sexual activity is limited. (Warner and Abegglen, 1959: 48–49)

This statement, which was written 15 years ago, remains true today. The corporation's specifications for a top job state that "this is not a nine-to-five job. The man we are looking for has to eat, live and breathe production."[3] He must be aggressive, for aggressiveness is a sine qua non

---

nurturant in the care of children, find it enormously satisfying. Of the 50 students—a fourth of them boys—put in the responsible position of operating day-care centers, many reported excellent results. One mother credited the experience for the return of her dropout son. She could not remember "when he was as enthusiastic about anything as he was about those little kids" (Rogers, 1974: 13).

3. Quoted by Lake, 1973: 28. The book from which the quotation is taken is *The Corporate Eunuch* by O. William Battalia and John J. Tarrant.

for success in this tiger race. He must be "achievement oriented." Two commentators note that although the specifications of the corporation may say it wants a stable man in a happy marriage, this is nonsense. "What management really wants is not stability but a monomaniacal involvement amounting to neurosis. . . . A successful career in management today is the deadly enemy of a happy marriage" (Lake, 1973: 30). Or, say two other commentators, a marriage in which husband and wife both "cope with the demands made upon them by the corporation" (Ibid.).[4] Hanna Papanek (1973) has devised the insightful term "two-person career" to describe the course these and other careerist men run.

One may concede that a dynamic society like ours demands a certain proportion of men of this ilk. But the proportion need not be large. And it is doubtful that most men have the qualities of ambition, drive, and aggression called for. They have become stereotyped as the very archetypical qualities of maleness; we define maleness in terms of them. But they are far from the qualities defining maleness in the sense of the male family roles. As husbands, according to the passage quoted above, their sexuality is flawed; and so, also, as fathers, their parenting.

The same kind of "monomaniacal involvement amounting to neurosis" characterizes all kinds of careerists, women as well as men. People who share this driving force are beyond mere role, and their families, like the families of alcoholics, with whom they are often compared, have to put up with their compulsion. Fewer wives today are willing to.

Most men are not so compulsive. They work hard because they are well socialized into the role of provider. That role need not demand "monomaniacal involvement amounting to neurosis" but the world of work in which it must be performed calls for a mentality, a style of relating to people which is not at all conformable to the world of the family. It is not merely a matter of work absorption on the part of the husband and father and domestic involvement on the part of the wife and mother that has maladaptive effects on the marriage and the family. It is also the kind of emotional styles of operating that go with such role differentiation. Quite apart from the hard-driving, achievement-oriented, aggressive momentum of the tycoon, there is an approach to relationships that separates the outside work world and the family.

THE UPPER-MIDDLE-CLASS FAMILY

In the 1950s and 1960s both a sociologist, Talcott Parsons, and a psychologist, Kenneth Keniston, contrasted the universalistic, rationalist type of mentality of the work world which played down emotional behavior with the more expressive style of the family. First Parsons:

4. The author is citing the work of Feinberg and Reichman, two psychologists who have studied executive marriage.

The American family is in a delicate state of balance and integration with the rest of the social structure, notably the occupational structure. . . . The most essential feature of our occupational system is the primacy of functional achievement as an ideal pattern. . . . This fact . . . implies that occupational roles are organized about standards of competence or effectiveness in performing a definite function. That means that criteria of effective performance in a role and of selection to perform it must be predominantly universalistic and must be attached to impersonally and objectively defined abilities and competence through training. . . . Functionally irrelevant elements must be subordinated or excluded. . . . Procedures must be continually subjected to rational criticism. . . . The functioning of our occupational system . . . is possible only by virtue of a relatively severe discipline. . . .
Broadly speaking, there is no sector of our society where the dominant patterns stand in sharper contrast to those of the occupational world than in the family. . . . (Parsons, 1959:260–262)

In brief, the better you fit into the occupational world the less well you fit into the family world. Keniston said the same thing:

There is an incompatibility of values and expectations that surround occupational and familial roles. To be very successful in occupational pursuits requires a fairly active acceptance of the modes of interpersonal interaction predominant in the occupational world. To be successful, one has to be competitive and aggressive; others have to be judged with some degree of rationality and calculation. The family, obviously, defines the modes of interpersonal relationship differently; individuals should mildly and cheerfully cooperate with others in the family group; family members are to be loved, to be treated as ends— and not as means. (1965: 485-486, 487)

Keniston speaks also in terms of "public cognition" and family feeling, and he sees "the problems created by our American family system" for middle-class fathers as arising "from the demand for a radical split between public cognition and family feeling, and from the human difficulty in complying with this demand" (Ibid.: 295).

The "normal" resolution of this conflict, according to Keniston, is compartmentalization. A man

expresses his feelings in family and fun, and satisfies his needs for achievement and cognitive performance in his job. . . . When it works, this compartmentalization almost literally permits psychic survival. A man can tolerate the cold unemotionality of his work because he can 'live for the weekends' and . . . he can put up with the sometimes vacuous round of family feeling and fun because his work— however meaningless in ultimate terms—permits him to use his highly developed cognitive skills. Work at least permits him to 'support' his family (Ibid.: 293).

When it succeeds, this "normal" compartmentalization makes possible at least some mitigation of the untoward effect of excessive role specialization. But, Keniston further notes, such "psychic compartmentalization is hard to maintain, and continually threatens to break down" (Ibid.). Two breakdowns are common: careerism and familism, a breakdown, that is, in one compartment or the other, with satisfaction resulting from neither.

Careerism in this form is a compulsive flight into work; it is not the same as genuine involvement in meaningful work (Ibid.: 299). It is damaging to family life, for the father has almost no chance at all to succeed as a father. Though he may be physically present, he is "emotionally detached from his family and children, secretly disappointed and embittered" so that "he is simply 'not there' for his children" (Ibid.). He is "psychologically absent." Keniston found that fathers of alienated youth were extremely successful in their careers if not in their families.

The sons of these men have sympathy for their fathers but they feel "a lack of basic respect." All that achievement, all that success, all that upward mobility has been, in their eyes, at too great a cost. It has, in effect, cost him his ability to be a normal human being. Descriptions by these sons of their fathers include such phrases as: "finds it hard to show emotions, no matter how deeply felt, in public"; "he is very difficult to talk to—he has no desire to talk"; "I loved my father, though with the restraint and inhibition that arises . . . from his having been away from home, and, more important, from his genuine inability to be relaxed and affectionate in our company." Keniston summarizes the main themes in the descriptions these sons give of their fathers as "related terms like 'unable to express himself,' 'withdrawn,' 'cold'—and yet at the same time these subjects sense (or perhaps wishfully imagine) some lost part of their fathers which wants to express itself" (Ibid.: 115–117). In brief, these were men so well specialized for the occupational world that they could scarcely function in any other.

The other form breakdown takes is familism, not in the sense of more involvement with children but in the form of a great many chores around the house, yard work, and home projects. The father putters and fixes and builds. This alternative can put great strain on the family for it cannot provide all the satisfactions an adult needs. "A man who expects his wife and children to provide the entire meaning for his life, will be filled with inordinate disappointment when they fall short" (Ibid.: 297), as they must for him as they do for women. It further gives the child the idea that work is something to escape. If there is no satisfaction in the provider role it cannot be made up for by the family. Neither the work role by itself nor the family role by itself can fill a life completely.

The sons hold their fathers "responsible for their failings" (Ibid.: 117), but Keniston is not so harsh. Not the individual fathers, struggling one by one to come to terms with the demands made on them, but something intrinsically unbalanced in the way we live, is "to blame." "The family constellations of the alienated . . . result in part from efforts to 'solve' problems inherent in the organization of American families and in their relations to the wider society" (Ibid.: 300). Not compartmentalization, not careerism, not familism—all of which are disintegrative forms of accommodation—but less extreme specialization, more genuine integration of work and family roles are, as we shall presently note, being increasingly called for by men, by women, and by youth.

BLUE-COLLAR FATHER

If individual upward mobility is the key for understanding the upper-middle-class father, its denigration is central for understanding him among blue-collar, and especially ethnic, groups. In a study published in 1962 and therefore researched in the 1950s, Herbert Gans tells us that the kind of mobility Italians of the West End in Boston approved of was group, not individual, mobility. The West Ender rejected "the conscious pursuit of status and the acquisition of artifacts that would require him to detach himself from his peers, and to seek ways of living in which they cannot share" (Gans, 1962:219). But in the third generation, external upward mobility for individuals was already becoming acceptable (Ibid.: 226).

Still, for most working-class families, with or without upward mobility, being a good provider has been a major imperative of the father's role. A man may not have had to be climbing up a ladder but he did have to be "bringing home the bacon," and the more the better. His position in the family depended almost exclusively on his success in this role. If his wife had to work, for example, because his earnings were not sufficient, he suffered in her eyes and in the community's. Indeed, not having a working wife was a status symbol. "In the old days," a report from England tells us, "if a Lancashire miner's wife was working, you knew that her husband had been disabled at the pits" (Ignatius, 1974). Today the supplementary income of the wives is needed; men cannot support their families without it. This is bad enough. But insult is added to injury when her work brings in more than his. "In the traditional society of a Northern town like Wigan, for a miner to depend on his wife's earning power to pay the bills is a profound humiliation" (Ibid.). But "what galls him is that if his wife were working full-time, she could bring home a bigger paycheck than he does." She beats him at his own—provider—game.

Mirra Komarovsky's study of blue-collar marriage documents how heavily being a good provider weighed in relations between parents and adult children (1964: 251ff.). And Alix Kates Shulman, reviewing books about the girlhood of two daughters reared in poverty, reminds us how bitter the failure of a father as provider could be for his children. The fathers, "withdrawn and depressed, are despised for their inability to provide adequately. Says Isabel of her father: 'I felt very little but contempt and disgust. He was weak physically and morally; he could not provide'"

(Shulman, 1974:34).[5] A basket—ability to provide well—so fragile that all the eggs—respect of community, love of family—can be broken in one mishap is a serious hazard.

Arthur Shostak (1971), reporting on blue-collar men, tells us that the men he studied "probably learned little about the possibilities of fatherhood from the old man they seldom saw—and genuinely feared. And many may have taken a note from his coolness to his own father [when he was a boy], and found at least that easy to emulate years after." They expected little intimacy, little warmth in their dealings with the old man. "Real men were hard, undemonstrative 'sons-of-bitches' " (Ibid.). If they brought home the bacon what more could anyone ask?

THE ABSENT FATHER

Nowhere is the effect of excessive role specialization seen in greater clarity than in the case of the "female-headed family." The provider role has become so specialized that when it is not being adequately performed by the father, the family is left stranded. Either the mother must assume both parental roles or some other person or agency has to assume one or the other of them. Either the mother is relieved of the child-rearing role in order to perform the provider role, or she remains in the child-rearing role and turns the provider role over to others. In any event, there is a severe rent in the social fabric.

In terms of the amount of time and talent invested in research on mothers, research on female-headed families is by far the most salient, for, in the absence of a provider they tend to be poor (Krause, 1974). A wide variety of ways for meeting this situation have been tried or proposed. One is to try to stabilize the family. If the father has deserted, he should be located and forced to perform the provider function. As it turns out, the cost does not warrant the effort (Ibid.:255-274). If the father is deceased, the mother should be provided for by the state. This policy was back of the so-

5. Schulman is reviewing Audry Thomas' *Songs My Mother Taught Me* (Bobbs-Merrill) and Merrill Joan Gerber's *Now Molly Knows* (New York: Arbor House). Elliot Liebow has revealed to us the pathos and destructiveness of father-child relationships when the father cannot live up successfully to the provider role: "The man who lives with his wife and children is under legal and social constraints to provide for them, to be a husband to his wife and a father to his children. The chances are, however, that he is failing to provide for them, and failure in this primary function contaminates his performance as father in other respects as well. . . . His occasional touch or other tender gesture is dwarfed by his unmet obligations. No matter how much he does, it is not enough. But where the man lives with children not his own, every gentleness and show of concern and affection redounds to his public and private credit; everything is profit. For him, living with children is not, as it is for the father, charged with failure and guilt. Since his own and others' expectations of him as father are minimal, he is free to enter into a close relationship with the children without fear of failure and uninhibited by guilt. It is as if living with your own children is to live with your failure, but to live with another man's children is, so far as children are concerned, to be in a fail-proof situation: you can win a little or a lot but, however small your effort or weak your performance, you can almost never lose" (Liebow, 1966:86–88).

called Mothers' Pension movement which began at the turn of the century and spread to a number of states before it was incorporated in the federal Social Security Act of 1935 as Aid to Dependent Children. With the change in circumstances that has taken place in the last 40 years, however, there is now disenchantment with this plan also. In any event, a third strategy is now being offered to meet this contingency: "reduce the dependency needs of women by encouraging them to become self-supporting" (Ross, 1973:13). This policy, in turn, calls for "the elimination of sex discrimination, for equal pay for equal work, no sex typing of jobs, equal access to education and training" (Ibid.).

A large part of the research on female-headed families has to do with the effect of the absence of a father on children. There are 78 "propositions" dealing with "father absence" in a propositional inventory through 1964 (Goode, Hopkins, and McClure, 1971: 247–250). These are largely horrendous in import. Among them: "children in families without a male head tend to have lower levels of intelligence than do children with fathers"; "absence of an adult male in the home is correlated with academic failure in the child"; "father absence is associated with exaggerated masculine behavior on the part of the son"; "boys who are reared in homes in which there is no father or father surrogate for the first six years of their lives tend to be more effeminate than do boys raised in normal homes"; "when the father is absent from the home, there is greater likelihood that the child will become alcoholic, homosexual, or totalitarian." It would seem that the presence of a father was, indeed, a sine qua non for socializing normal, at least conforming, children (Ibid.).

But another study, this time limited to 60 out of 400 studies of children (primarily boys) from fatherless homes in which control groups were built into the design gave quite equivocal results. Among them, 16 reported results too mixed or qualified to be of much help. Among the remaining 44 studies, 23 were judged sound enough in method to warrant the acceptance of findings. Of these, about half supported the classic view of the dire effects of father-absence, about half challenged it (Herzog and Sudia, 1970: 5). The authors of this careful evaluation conscientiously catalog all the pitfalls involved in generalizing the results of these studies. But the implication is that all too often it is not so much the absence of the father in and of itself that is harmful, as it is the absence of the income he would have provided (Ibid.: 69–70, 97–98).

The implications for the value of fathers is unflattering. Except as providers they are quite expendable, for it appears that what fatherless families mainly suffer from is low income or poverty, deprivation due to lack of income, not lack of his presence. Fathers who are good providers are nice to have around. They may even be fun and useful around the house. Conceivably they might occasionally play ball with you or read to you or take you to the circus. And if everyone else has a father it is a good idea to have one yourself so you are not different. If, however, he drinks a lot or beats up the kids or yells, it is just as well not to have him around. In brief, it is the income the father provides that is important for his family. Anything beyond that is gravy. And if he is a heavy drinker or abusive even the income may seem a pretty stiff price to pay for having him around the place, as many wives and children learn. But in a world where he is the sole provider they have no choice.

Well, so what? Why go over all this familiar ground? It is not new. It is well reported every day in the press. Everyone knows about the costs to the family of the achievement-driven father, of the importance of a good provider, of the destructive effects of father unemployment, of poverty. What is now new about all this is that women and young people of both sexes are no longer willing to accept it. They are looking for new ways to organize life, to integrate family and work roles, to overcome the extreme specialization of roles which has now become dysfunctional for all concerned.

III. The Tides of Change

ARE THE NATIVES BECOMING RESTLESS?

An increasing number of women have been coming to reject the reductio ad absurdum of the traditional role specialization imposed on them. They want to be mothers, to be sure, but they want to be more than mothers. And they want husbands who are more than providers. Wives of successful executives interviewed in one study "were questioning a marriage that so frequently offered neither shared joy nor shared responsibility. . . . One new and persistent question among thoughtful company wives is, Is success worth it?" (Lake, 1973: 30). And, apparently, corporations are coming to recognize that the men they hire have to be more than good providers, that they have to be good husbands and fathers as well as loyal company men.

Sons of many of the hard-driving men are concluding that their father's success was not worth the effort. Individual-by-individual efforts to achieve whole lives are always being "frustrated by the dissociation of work and family. . . . Social fragmentation pushes toward psychic fragmentation; without institutions or ideals to support psychic wholeness, inner division is a continual danger" (Keniston, 1965: 269). A notable, if not large, number of them seek integration in communities of their own, in urban or rural communes, in small enterprises that do not make them such good providers but do prevent alienation from their families. Keniston tells us that, perhaps as a reaction against the distant and nonexpressive work-absorbed father they have known, young men today say they themselves look forward to greater participation in the rearing of their own children (Ibid.: 117).·A study at the University of Rhode Island by Bernice Lott found that over a third of the young men were not only eager to have children but also to participate actively in rearing them (Lott, 1973: 577). The fact that research on fatherhood is now attracting attention reflects a new definition of the father role now in process of emerging.

Children of blue-collar fathers are not likely to look to communes or handicraft industries but they are, nevertheless, as troubled as the upper-middle-class young about the changing definitions of their roles. "Blue-collar men," Arthur Shostak tells us, "appear deeply confused about what to really and reasonably expect of themselves as husbands, as lovers, as fathers, and as sons" (Shostak, 1971). They are uneasy about the "open parental affect" being asked of them for the first time. "Role expectations of blue-collarites and fathers and sons are confused and unsettled." The father's authority has been eroded "almost beyond significance." And the old conception of manliness has gone with it. "Few now believe the 'real man' is . . . a cold fish . . . a crummy father, and a callous son." TV programs have done their part: "the worker's children . . . absorb from popular shows like *Bachelor Father* and *My Three Sons* new models of parenthood more sensitive, more communicative, and more constructively emotional than what they presently experience" (Ibid.). And the father knows it.

> A sweeping re-definition of what is reasonably expected of the blue-collar male by his loved ones and himself is being called for. Where once he was free to be a moody, enigmatic, and male-centric cowboy, he is now expected to strive for expressive, open, and genial affability with most, deep-coursing personal intimacy with some, and erotic artfulness with a very select few. . . . Expectations . . . appear much richer, and seem to go far in explaining the painful transitional situation of the worker caught today between his own outmoded role performance and his new and demanding role-standards. (Ibid.)

Like so many of their college-educated peers, these young blue-collar men were unhappy with the role of father as defined in the past; they were less certain about what to do to change it. Communes were not the answer for them, but hours of work were part of it. It is interesting, for example, as an index of change to note the emergence of required overtime as an issue among workers in the automobile industry. Young men were telling us on television that they rejected enforced overtime because they wanted more time to spend with their families.

A study made in the early 1960s at the Stanford Institute for the Study of Human Problems by Marjorie M. Lozoff concluded that "men must be brought back to center stage in their roles and responsibilities" both as husbands and fathers, and not merely as providers. The study demonstrated "the need for changing the male stereotype role in our Western society and other societies." The author recognized that this would be most difficult to achieve despite the benefits to both physical and mental health, for "it would involve modification and reassessment of institutions and of social attitudes and practices, particularly our concept of success" (1973: 105). This study was made more than a decade ago. What are we waiting for?

A NEW STAGE IN ECONOMIC DEVELOPMENT

For some time, suggested solutions for the dysfunctions associated with the extreme role specialization of our society have taken the form of role integration. In the 1960s, Keniston was searching for ways to achieve such integration for fathers with full recognizion of its difficulty:

> We all marvel at the complexity of our society's organization and at the high levels of technological productivity it has achieved. But a society which "works" well, as ours does in many ways, may nonetheless create great stresses on individuals by virtue of *how* it works. And no psychological adaptations are more burdensome than the maneuvers required to integrate individual life in a fragmented society. Men and women need a sense of coherence, integration, and wholeness; but to attain such personal wholeness in our technological society is not an easy task. (1965: 264)

Keniston was writing about the lives of men; how could they be both good fathers and good providers? And now the problem of integration is hitting an increasing number of women also. How can they perform both their mother and their worker roles without too great a cost?

My own preoccupation for several years has been with more sharing of roles, a pattern in which both fathers and mothers perform both parental and provider roles (Bernard, 1972: Chapter 11). Now come three economists who offer a model of economic development as related to the family which suggests that the tides of change are, indeed, clearly on the side of some such pattern as this. Sawhill, Ross, and MacIntosh propose a three-stage theory of the family in terms of the salience of production, distribution, and consumption in the economy. The type of family suitable for one stage is not necessarily suitable for another. In preindustrial societies, a great deal of the economic production is performed by the family as a whole, including the mother, and parental roles accommodate themselves to that pattern. In the distributive stage of economic development, most productive work is done outside the family and the income from the paid work is channeled to the father who then "provides" for the wife and children. In the third, or consumption stage, both husband and wife contribute to the maintenance of the household and pool their incomes for consumption purposes.

The idea that economic development has been responsible for a number of basic changes in the structure of the family is not new. Although there is undoubtedly a rather complex interaction between economic variables and family organization with the latter often operating independently of the former, it will be useful to trace out what seem to be the broad consequences of industrialization for family life. We will postulate three "stages" of development for this purpose.

In the first, or preindustrial stage, technology is limited and unchanging, most economic activity takes place within the household and production and distribution are organized by custom and tradition. . . . In this type of society the family plays a central role, since economic and social status are defined by birth, family ties, and social custom.

In the second, or industrial, stage of development, new technology and the benefits of specialization cause production to shift from home to factory. . . . Status is determined increasingly by one's position in the market and less and less by membership in a particular family. To some extent, the family itself becomes a more specialized unit with its major responsibility being the production and socialization of children. But because it has been stripped of some of its earlier functions, the family is no longer the central institution in society. Declining fertility, the loosening of kinship ties, and the streamlining of the extended family into its present nuclear form may be viewed as adaptations to industrialization. . . . As a vestige of an earlier, preindustrial era, the household remains an economically primitive organization and family relationships and roles continue to be dominated by custom and tradition—examples being the rigid division of tasks between men and women and the continued authority of the male head of the household. During this stage of development, although there is little market production within the home, the family continues to play a crucial economic role in re-distributing resources from one group of individuals (primarily male breadwinners) to another group (primarily market-dependent women and children)—a situation which helps to maintain the superior status of the former vis-à-vis the latter.

The third stage of development is still unfolding and lies mostly in the future. We may speculate that its inception came with the extension of technology to those responsibilities which have remained the responsibility of the family, especially control over reproduction, and that its fruition will be marked by equality between the sexes, companionate marriages, and families operating largely as consumption (income-pooling) units. . . . More specialized institutions to socialize children open up to women the kinds of market opportunities and control over their destiny that became available to men during the "first" industrial revolution. . . . Men will have been freed from the full burden of family support. . . . To the extent that the family survives at all, its major raison d'être will be to meet the expressive or psychological needs of individuals—its more utilitarian functions having been transferred to other institutions (Sawhill, Ross, and MacIntosh, 1973: 7–9).

It goes without saying, of course, that this model does not imply that any one type of family is intrinsically better than any other. (I confess I quail a bit at "specialized institutions to socialize children," preferring role-sharing by parents myself.) It implies only that one is better suited to the economy in which it functions than any other. Nor does the consumption-based pattern imply role sharing for *every* father and mother. There are men who cannot stop running; they are hooked rat-race runners. There are women who do not wish to share the provider role. But for an increasing number there is already convergence between the demands of men and women for more part-time jobs, more flexibility in the uses of time. At least the availability of options is being called for. More and more people of both sexes seek integrated lives in which both their parental and their work roles can mutually relieve and enhance one another.

Sex-role specialization in our society has, in brief, been carried to such an extent as to wreak havoc on all of us. Men and women have been role-specialized out of all reasonable proportion. If such extreme specialization was ever adaptive—as, no doubt, it may once have been—it no longer is. In fact, a good case can be made to the effect that it is maladaptive, that it reduces rather than enhances adaptation. A species that becomes too specialized for a given environment suffers when the environment changes, as both our ecological and our technological environments are changing. A sex-role specialization that was adaptive for a certain economic stage of development in a given ecological environment is in process of becoming maladaptive for the world we are now moving toward. It is fine to have nurturing mothers; but if they do nothing else than bear and rear children, the result is not good. It is just as fine to have providing fathers; but if they do nothing else, the result is not favorable. Does it have to be like that? Quite the reverse. If probably has *not* to be like that.

References

1969. Career and family orientations of husbands and wives in relation to marital happiness. *Human Relations* 23: 97–113.

Bales, Robert F. 1950. *Interaction process analysis: A method for the study of small groups.* Reading, Mass.: Addison, Wesley.

Bernard, Jessie. 1964. *Academic women.* University Park: Pennsylvania State University Press. New York: Meridian, 1966, 1972.

———— . 1972. *The future of marriage.* New York: World. New York: Bantam, 1973.

———— . 1974. *The future of motherhood.* New York: Dial.

Bowlby, John. 1951. *Maternal care and mental health.* World Health Organization Monograph.

———. 1969. *Attachment and loss.* London: Hogarth.

Brenton, Myron. 1966. *The American male.* New York: Coward-McCann.

Bronfenbrenner, Urie. 1973. Testimoney presented at the Hearings of Senator Walter Mondale's Subcommittee on Children and Youth. *Congressional Record,* vol. 119, no. 142, September 26, 1973.

Coles, Robert. 1973. Testimony presented at the Hearings of Senator Walter Mondale's Subcommittee on Children and Youth. *Congressional Record,* vol. 119, no. 142, September 26, 1973.

Dizard, Jan. 1968. *Social change in the family.* Chicago: Community and Family Center, University of Chicago.

Gans, Herbert. 1962. *The urban villagers.* New York: The Free Press.

Goode, W. J., Hopkins, Elizabeth; and McClure, Helen M. 1971. *Social systems and family patterns: A propositional inventory.* Indianapolis: Bobbs-Merrill.

Gronseth, Erik. 1971. The husband provider role: A critical appraisal, in Mitchell, A., ed., *Family issues of working women in Europe and America.* Leiden: Brill.

Herzog, Elizabeth, and Sudia, Cecelia E. 1970. *Boys in fatherless families.* Children's Bureau.

Ignatius, David. 1974. Down and out in Orwell's Wigan. *Washington Post,* March 3, 1974.

Keniston, Kenneth. 1965. *The uncommitted.* New York: Delta.

Komarovsky, Mirra. 1964. *Blue-collar marriage.* New York: Random House.

Krause, Harry D. 1973. Child welfare, parental responsibility, and the state, in *Studies in public welfare,* paper no. 12, part 2, The family, poverty, and welfare programs: Household patterns and government policies. Washington, D. C.: U. S. Government Printing Office.

Lake, Alice. 1973. The revolt of the company wife. *McCall's* (October).

Lederer, Wolfgang. 1968. *The fear of women.* New York: Harcourt Brace Jovanovich.

Liebow, Eliot. 1966. *Tally's Corner: A study of Negro streetcorner men.* Boston: Little, Brown.

Lott, Bernice E. 1973. Who wants the children? *American Psychologist* 28 (July): 573-582.

Lozoff, Marjorie M. Fathers and autonomy in women, in Kundsen, Ruth B., ed., *Successful women in the sciences.*

Malinowski, Bronislaw. 1930. Parenthood—the basis of social structure, pp. 113–168, in Calverton, V. F., and Schmalhausen, S. D., eds., *The new generation.* New York: Macauley. This paper is sometimes referred to under the title, The principle of legitimacy.

Minturn, Leigh; Lambert, William W.; and Associates. 1964. *Mothers of six cultures: Antecedents of child rearing.* New York: Wiley.

Papanek, Hanna. 1973. Men, women, and work: Reflections on the two-person career, in Huber, Joan, ed., *Changing women in a changing society.* Chicago: University of Chicago Press.

Parsons, Talcott. 1959. The social structure of the family, in Anshen, Ruth Nanda, ed., *The family: Its function and destiny.* New York: Harper.

———. 1955. The American family. Parsons, Talcott and Bales, Robert F. 1955. *Family, socialization and interaction process.* New York: Free Press.

Pollak, Otto. 1950. *The criminality of women.* Philadelphia: University of Pennsylvania Press.

Radl, Shirley. 1973. *Mother's Day is over.* New York: Charterhouse.

Rheingold, Joseph. 1967. *The mother, anxiety, and death: The catastrophic death complex.* Boston: Little, Brown.

Rogers, John G. 1974. These students are learning to be good parents. *Parade*, April 7, 1974.

Ross, Heather L. 1973. *Poverty: Women and children last*. Washington, D. C.: Urban Institute.

Sawhill, Isabel; Ross, Heather L.; and MacIntosh, Anita. 1973. *The family in transition*. Washington, D. C.: Urban Institute.

Shostak, Arthur B. 1971. Working class families at home: Changing expectations of manhood. Paper prepared for Conference on Problems, Programs, and Prospects of the American Working Class in the 1970s, October, Rutgers University.

Shulman, Alix Kates. 1974. Surviving childhood. *Ms* 2 (April): 34.

Talbot, Stanley. 1952. *Time*. November 10, 1952: 109.

Warner, W. Lloyd, and Abegglan, James C. 1959. Case histories of two "unsuccessful" men, in Warner, W. Lloyd, and Martin, Norman H., eds., *Industrial man, businessman and business organizations*. New York: Harper.

Zigler, Edward. 1973. Testimony presented at the Hearings of Senator Walter Mondale's Subcommittee on Children and Youth. *Congressional Record*, vol. 119, no. 142, September 26, 1973.

TWELVE

Policy-Relevant Research on Motherhood: The State of the Art

"A Great Hiatus"

Jean Lipman-Blumen (1974) has noted that there is "a great hiatus . . . between research results and the development and implementation of social policy." It is this hiatus that I investigate in this paper.

The application of science to policy to promote human welfare is a great American tradition.[1] In the nineteenth century reform was one of the major objectives of the new discipline known as Social Science (Bernard and Bernard, 1941:Part 8), and some of its devotees, in the first fine frenzy of the discovery of statistics as applicable to sociological phenomena, looked forward to the day when the figures of arithmetic would take the place of the figures of rhetoric in the formulation of policy (Hine, 1848:398). In that age of scientific innocence there were those who did not see the hiatus. They believed that science offered policy makers ready-made solutions; one need only present the facts and the policy answers would be forthcoming. As recently as 1947, in fact, George Lundberg still believed that the art of research could achieve that goal. He answered the question, Can science

1. The dream of a marriage between science and policy is of long standing. Francis Bacon was the forerunner of this science-in-the-service-of-human-welfare tradition. And we cannot forget that Comte's *Positive Philosophy*, one of the cornerstones of the discipline of sociology, was only the prolegomenon to his real concern, the *Positive Polity*, a polity modeled after the Catholic Church, with scientists serving in the role of priests.

240

save us? with a resounding yes—if we wanted it to. We have become considerably more sophisticated since then on both the research and the policy side of the hiatus; some of us have become disillusioned. There are, in fact, "active groups . . . who think science and technology deserve *less* attention, who see science and technology as a threat, not as a hope" (Platt, 1973:16). But not everyone is discouraged, and especially not women who are only now beginning to learn the art.

An Omission

Before continuing let me point out that a very considerable amount of research dealing with motherhood will not be commented on here, namely, the spectacular series of achievements in biology and biochemistry which affect the control of conception, give rise to genetic engineering, artificial insemination, enovulation, and fetal transplants, all with potentially profound effects on the maternal role. Policies ranging from the licensing of parenthood to the legitimization of motherhood in cases of enovulation, from sterilization to compulsory genetic screening are increasingly called for.[2] The intensely emotional impact of these policy decisions was adumbrated in the controversy over the legalization of abortion. As yet the proto-Nazi policies made possible by this research have surfaced only remotely and discreetly. Thus one author proposes 10 principles to guide policy in answer to the question, Who should have children? Among them are:

> Some couples should remain childless because of the high risk that their children would inherit biological bases of poor health and incompetence; some couples should remain childless because they cannot offer children the sort of environment needed for good health, citizenship, and self sufficiency; programs of selective population control should be in the hands of the medical profession and a new professional class of social scientists trained to judge qualifications for parenthood. The evolution of programs should be guided by the outcomes of experiments with small pilot studies. (Ingle, 1973)

What form such principles should take in actual policy formulation and implementation is not concretely spelled out.

There is widespread concern that a strong ethos against too brave new worlds should be hammered out, so that when the hiatus is bridged and policy makers turn to drawing up legislative guides for administrators the results will be humane. To this end, Senator Walter Mondale has

2. Francoeur, 1970; Williams, 1973; and Etzioni, 1973 deal with the policy implications of this stream of research. See also Bernard, 1974:Chapter 13.

introduced a so-called bioethics bill to provide a mechanism for bridging the hiatus so as to render policy makers' judgments with respect to the uses of such research as enlightened as possible. A 15-member Congressional bioethics commission is provided for in this bill to deliberate on ethical issues precipitated by research, and to formulate appropriate guidelines. Law, medicine, theology, and technology would all be represented. (But not, interestingly enough, mothers.) An annual budget of a million dollars would be granted the commission to engage a research staff.

By electing to comment on research that deals with old leftover, nonglamorous, nonspectacular policy issues having to do directly or indirectly with "women's two roles," I hope I do not seem to denigrate the importance of this new corpus of research for motherhood. I may add parenthetically that much of the research on women's two roles has suffered from what I have called the Pickwick fallacy. When Mr. Pickwick had to write a paper on Chinese metaphysics, he read everything in the *Britannica* on China and everything on metaphysics. He was then well prepared to write his paper on Chinese metaphysics. A growing research literature tells us about women in the labor force; another tells us about women in the family. Just as we need policies that help women themselves integrate their two roles, we need an integrated research approach that will help us see the lives of women as unitary wholes.

The Policy Side of the Hiatus

On the policy side of the research-policy hiatus we still have to face up to the fact that the old laissez-faire dogma lingers on in some quarters. It is alleged, for example, that everything we have tried to do in behalf of the family has been in vain, at least so far as benefitting children is concerned. Edward Zigler (1973) reminds us, for example, that "a scholarly, but nevertheless questionable, literature has developed asserting that children's destinies reside in their genes, that admired preschool programs such as Head Start are failures, that variations in the quality of schooling make no real difference, and that a variety of recommended intervention efforts would probably be failures if implemented." And there have been enough ears willing to hear this message. It has, in fact, become fashionable among some to insist that all the Great Society programs of the 1960s were colossal failures.[3]

It is argued, further, that even when we do intervene, we do not know what the effects are. With respect to tax and other programs as related to reproduction, for example, "a brief review . . . indicates how scant our knowledge is of the demographic effects" (Commission on Population, 1972:158). It is argued also that even when research produces the

3. For a less pessimistic assessment, see "The Great Society: Lessons for the Future," Special Issue of *The Public Interest* 34 (Winter, 1974).

knowledge, it can lead different policy makers to different policy conclusions. If, for example, research shows that labor-force participation by women is ecologically correlated with a high suicide rate (Newman, Whittmore, and Newman, 1973) one policy maker recommends that women be discouraged from entering the labor force, another that whatever produces the correlation be removed.

It is argued, finally, that the present form of the family is profitable to those who benefit from the status quo and that changing it would cost too much not only in monetary terms but also in terms of the principles on which our free-enterprise, profit-motivated, work-ethic economy rests. If guaranteeing family stability, for example, is "at the expense of drastic reduction in the productivity of our economy and drastic limitations on the realizability of our democratic values," some along with Talcott Parsons, ask, "is it worth the price?" (Parsons, 1959:273). In Parsons' opinion, "some such consequences would in fact be the price of the realization of some current programs for the restoration of the strong family" (Ibid.). And another observer asks, "How do we eliminate poverty and discrimination while committed to an economic system built on capitalism, free enterprise and heavily tinged with materialism?" without "a radical shift in our values" (McHugh, 1973).[4] How, indeed, for values are in fact the heart of the matter of both policy and research.

One may grant all these objections and still not accept the laissez-faire implications. For having no policy is itself a policy. The choice is not between a policy and no policy. It is between a deliberate policy and policy by default, or between a consistent, thought-through policy and a congeries of casually thrown in incidental policies, often working at cross-purposes.

At the present time two major paradigms have guided policy-relevant research on motherhood, the demographic and the functionalist. They tend to produce quite different results leading to differing, even opposite, policy recommendations.

The Research Side of the Hiatus: Policy Implications of Research Based on the Demographic Paradigm

The demographic paradigm traces back to Thomas Malthus, who first stated it in the late eighteenth and early nineteenth centuries. The policy recommendations that flowed from it dealt with the dole, with birth

4. The Reverend Monsignor McHugh is on the firing line in his position as Director of the Family Life Division of the United States Catholic Conference. He calls for a radical shift in our values.

control by way of celibacy, delayed marriage, and continence, and with workhouses. Today we are still speaking of the dole, which we now call welfare, of birth control by way of contraception, and of workfare instead of workhouses. From its first appearance on the scene, in brief, the type of family which Sawhill, Ross, and MacIntosh (1973) call the "distributive" was already showing the same weaknesses as those it shows today.

Although the demographic paradigm today deals largely with the reproductive component of motherhood,[5] its policy recommendations have also had to do with the work component. By and large research has shown an inverse relationship between the number of children women have and female labor-force participation (Commission on Population, 1972: 153–154), and, although this relationship seems to be in process of attenuation (Bernard, 1971), there are still a great many unanswered questions. What is needed, for example, is:

> additional analysis of why these changes in fertility and labor force participation by women are occurring. . . . Additional analysis of all of these linkages—increased employment, expansion of job opportunities in white-collar work, decisions about family size, market substitutes for such services as day care, prepared foods, commercial laundries—is needed before we can make intelligent extrapolations of the future. It would also be useful to know more about the impact of changes in attitudes, the rise in educational attainment, and increased life expectancy on the lives of women and their role within the family and the economy. (Sawhill, Ross, and MacIntosh, 1973: 11)

Still, enough is known about all these phenomena to support a policy recommendation by the Commission on Population Growth and the American Future that women be encouraged to enter the labor force. "We believe," the authors of the Commission's report tell us, "that attractive work may effectively compete with childbearing and have the effect of lowering fertility, especially higher-order births" (1972: 154).

Having arrived at this policy conclusion, the authors proceed to sketch some of the role modifications it calls for and some of the policy changes needed to effect them:

> There is, despite the number of working mothers, considerable ambivalence in our society as to whether women with children should be working outside the home. If the notion is to receive greater social acceptability, some redefinition of the family roles of men and women will be required. Under such conditions, both husband and wife would

---

5. The concept of motherhood is used rather than the term *maternal role* in order to indicate more clearly the perspective implied. *Motherhood* involves the whole institutional framework in which the bearing, raising, and socialization of children takes place; the *maternal role* bears down more specifically on the woman vis-à-vis her children.

share more equally in both economic and domestic functions. Women who now work outside the home often receive little assistance from their husbands in domestic functions. Greater participation would also provide fathers more opportunity to participate in the rearing of their children and give children the opportunity to know their fathers better. Many young couples are striving to develop this pattern of family life, but it is difficult to achieve within the present American context. A reworking of family roles would necessarily involve changes in institutional practices—different sets of working hours and provision for some sort of paternity leave, for instance. Certainly, more study of the effects of changing family structures and roles is necessary. (Ibid.)

This policy recommendation was a major advance over earlier recommendations dealing with the work roles of women. In 1949, a Royal Commission on Population in Great Britain stated that it would be harmful to restrict the contribution that women could make to the economy and there should be "a deliberate effort . . . to devise adjustments that would render it easier for women to combine motherhood and the care of a home with outside activities" (Royal Commission on Population, 1949). Both Presidents Kennedy and Johnson went along with this point of view. In a statement establishing a Commission on the Status of Women in 1961, Kennedy even recommended services to women to enable them "to continue their role as wives and mothers" while at the same time "making a maximum contribution to the world around them." In 1956, Alva Myrdal and Viola Klein provided the research support for this two-role ideology in their classic book on the subject.

Only recently have women begun to wonder if they may not, after all, have been sold a bill of goods without actual delivery of the goods. They have even begun to wonder about the goods themselves. For although they have been given sanction for labor-force participation they have not been correspondingly relieved of any portion of the mother role. They are left, therefore, doing more than their share of the total amount of work in our society (Subcommittee on Employment, 1973: 52).

This is why the role-sharing policy recommendations of the Commission on Population and the American Future represent a great advance. If women are to be encouraged to enter the labor force, for whatever reason—as a way to increase the labor force or, as sometimes argued, as a form of birth control (although this allegation is disavowed by advocates) (Commission on Population, 1972: 152)—they must be relieved of other obligations. If they are to share the provider role, their husbands should share the child-rearing role, even if such a "reworking of family roles would necessarily involve changes in institutional practices," including the hours of labor.

Although the policies based on research guided by the demographic paradigm point in the direction of a shared-role pattern of marriage, they do not go all the way to the model of the consumption-oriented pattern sketched by Sawhill, Ross, and MacIntosh, in which child rearing is turned over to specialized agencies designed for that purpose. But neither do they shore up the nuclear family so characteristic of the distributive stage of economic development.

Policy Implications of Research Based on the Functionalist Paradigm

The functionalist paradigm, which in its most general form states that any society has the kind of family that is suitable for its structure, has taken the form articulated by Talcott Parsons (1959; Parsons and Bales, 1955), whose formulation has become the standard one for the nuclear family today.[6] For our particular society that formulation states that the isolated nuclear family (which corresponds to the type suitable for the distributive stage of economic development), though hard on women (Parsons, 1959: 267),[7] is the most appropriate form.

This paradigm held that there was both a clear differentiation of function between mothers and fathers—mothers performing the expressive, fathers the instrumental—and a division of labor as well—mothers running the household under the father's general oversight and fathers providing economic support. The function of the family, and especially of the mother, was to socialize children and stabilize adult personalities. This involved (1) strict sex-role segregation to keep women out of the occupational structure, with policy consequences in the form of discrimination in work and education; (2) socialization of boys and girls into their proper occupational and domestic sex roles; and (3) protection of men in the provider role as a necessary support for the male ego. The emphasis on role segregation and specialization was not so much on the utilitarian or work aspect of the woman's role in child care and housework, though both were included, as on the psychological aspect of protecting the male ego:

> Structurally the most fundamental aspect of the segregation of the roles
> seems to be with reference to the occupational system. Especially in the

6. Although the term *functionalism* has become almost a dirty word in sociology, it is, as Kingsley Davis (1959) has pointed out, the basic sociological paradigm. The attack on Parsons was not an attack on functionalism but on his analysis of the kind of family that was suitable for a particular society.

7. Parsons finds the major role conflict among middle-class women to be not in the mother-worker roles but in the mother-glamor roles and believes that "a constructive synthesis of these two often conflicting tendencies in the feminine role . . . to be one of the most urgent needs of the American family" (1959:270).

structurally crucial middle-class area of our society, the dominant mature feminine role is that of housewife or of wife-and-mother. Apart from the extremely important utilitarian problems of how adequate care of household and children are to be accomplished, the most important aspect of this fact is that it shields spouses from competition with each other in the occupational sphere. (Ibid.: 264–265)[8]

(It may be noted in passing that already the "utilitarian" functions of the female role were being subordinated to the psychological.)

In addition to these components of the Parsonian paradigm, other researchers included also a maternal instinct of sorts, which made women want children and find complete fulfillment in caring for them. If women were not completely fulfilled in the maternal role there was something wrong with them. They were to be dealt with as though they were sick, or they were simply to be tranquilized,[9] or made to feel guilty and unnatural, especially if they sought outside careers (Helson, 1972: 33–46).

So far as policy was concerned, this model was taken to be normative, as evidenced by policies of (1) socializing "the young into sex-typed roles, with the boys pointed toward jobs and the girls toward home and motherhood; (2) discrimination against the working women and even more, the working mother; and (3) restrictions on higher education for women" (Commission on Population, 1972: 149). The discrimination in favor of men was justified on the grounds that they were the providers.

Parsons stated that trying to make the family more stable by moving back to the productive family type would be at the cost of lowered productivity; permitting it to become less stable by moving toward the consumption type, for example, would prevent it from performing any stabilizing function for the total society at all.[10]

Research, expectedly, validated the paradigm, proving almost unequivocally that families which fit the model were better off on almost any criterion than families that deviated from it; conformity almost guaranteed well-socialized children, nonconformity guaranteed sick ones. Thus, for example, one study of the families of emotionally healthy college students found that "where both parents fully accepted their spouse roles, more than half of the children were emotionally healthy, and where both rejected these roles, more than half were emotionally disturbed" (Westley and

8. A slightly different statement of this same idea appeared in George Gilder's *Sexual Suicide* (New York: Harper & Row, 1973).

9. Case in Point: "Dear Dr. Steincrohn: Now that I am in my late 40s I've become depressed. . . . Our two children are married. . . . My husband and I are alone as when we first married. Is it abnormal to feel so dejected?" Reply: " . . . not accepting what nature offers presumably indicates that you are suffering from an unnatural depression. . . . Hormones or tranquilizers (or some good old-fashioned advice) will probably disperse the clouds and let some sun shine through" (*Washington Star-News*, September 28, 1973).

10. Even so, Talcott Parsons thought that "there is some legitimate doubt whether the American type of family system is in the long run capable of sufficient stability to perform its extremely essential functions on behalf of our type of society" (1959:273).

Epstein, 1969: 163). Father-led families produced most emotionally healthy children, followed by father-dominant families, equalitarian, and mother-dominant, in that order. These authors found, "in agreement with most other studies . . . that the mother-dominant form was extremely destructive of family authority and that almost none of the children in these families were emotionally healthy" (Ibid.). Such families were extremely unhappy; the mothers were cold, and family relations were impersonal. (It would be interesting to know more about these unhappy mothers in the families where they were dominant; what were they unhappy about?)

Understandably, in view of the power of the paradigm, it has remained as the basis for recommended policy:

> If our society provided stable employment at above-poverty level wages for all men, and if all women could therefore look forward to marrying men who could serve them in the provider role and for whom they could serve in the homemaker role, then it is likely that fewer girls would become pregnant before marriage, that lower-class couples would marry at a somewhat later age, that relationships in lower-class marriages would be less tense, that fewer lower-class marriages would break up, and for those that did, remarriage would take place more quickly. (Subcommittee on Employment, 1973: 149)

Although it was recommended that policy should seek to mollify the difficulties in the role of mother by providing her more services and seek to make it possible for fathers to contribute more to child rearing, the basic recommendation was that policy should confirm the role-segregating specialization of the past. Women should be in the home taking care of the children, men should be in the labor force providing the income that made this possible (Bronfenbrenner, 1973).

The contrast between the policies flowing from the demographic paradigm and those flowing from the Parsonian statement of the functionalist paradigm could hardly be more extreme. One calls for the sharing of both the provider and the child-care roles by both mothers and fathers, whatever institutional changes such sharing may require; the other calls for a shoring up of role specialization. One calls for encouraging women to enter the labor force; the other for strengthening the provider role, and keeping women out of the labor force.

The Feminist Critique: A Different Reality

The Parsons statement of the functionalist paradigm recognized the costs to women it involved. The housewife's role embodied "relatively little that can be taken seriously and importantly rewarded in terms of the American system of achievement values" (Parsons, 1959: 271). Our type of family does deny equal opportunity to married women (Ibid.: 267). Despite these costs to women of the nuclear family as he defined it, however, Parsons believed the family was doing a good job (Ibid.: 274). Understandably, therefore, the Parsonian statement of the paradigm became one of the first targets of the feminists. Betty Friedan was among the first to offer a critique, which has been extensively elaborated since then (1963: 131–132). The nuclear family was bad not only for women but also—and this was new—for children.

The ace-in-the-hole for those defending the nuclear family had been that no matter how hard it might be on mothers or fathers, it was after all the best possible way to rear children. Witness after witness appearing before Senator Mondale's hearings on the family in the fall of 1973 hammered out the same theme: there is no substitute for the nuclear family for rearing children.

Actually, although we know how bad other ways of rearing children can be, we do not know nearly so much about how bad the nuclear family can be. The family has been strongly protected from legal as well as research scrutiny, and the law has been hesitant to do anything that violated its privacy. For years we have known that children were abused in their families but no one was willing to interfere. In any event, what could we do with children if we took them from such homes? We had put all our eggs in the one basket of the nuclear family. We have, therefore, had only jerry-built fallback systems, to change the figure of speech. We know that children have moldered in detention "homes" or even jails for lack of suitable facilities. We have "warehoused" children in what were once called "asylums," but which were in no sense asylums. Our fixed belief that "there is just no substitute for a healthy family" has guaranteed that there be none; it has inhibited us from providing substitutes for "unhealthy" families.

As long as our thinking was in terms of the nuclear family this was a self-fulfilling prophecy. We have traditionally spoken of women as "good" or as "bad" mothers but no one has systematically gone about observing and evaluating them in their homes to see just what kind of care they were giving their children. We are having to do precisely that with respect to child care outside the family. We have permitted women we would never employ to take care of other children to take care of their own children. Believing that even a bad mother was better than a good substitute, we have permitted women to take care of children when we knew they were harmful, even dangerous, to children. We have insisted that mothers, regardless of their own needs, regardless of their attitudes toward their children, take care of them. Since we had few if any decent alternatives, a home with almost any kind of mother was as good as we could provide the child, whatever the cost to either mother or child. All this despite the fact that, as Edward Zigler points out, his own research "as well as the

experience of the Scandinavian countries indicates that humane in-
stitutionalization constructive to the child's development is possible if we
would simply commit ourselves to such a policy" (Zigler, 1973).

Parsons' statement of the nuclear family paradigm had not emphasized
the child-care function of the feminine role so much as the male-ego-
support aspect. He had recognized "adequate care of household and
children" as "extremely important utilitarian problems," but "the most
important aspect" had been protecting men from competition. In recent
years there had been increasing emphasis on the child-rearing function.
And it was the feminists who attacked this very citadel of conservative
thought.

Women psychologists were not the first since Plato to attack the nuclear
family as the best matrix for human development (Moore, 1958), but they
were certainly among the most vehement. Unlike Urie Bronfenbrenner
(1973), they did not see the nuclear family as "the most humane, effective,
and economical system of child care known to man [sic]." They had in
mind a perspective that was almost a mirror image of the classic one. Zelda
S. Klapper, for example, specified five propositions held by feminists
relevant to the child-care component of motherhood:

> (1) The nuclear family is an arbitrary development that may obstruct a
> child's optimum development; (2) early growth processes are not
> critically dependent upon the biological mother; (3) traditional
> gender-roles are artificially imposed upon children by the culture; (4)
> the assumption of gender-roles by children is counter-productive to
> their developmental health; and (5) mental health may be better
> ensured by the early transfer of responsibility for child-rearing from
> mother to the community. (1972: 21–22)

The feminists were no longer on the defensive; they were very much on the
offensive.

The entrance of the feminists into the area of policy-relevant research
opened up a new and different reality. As Alice Rossi (1968) has pointed
out, research in the past made the child the major focus of attention. The
new perspective made the mother equally focal. Now the components of
good motherhood included satisfaction of the legitimate needs of mothers
as well as of their children (Safilios-Rothschild, 1973: 39–40). New
questions were asked, including: Is motherhood as now institutionalized
in our society a good way? And surprising answers were being offered: No,
it is not. It is a product of affluence and it may be the worst possible way,
good for neither mothers nor children (Bernard, 1974).[11] Nor, for that
matter, for fathers either.

The feminist critique raised consciousness about the defects in the classic
formulation of the nuclear family paradigm. One of its major con-

11. See also Bernard, 1974: Chapter 5.

tributions was to turn the spotlight on the women who were mothers. Most of the policy-relevant research on mothers had had to do with solo parents, who had appeared as background variables or factors explaining the behavior of children. Even traditional mothers had appeared as villains to blame for all human defects.

It was not the feminist researchers alone, however, who forced us to look at mothers rather than exclusively at children. For the first time mothers themselves were also in the act. They were shouting out loud and clear that although they loved their children they did not love motherhood (Radl, 1973).

Serious as these critiques were, it was not the women who made them who were undermining faith in the nuclear family so much as it was its supporters, people who believed in it, who wanted to protect and preserve it—people who believed in it enough to prepare long statements for Senator Mondale's hearings on the family. It was precisely *their* attacks on the way the nuclear family was functioning, or rather not functioning, that cast doubt on its adequacy. If so much was needed to shore it up—almost a restructuring of our whole society—where did that leave the classic concept of the nuclear family? It was precisely the effort required for this end that demonstrated its inadequacy. If it took this, and this, and this to make it function, how could one judge it suitable? The question was precisely the long list of structural requirements for change called for to make the nuclear family a good place for children.

A Paradigmatic Crisis?

It seems to me that we are in the presence of what Thomas S. Kuhn has called a paradigmatic crisis. He has described such a crisis as the process by which a paradigmatic shift takes place. When an old paradigm accumulates such a weight of "anomalies of fact" that it becomes unwieldy, a scientific revolution is called for. In time a more suitable paradigm appears, one that more adequately deals with the new data, which shifts the focus so that a new reality becomes visible (Kuhn, 1962). We have two paradigms—the demographic and the nuclear family—that lead to research which generates quite different policy orientations. We have not yet achieved the perspective we need to design a model for motherhood that will suit the kind of society now emerging.

One candidate for such a paradigm is the one proposed by Sawhill, Ross, and MacIntosh. It falls within the orbit of the general functionalist paradigm in that it describes the form of family organization that is called for in different stages of economic development. The nuclear family as we have known it was the kind of family that fit the distributive stage of economic development. It does not seem equally suitable for the stage of economic development we are now approaching.

But even though there may be, as Sawhill, Ross, and MacIntosh suggest, a technologically based development of our economy which calls for a type of marriage with pooled income and consumption—shared roles at a minimum—still we may choose policies to move with this trend or against it. Our values will greatly influence which path we choose. If our values center in the nuclear family which, in its nineteenth century form, was well suited to the distributive stage of economic development, we will look for policies and societal structures that shore it up. If, on the other hand, we see the writing on the wall with a message of new ways of organizing both work and family, we will lean toward policies that help women share the provider role, and that distribute the total national income not by way of the father's earnings alone but by way of the mother also; we will do what we can to see that women can have incomes of their own.

What form will the writing on the wall take? How can we read its message? Three criteria are suggested by Sawhill, Ross, and MacIntosh as indexes of change:

> We may hypothesize that the present distributive family will become at least partially obsolete if and when (1) fertility declines to the point where a large proportion of families contain few or no children, (2) female opportunities in the market increase to the point where the present division of the labor has little economic justification, and (3) child care and other household tasks are increasingly turned over to more specialized institutions or living arrangements change the focus of such activities. (1973: 11)

The first of these criteria is a present reality. With respect to the second, although female labor-force participation has been increasing rapidly, there is probably a limit not too far off (Bernard, 1974: Chapter 8). At what point "the present division of labor has little economic justification" we cannot yet say with certainty. The third criterion is still far from being met, but a great deal of thinking and experimenting is going on to serve as measures.

My own biases are, I believe, quite clear. I believe that the kind of society we are living in calls unequivocally for some variant of the shared-role model. We are no longer dealing with a generation of Cornelias whose children were her jewels. Nor do we have an economy that can support a large proportion of its members in non- or underemployment while weighting another considerable proportion with overwork. Achieving a shared-role pattern can, I am confident, be worked out on the basis of policy-relevant research.

Whether we are in a paradigmatic crisis, whether a new paradigm more useful for guiding research relevant for policy is in process, whether the great hiatus between research and policy is bridged, the effort involved has alerted us to the fact that we are engaged in a structural revolution as profound and as drastic as the revolution in the class structure that began with industrialization and urbanization in the late eighteenth century, transforming stable estates into mobile classes and reordering their status relationships. The sex-role restructuring now in process is as revolutionary as the shake-up in the class structure was then. Policy makers at that time were still thinking in terms of agriculturally-based physiocratic paradigms, while Adam Smith was presenting a market-oriented paradigm interpreting how all the factors of production—including land, of course, but not limited to it—operated in a free market. We seem to be like the physiocrats but have, as yet, no Adam Smith. We are still casting about for the most appropriate way to view our world, for the most suitable paradigm that will help us structure the fundamental functions of reproduction, child care, and socialization.

Appendix

SELECTED EXAMPLES OF RESEARCH RELEVANT FOR POLICY

I do not claim to know all the policy-relevant research on the family or motherhood going on today. The examples given are certainly far from exhaustive; nor do they add up to a systematic new model to guide policy. Still, they are all, in my opinion, interesting, useful, and worthy of attention. Some of this research is experimental, some is exploratory. Some is designed explicitly to answer questions raised by policy makers; some is designed to answer theoretical questions the researcher is concerned with. Whatever the context, the signficance is unquestionable.

EXPERIMENTAL STUDIES

The most interesting experiments relevant for policy with respect to the family and motherhood deal with (1) the provider role, (2) shared roles, and (3) alternative life styles.

The New Jersey-Pennsylvania Income Maintenance Experiment. In August, 1968, a three-year experiment was launched in four cities in New Jersey and one in Pennsylvania to determine what effect a *negative income tax* would have on family stability and on the work lives of 741 (out of an original sample of 1350) intact families below the poverty level. They were divided into a control group and eight experimental groups, the first receiving no supplementary income and the other eight receiving different guaranteed income supplements. They were interviewed every three months. The major impact of this income supplement was on the number of hours white—but not black—women worked. They reduced their working hours by 15 percent. There was little effect on the work of men; they did not quit work when they received the supplementary income but they did work slightly fewer hours (Garfinkel, 1974: 6–13). Although they stayed on the job, however, they did not become more stable in their family roles.

The Norwegian Shared Role Experiment. An experiment reported by Erik Gronseth in Norway was designed to see how shared role patterns might operate:

> In 1971, Norway's Family Council and the Institute of Sociology in Oslo launched their experiment on "work-sharing" families. In these families both wife and husband should work only part-time in occupational life . . . while supposedly they should then share the home and family work. The general idea was that such a work and family pattern could contribute to the solution of some of the mounting troubles, stresses and frustrations within families of both the traditional type with home-staying wives, and within the families of the now rapidly spreading type in which both parents work outside the family. (Gronseth, 1972)[12]

The original design called for 25 experimental families and a matched control sample of 25 families. Five companies made 10 half-time positions available for participants. But the results were disappointing. Only one working family could be recruited and eight middle- or lower-middle-class families, two of which were already sharing roles. They were not motivated by feminist ideology but rather by "a wish for more father-child contact." Gronseth faces up to the limitations of the experiment and recognizes all the obstacles that would have to be overcome in order to make it succeed. At least we learn that much.

Alternate Life Styles. I am encouraged to note that research on motherhood in alternate life styles is improving. My own brief and sketchy glance at research on motherhood in the communes was not very encouraging (Bernard, 1974: Chapter 16). I concur with Joan Aldous's plea that these studies of alternatives to the family be related not only to policy-relevant but also to theoretically-relevant issues. Aldous asks researchers to

---

12. Gronseth is one of the more radical proponents of the feminist point of view. He is especially critical of the male-provider role, his analysis constituting a mirror-image of the critique of the female-housewife role.

tell policy makers "how these family variants . . . attempt to fulfill the widening horizons of women and children within societal constraints" (1973: 478).

Rosabeth Moss Kanter's work on urban communes does just that (1973; Kanter and Halter, 1973; Halter, 1973). It presents evidence that drastically modifies the old sex-role stereotypes. Her studies show that the weight of the maternal role can be lightened by cooperation in urban communes; but they also show that sex-role specialization, though attenuated, remains so far as motherhood is concerned. The major responsibility for child care is still assumed by women, almost entirely by mothers. Housekeeping and food preparation become desexed but not the parental roles.

> Though the urban communes in our sample can be said to be uniformly striving to minimize sex roles, child-rearing remains a most glaring area of daily life in which holdovers from traditional male-female role behavior are in evidence. (Kanter, 1973.)

Bennett Berger and his associates have reported on motherhood in rural communes (Berger, 1972: Berger, Hackett, and Millar, 1972). Although it is of tangential interest to their major concern, child rearing, it is relevant for policy, especially AFDC policy, since the availability of AFDC grants does seem to influence the willingness of unattached women in these communes to have babies and to relieve the fathers of feelings of responsibility.

In the one rural commune I know best, Twin Oaks, the pooled-income-and-consumption pattern is achieved and both work and family roles are shared on the basis of preference, not sex. Men and women work together and share a common home. There are as yet only three infants in this particular community so it is difficult to determine how the parental roles will function. Care of the children is counted as work and given credit. The proportion of men who select this work is low—originally one in eight, upped to two some months later—and fathers are not among them. But since the infants are thought of as belonging not to parents but to the community as a whole this may be unimportant. I am reminded of Claudia Lewis's study of rural children in the Cumberland mountains in the 1940s. There "where the family is close-knit," the child's life "has some of the integration so characteristic of our preindustrial era, an integration that has been called [by James S. Plant] essential for healthy development. . . . Furthermore, the actual physical presence of . . . parents is a reality to him, from early babyhood, when he is constantly being cuddled in someone's arms, up through later years when his dad lets him tag him around" (1946: 158). We have here both the productive and the pooled-income-consumption families illustrated. What they teach us about policy is not so clear.

I suppose what both Twin Oaks and the urban communes analyzed by

Kanter do show is that it is possible to mitigate sex-role specialization without untoward results, and quite possibly with very good results.

"Flexitime." An experiment only now underway has to do with the uses of time. It deals with ways in which not only hours of work but also days, weeks, months, and even years can be planned to dovetail work with family roles for both parents and thus facilitate role-sharing. So far it has attracted more attention in Europe than it has in this country, and its impact on industry has been more researched than its impact on families (Rehn, 1973).[13] (Gronseth's experience illustrates why.) Meanwhile cases accumulate of families that work out individual solutions to the allocation of time that makes role-sharing feasible (Bernard, 1972: 258–263), and the Social Security Administration in Baltimore, which works round the clock, was planning to introduce a "flexitime" system under which "a limited number of workers could fix their own eight-hour schedules with a standard workday of 6 A.M. to 6 P.M." (Causey, 1974). Some workers at the Federal Reserve Board are also on flexitime, and Senator John Tunney has introduced S2022 into the Senate this year, called The Flexible Hours Employment Act. It provides that wherever feasible and after a 5-year phase-in period, 10 percent of all positions at all levels of the federal civil service shall be made available on a flexible-hours basis for those who either cannot or do not wish to work full time. These positions would have all the protections and fringe benefits of regular jobs. Congresswomen Burke and Abzug have introduced identical bills (HR9699, HR9116) in the House. When or if flexitime becomes widespread it will, I believe, have great impact on the work lives of women. Such freedom would facilitate the sharing of the child-care function by both parents during the first few years of the children's life and offer an alternative to child-development centers for those who preferred it.

STATE-OF-THE-ART STUDIES

In addition to experimental research, there has been important work on the state of the art, two books on child care and one on female-headed families.

Pamela Roby's *Child Care—Who Cares?* (1973) is "an indispensable guide . . . to the on-rushing revolution in child care and development" through which all industrialized nations are now passing, and Sarane Spence Boocock's work reminds us of what more is needed and assigns us four research problems:

(1) We still know very little about people's reasons for wanting—or not wanting—children. Nor do we know what kinds of child care

13. In 1972 the Organization for Economic Cooperation and Development held a conference on Patterns for Working Time.

arrangements they would choose if they had knowledge of and access to a wide range of choices; (2) we still do not know enough about what children do all day . . . (3) we have not figured out a way to balance the expectations and obligations of the major roles in the system, so that the improvement of one role (e.g., the mother) is not at the expense of another (the child); and (4) we lack the social inventions which would allow responsible child care in a society in which fewer people are willing to devote large amounts of time to children. (1973: 81)[14]

Heather L. Ross and Anita MacIntosh have put us all in their debt by their organization and critique of existing data and research on the formation, existence, and disappearance of female-headed households (1973; see also Ross, 1973; Sawhill, Ross, and MacIntosh, 1973), including a 60-item annotated bibliography. It deals with "empirical patterns of demographic change and household makeup" as a background for explanations for the rise in female-headed households, "including attention to intended and unintended effects of government policy." In addition, Ross (1973) has analyzed the factors at work to increase the growth of female-headed families, proposed strategies for dealing with them, and concludes that improving the opportunity and capability of women for earning a decent living is the most auspicious.

Finally, Constantina Safilios-Rothschild has recommended social policy for liberating women, men, marriage, the family, family life, and society as a whole on the basis of a "synthesis of research findings and factual evidence about sex roles and sexism" (Safilios-Rothschild, 1974).

References

Aldous, Joan. 1973. Letter to the editor. *The Family Coordinator* 22 (October):478.

Berger, Bennett, 1972. The decline of age grading in rural anarchist communes. Paper presented at meetings of the American Sociological Association, New Orleans, August.

Berger, Bennett; Hackett, Bruce M.; and Millar, R. Mervin. 1972. Child rearing in communes, in Howe, Louise Kapp, ed., *The future of the family*. New York: Simon and Schuster.

Bernard, Jessie. 1971. Changing family life styles: One role, two roles, shared roles. *Issues in Industrial Society* 2 (January):21–28.

———— . 1972. *The future of marriage*. New York: World.

———— . 1974. *The future of motherhood*. New York: Dial.

14. An international conference on the economic role of women sponsored by the Organization for Economic Cooperation and Development expressed concern about adequate day care, the focus of attention being "whether in centers or in the home" the educational benefits of the child were the center of attention. The Conference recommended that OECD set up a work group to evaluate the benefits to the economy as a whole of day care (Levy, 1973). The interests of working women, of children, and of the economy were given attention but not specifically, of mothers per se.

Bernard, Jessie, and Bernard, L.L. 1941. *Origins of American sociology*. New York: Crowell. New York: Russell and Russell, 1965.

Boocock, Sarane Spence. 1973. *Crosscultural analysis of the child care system*. New York: Russell Sage.

Bronfenbrenner, Urie. 1973. Testimony presented at the Hearings of Senator Walter Mondale's Subcommittee on Children and Youth. *Congressional Record*, vol. 119, no. 142, September 26, 1973.

Causey, Mike. 1974. Flexi-time test sought by agency. *Washington Post*, February 6, 1974.

Commission on Population Growth and the American Future. 1972. *Population and the American future*. New York: Signet.

David, Kingsley. 1959. The myth of functional analysis. *American Sociological Review* 24 (December):757–771.

Etzioni, Amitai. 1973. *Genetic fix: New opportunities and dangers for you, your child, and the nation*. New York: Macmillan.

Francoeur, Robert T. 1970. *Utopian motherhood*. Garden City: Doubleday.

Friedan, Betty. 1963. *The feminine mystique*. New York: Norton.

Garfinkel, Irwin. 1974. Income transfer programs and work effort: A review, in *Studies in public welfare*, paper no. 13 of the Joint Economic Committee of the Congress of the United States. Washington, D.C.: U.S. Government Printing Office.

Gronseth, Erik. 1972. Work-sharing families: Husband and wife both in part-time employment. Paper prepared for Conference on Partnership Tomorrow, Gottlieb Duttweiler Institute, Zurich.

Helson, Ravenna. 1972. The changing image of the career woman. *Journal of Social Issues*. 28:33–46.

Hine, L. A. 1848. A general statistical society for the United States. *Merchant's Magazine* 18.

Halter, Marilyn B. 1973. The Swan family. Preliminary case report I for Kanter, Rosabeth Moss, Structure, functions, and impact of urban communes.

Ingle, Dwight J. 1973. *Who should have children? An environmental and genetic approach*. Indianapolis: Bobbs-Merrill.

Kanter, Rosabeth Moss. 1973. Structure, functions, and impact of urban communes. Progress report to NIMH on Study of historical context and social role: Boston urban communes: The domestication of the counterculture.

Kanter, Rosabeth Moss, and Halter, Marilyn B. 1973. The dehousewifing of women: Equality between the sexes in urban communes. Paper presented at meetings of the American Psychological Association.

Klapper, Zelda S. 1972. The impact of the women's liberation movement in child development books, in Wortis, Helen, and Rabinowitz, Clara, eds., *The women's movement*. New York: Wiley.

Kuhn, Thomas S. 1962. *The structure of scientific revolutions*. Chicago: University of Chicago Press.

Levy, Claudia. 1973. OECD is urged to aid working women. *Washington Post*, December 9, 1973.

Lewis, Claudia. 1946. *Children of the Cumberland*. New York: Columbia University Press.

Lipman-Blumen, Jean. 1974. Introductory statement to her program on sex roles at Feb., 1974, meetings of AAAS.

Lundberg, George. 1947. *Can science save us?* New York: Harper.

McHugh, James T. 1973. Testimony presented at the Hearings of Senator Walter Mondale's Subcommittee on Children and Youth. *Congressional Record*, vol. 119, no. 142, September 26, 1973.

Moore, Barrington. 1958. Thoughts on the future of the family, in *Political power and social theory*. Cambridge: Harvard University Press.

Myrdal, Alva, and Klein, Viola. 1956. *Women's two roles*. London: Routledge and Kegan Paul.

Newman, John F.; Whittmore, Kenneth R.; and Newman, Helen G. 1973. Women in the labor force and suicide. *Social Problems* 21 (fall):220–230.

Parsons, Talcott. 1959. The social structure of the family, in Anshen, Ruth Nanda, ed., *The family: Its function and destiny*. New York: Harper.

Parsons, Talcott, and Bales, Robert F. 1955. *Family, socialization and the interaction process*. New York: Free Press.

Platt, Joseph B. 1973. The value of science and technology to human welfare. *Science and Public Affairs* (October):

Radl, Shirley. 1973. *Mother's Day is over*. New York: Charterhouse.

Rehn, Gösta. 1973. For greater flexibility of working life. *OECD Observer* (February):3ff

Roby, Pamela, ed. 1973. *Child care—Who cares?* New York: Basic.

Ross, Heather L. 1973. *Poverty: Women and children last*. Washington, D.C.: Urban Institute.

Ross, Heather L., and MacIntosh, Anita. 1973. *The emergence of households headed by women*. Washington, D.C.: Urban Institute.

Rossi, Alice. 1968. Transition to parenthood. *Journal of Marriage and the Family* 30 (February):26–39.

Royal Commission on Population. 1949. *Report*. Cod. 7695. London: Her Majesty's Stationery Office.

Safilios-Rothschild, Constantina. 1973. Parents' need for child care, in Roby, Pamela, ed., 1973.

——— . 1974. *Women and social policy*. Englewood Cliffs: Prentice-Hall.

Sawhill, Isabel; Ross, Heather L.; and MacIntosh, Anita. 1973. *The family in transition*. Washington, D.C.: Urban Institute.

Subcommittee on Employment, Manpower, and Poverty. 1973. *Work in America*. Washington, D.C.: U.S. Government Printing Office.

Westley, William A., and Epstein, Nathan B. 1969. *The silent majority*. San Francisco: Jossey-Bass.

Williams, Preston, ed. 1973. *Ethical issues in biology and medicine*. Cambridge, Mass.: Schenkman.

Zigler, Edward. 1973. Testimony presented at the Hearings of Senator Walter Mondale's Subcommittee on Children and Youth. *Congressional Record*, vol. 119, no. 142, September 26, 1973.

THIRTEEN

New Societal Forms

The Current Scene

Despite the present antinatalist ambience that has been accompanied by a tripling of the proportion of women who say they want no children, that proportion remains minute—only 3.9 percent as of June, 1972. For the foreseeable future, motherhood will thus remain a certainty in the lives of most women. That, of course, is not news.

Equally important, however, is the fact that the chances are more than even that when their children are of school age, women will be both mothers and labor-force participants. And this is news. We are, in fact, living through precisely the tipping point at which the woman with school-age children who is not in the labor force becomes part of a minority. The "typical" woman in the 35 to 44 age bracket, if there is such a person, is both a mother and a labor-force participant.[1] This, it seems to me, is an extremely important fact.

These trends are encapsulated in the three "feminine curves" shown in

1. When we speak of mothers in the labor force are we referring to a minuscule proportion of the female labor force? In 1970, women constituted 36.7 percent of the labor force. Among these 31,560,000 women, 18,377,000 or 58.2 percent were married and living with their husbands. Among these married women only 8,174,000 or 25.9 percent had no children under 18; the other three-fourths did. There were 8,339,000 or 26.4 percent who had school-age children and 3,914,000 or 12.4 percent who had preschool children. When we speak of mothers of children under 18 in the labor force, then, we are referring to 10,203,000 women who constitute a third (32.3 percent) of the female labor force and about 12 percent of the total labor force. If mothers in other marital statuses were included the proportion would be higher. In 1973, for example, 64.0 percent of women 25 to 34 years of age who were widowed, divorced, or separated were in the labor force, most of whom were doubtless mothers; among women 35 to 44, 70.7 percent were in the labor force.

Figures 13.1 and 13.2. The top curve describes the trends in fertility; the middle one, the proportion of mothers of school-age children, but no preschoolers, in the labor force; and the third, the proportion of mothers of preschool children in the labor force. The relationship among these curves deserves comment. The fertility rate peaked in 1957 and since then it has been declining. The other two curves have, with only minor fluctuations, been rising steadily, until today about half of the mothers of school-age, but no preschool, children, and about a third of the mothers of preschoolers are in the labor force.

There is a high-level research literature trying to figure out the direction of the relationships here. Does labor-force participation depress the birth rate? Or are women with fewer children more likely to enter the labor force? The three curves in Figure 13.1 suggest that the answer is yes to both questions. Labor-force participation went up when the fertility rate was going up in the early 1950s; it went up also when the fertility rate was going down as it has been doing since 1957. Stewart Garfinkle has noted that although motherhood remains a major factor in female labor-force participation, it is having a declining effect:

> The birth of a child is undoubtedly the single most important factor in bringing about the discontinuity in the work careers of women. But the rather astonishing change which is taking place in the work lives of women is that the effects of the birth of a child on work life continuity is rapidly diminishing. This writer's own observations have included numerous instances of married women working virtually until their child is born and then returning to work after a time lapse hardly longer than a somewhat lengthy vacation or the time their husband might require to recover from a fairly minor illness (1969; see also Bernard, 1971a:23–25).

Because having children takes less time out of the work-force the difference that labor-force participation makes is declining. The difference in fertility between women in the labor-force and those not in it was less in 1970 than it had been in 1960 (Bernard, 1971:23-25). Women were learning how to cope with both motherhood and labor-force participation. This point is especially relevant for the discussion of flexible work schedules below, which presupposes a predictable and continuous work life.

What is important also is the rate of rise of the two lower curves, those of labor-force participation by mothers. In 1973, the rates were 50.1 percent for mothers with only school-age children (down from 50.2 percent in 1972) and 34.3 percent for mothers with only preschool children (up from 31.1 percent in 1972) (*President's Manpower Report*, 1974: Table B-4). (The rate for mothers with both preschoolers and school-age children has tended to be slightly lower since 1963.)[2]

2. The proportion of mothers in the labor force may be leveling off. For women in the ages

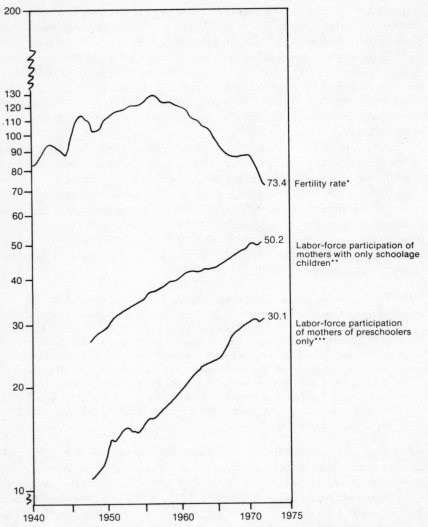

SOURCES: *Bureau of the Census, Series P-24, #499, May, 1973, p. 2 (estimates of the Population of the U.S. and Components of Change, 1972) . **President's Manpower Report, 1973, p. 168. This category does not include divorced, separated or widowed mothers.

Figure 13.1
Fertility Rate (1940-1972) and Labor-Participation Rates (1947-1972) for Mothers in Specified Categories.

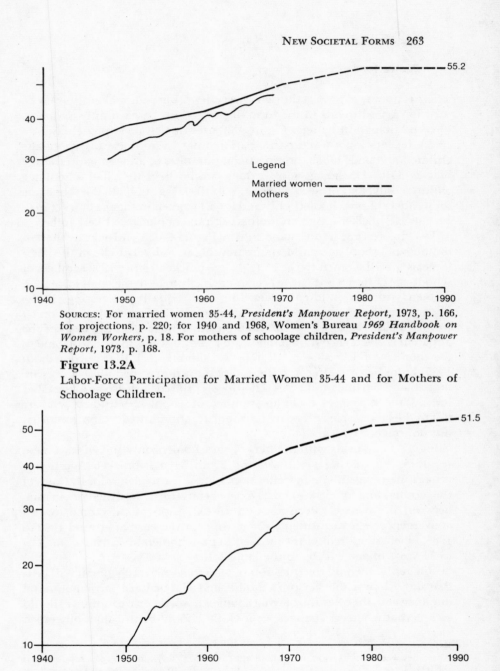

SOURCES: For married women 35-44, *President's Manpower Report*, 1973, p. 166, for projections, p. 220; for 1940 and 1968, Women's Bureau *1969 Handbook on Women Workers*, p. 18. For mothers of schoolage children, *President's Manpower Report*, 1973, p. 168.

Figure 13.2A
Labor-Force Participation for Married Women 35-44 and for Mothers of Schoolage Children.

SOURCE: same as for Figure 2A

Figure 13.2B
Labor-Force Participation for Married Women 25-34 and for Mothers of Preschool Children.

Projections

There is no way to project the two lower curves, but rude makeshifts may be used to suggest trends in the form of projections based simply on labor-force participation by age. Figure 13.2 uses this crude approach. Figure 13.2A repeats labor-force participation rates by mothers of school-age children and adds labor-force participation rates of all women in the age bracket 35 to 44, the age most women would be if they had school-age children only, and projects these rates to 1990. Figure 13.2B does the same for mothers of preschoolers only and for all women in the age bracket 25 to 34, the age bracket in which mothers of preschoolers are likely to be.

Two interesting trends stand out in Figure 13.2A. It looks as though mothers of school-age children are now about as likely to be in the labor force as are all women in the 35 to 44 age bracket. (Since 1952 mothers of school-age children only have been more likely to be in the labor force than women with no children under 18.) And, equally interesting, is the apparent ceiling we are now approaching in labor-force participation by women in the 35 to 44 age bracket, a ceiling which, on the basis of the apparent convergence shown in Figure 13.2A, it seems logical to extend to the mothers of school-age children. We should reach that ceiling about 1985. From here on almost to the end of the century, then, the chances are more than even that mothers of school-age children will also be in the labor force. Women 35 to 44, including mothers of school-age children, who are not in the labor force will be in the minority, an admittedly large minority, but no longer "typical."[3]

Figure 13.2B deals with mothers of preschoolers only and with women, regardless of marital status, in the 25 to 34 age bracket. Again two interesting trends invite our attention. One is the tendency for the rates of the mothers and for all women 25 to 34 to converge. The difference in rates between the two sets declines, and an extension of this trend toward convergence seems legitimate, suggesting convergence at around 1980 to 1985, when about half of the mothers of preschoolers and of all women 25 to 34 years of age will be in the labor force.

One reply, then, to the question of who the American woman will be is that she will probably be both a mother and a labor-force participant. And one answer to the question of what changes in social institutions we should seek is that whatever changes we look for should be in behalf of women

---

when they were most likely to have school-age children, 35 to 44, the projected proportion in the labor force in 1990 is only slightly higher than in 1973, that is, 55.4 percent; for women in the age bracket when they are most likely to have preschoolers, 25 to 34, the projected proportion in the labor force for 1990 is only 51.6 percent, about the same as in 1973 (*President's Manpower Report*, 1974: Table E-7).

3. The women in this "other half," that is, mothers not in the labor force are discussed at length in Chapter 11 of Bernard, 1974.

who are both mothers and workers, changes that help them carry this double load.

The subtitle of my book on the future of motherhood is "the severence and attrition of a role." The role of mother has been severed from the role of worker and it has been in process of attrition for some time. How to reintegrate the two roles psychologically as well as structurally is a major theme of that book. The approach there is to help women perform both roles with a minimum amount of strain by way of structural changes. Among the more obvious ways that have been suggested are such proposals as supplying more services of many kinds—child-care centers, role sharing, part-time jobs, and the like—to provide relief from overload which, as all studies of dual-career families both here and abroad show, tends to be universal (Holmstrom, 1972; Rapoport and Rapoport, 1971). I would prefer to approach the problem from a somewhat different point of view— not how to help women individually integrate their mother and their worker roles but how to integrate two worlds. Or, perhaps, how to incorporate mothers into the economy and thus help to spread the costs of motherhood.

Woman's World

The concept of a "woman's sphere" is a very old one and it lingers on today in both the media and in popular culture. Even academic researchers discuss what they call "female culture" (LeMasters, 1957:Chapter 23; Battle-Sister, 1971). In most societies women do, in fact, live in quite different societal structures from those men live in. The wife's marriage is different from the husband's in terms of the norms, written and unwritten, articulated and unarticulated, involved and the functions performed (Bernard, 1972:Chapters 1–3). Girls and boys may sit side by side in the same classroom, but they are attending different educational institutions, with different facilities and equipment, and different latent as well as manifest curricula. The religious institutions women are involved in, including churches, are different for men and women. The legal institutions in her world differ from those in his, and so on for recreational institutions, the work world, or any other societal structure. The rules in the world women inhabit are different from those in the world men inhabit. Men and women march to different drummers. They are not even in the same parade.

A case in point, illustrating how women's worlds operated in the past, was the female support network that young women historians are now revealing. Women could help one another in performing their roles. They could spell a mother off or relieve her from time to time, sit with sick children, take over the kitchen in an emergency, perform whatever needed services were called for. There was no thought of monetary pay for such help; it was offered out of love or a sense of duty. Sisterhood in this sense was powerful even then.

> One of the most interesting discoveries we made in these letters [the Jeffries-Sheppard papers, 1830–1860] was the existence of an elaborate female ritual and support system around virtually every important event in a woman's life, from birth to death. . . . [Such] female support systems centering around child birth are familiar to many of us . . . but far less familiar is the ritual . . . revolving around death and dying. . . . We found that when a child or an adult female was in the danger of death, as many of her female relatives as geographically possible would gather. Their purpose was to support the dying woman through these stages. . . . These women regularly bridged a number of generations—unmarried younger women came as well as married and older women. Husbands and children would be left for weeks, even months, at a time. ·. . .
>
> The Jeffries-Sheppard papers indicate the existence of other female rituals surrounding courtship, marriage, birth and nursing—which rendered women central to all these events. . . . The women of the Jeffries-Sheppard family along with their Sharples and Biddle cousins formed a closely bonded unit. . . .
>
> Mothers and daughters composed one intimate network. But so did friends and cousins. (Smith-Rosenberg)

Although these female networks were the most clearly defined, the services women performed were not limited to women. They served the church, the community, and voluntary organizations with similar dedication, out of love or a sense of duty. The functions these activities performed were integrative, centripetal, stabilizing, and conserving. They were not part of the economy, not operated on the basis of monetary exchange. Women's world was not run on "business principles." As a component of the societal structure it was a system in which mercy tempered justice if justice was too painful, in which the weak had to be protected and allowances made, in which the welfare of the group as a whole was felt by individuals to be more important than their own and the individual more important than the principle, in which no one had to achieve or earn or win or deserve or prove himself or herself in order to be accepted, cherished, and protected. All gave according to their ability, and received according to their need. The question of why does not even arise in such a world. It is not a world in which one seeks to strike bargains and maximize gains or minimize losses. One helps others because they are members of *our* family, *our* neighborhood, *our* church, *our* city. Such a system holds the total structure together; without it the total structure would fall apart. It is for this reason that, with modifications, I have co-opted Kenneth Boulding's terms *integry* (1969:4) to refer to "woman's world."

The Integry

"[The] integry," Boulding tells us, "is that part of the total social system which deals with such concepts and relationships as status, identity, community, legitimacy, loyalty, love, trust, and so on" (Ibid.). We do not yet understand how the integry operates:

> We are barely beginning to understand the processes by which a community is built up or destroyed, by which unions or schisms take place, by which loyalty is created, legitimacy accepted, and love fostered. One important element in the building up of an integrative structure is cooperative endeavor, that is, doing things together. (Ibid.:5)

I had originally called the world women live in a "status world" in contrast to the male cash-nexus world because these were the terms used in the nineteenth century to differentiate between the preindustrial world and the world shaped by the industrial revolution. I now prefer to call the status world of women an integry.[4]

The two worlds of the integry and the economy operate on quite different principles, one on the basis of love or duty and one on the basis of monetary incentives. The saying "I wouldn't do it for love or money" is a folk recognition of the differences between the two systems. "You can't buy love" is a recognition of the incompatibility of the major principles of the two worlds. "I wouldn't take a cent for my child nor give a cent for someone else's" also highlights folk recognition of the distinction between them.

The differences were first called to our attention by scholars who emphasized different aspects of the polarity. Sir Henry Maine contrasted "status" with "contract," noting that in the preindustrial world the relationships among people were based on one's ascribed position in the group or community, but that increasingly they were becoming contractual, based on rational, purposive deliberations, and determined on the basis of achievement rather than on age, sex, and other status characteristics. Such dissimilar writers as Thomas Carlyle and Karl Marx

4. I feel justified in pilfering Boulding's term because after this early reference to the "integry" which he defined as "that part of the total social system which deals with such concepts and relationships as status, identity, community, legitimacy, loyalty, love, trust, and so on"—all of which fit the women's world—he proceeded to develop his concept of the grants economy which, though performing an integrative function, had little if any resemblance to the integry.

both used the descriptive term *cash-nexus* to specify the nature of the relationships among people in this contractual world.[5]

My own statement of the sociological characteristics of the integry was based on Talcott Parsons' paradigm of the so-called five pattern variables:

> Even when the work of both women and men was in the home, they lived in different worlds; there was a sphere for men and a sphere for women. . . . These worlds can be described in terms of several dimensions or variables that those sociologists who follow Talcott Parsons have found useful in describing social systems. . . . A community can, first of all, make one's position rest on what one *does* or on what one *is*; it can be the result of achievement or of ascription. Second, the expectations that parties in any relationship share may be specific or diffuse. Duties, obligations, and responsibilities may be defined specifically and contractually or they may be left unspecified. If they are specified, each party knows precisely what is expected of him and of others; nothing more can be demanded than what is specified and nothing less can be supplied. . . . A community can require that all relationships be governed by general universalistic principles or it can permit them to be governed by particularistic personal loyalties and obligations tailored to the particular individuals involved. Fourth, it can permit behavior to be oriented toward furthering one's own interests or it can require that actions be oriented toward a larger group or the collectivity as a whole, regardless of individual wishes. Finally, the community can admit a wide range of relationships in which there is a minimum of affect or emotional gratification (in which relationships are neutral) or it can allow a wide range of relationships in which affectivity or emotional gratification plays a large part. It is quite clear that a society in which the first of each of these five pairs of variables prevails will be quite different from one in which the second of each does. . . .
>
> It is not too fanciful to view the . . . sphere in which women live as characterized . . . by ascription, diffuseness, particularism, collectivity-orientation, and affectivity. . . . Here relationships are diffuse rather than specific or contractual. Even in a work situation, where presumably relations are contractual and specific, the secretary has diffuse expectations to live up to, such as the variegated services expected of an "office wife" or "girl Friday." The sphere of women is expected to be characteized by particularistic morality more than by universalistic morality, by intense personal loyalty more than by principles. Women are to protect their children even when the children

5. Later on a German sociologist, Ferdinand Tönnies, contrasted what he called *Gemeinschaft* with *Gesellschaft*, the first referring to the blood-and-soil kind of relationship in which kinship ties and common ties to the land characterized human relationships. The second referred to capitalist society in which cold, hard-nosed, nonemotional considerations determined human relationships. Other social scientists have elaborated different aspects of these polarities in different ways, but all imply a basic and fundamental difference between the two ways of relating.

are delinquents or criminals, to do everything they can for those near and dear to them rather than be blindly just or impartial. On the job, women . . . are expected to be more loyal to their employers than are men. . . . In the women's sphere, women are expected to be oriented toward the larger group or the collectivity and to make sacrifices for it. We know that in marriage it is wives who make more of the adjustments; it is taken for granted that mothers make sacrifices for their children; it is expectable that if necessary, the daughter rather than the son will sacrifice marriage to take care of elderly parents. Yet the pursuit of self-interest is almost a virtue in the world men inhabit . . . the personal characteristics of the individuals involved are not the focus of attention; it is rather the shared expectations built into the situation. A social system leads to certain kinds of behavior on the part of its members regardless of their personal qualities or traits. We tend therefore to attribute to the individuals the qualities expected in them by the system. (Bernard, 1971b:24-27).

And, we might add parenthetically, the person shaped by and for the integry develops one kind of mentality, the person shaped by the market world, another. To one, need is an important determiner of what one receives, to the other the question of who is going to pay the bill looms large. People reared in the integry are at a special disadvantage in the economy. And most women, at least until now, have been reared for life in the integry and shaped to follow its principles.

We might, again parenthetically, add that there has been increasing, though usually reluctant, recognition of the need for the principles of the integry even in the market world. Industry has found it necessary to "humanize" the work situation. In fact, for half a century the importance of "human relations in industry" has been a recognized personnel principle. Overcoming "alienation," that is, failures of integration, has become a government concern.[6]

The Economy: Grants to the Rescue

The economy is an exchange system operated by rational "economic men" who, according to the classic model, make decisions on the basis of market signals only: profit signals "advance" and loss signals "withdraw."[7] It is characterized by competitive rules; one has to achieve. Rank is important;

6. A bill introduced into the Ninety-Third Congress (S736) stated that "it is in the national interest to encourage the humanization of working conditions and the work itself so as to increase worker job satisfaction.

7. Peter Blau, a sociologist, distinguishes economic from social exchange in terms of the degree of specification of the obligations incurred: "the most basic difference is that the obligations incurred in social transactions are not clearly specified in advance. In economic

inequality is built in. Justice, not mercy, is emphasized regardless of the costs that may attend it. A certain degree of ruthlessness is expected; no one can be coddled, no allowances made. The individual person or firm is supposed to prevail on the basis of merit alone; one neither gives nor expects others to give.

The solidarity principles on which the integry operates and the competitive, Social Darwinian principles on which the economy operates fought it out for a long time. Throughout the nineteenth century men like Kropotkin fought for the solidarity vision and classical economists for the competitive version. But though the exchange theorists won, it was found in practice that modifications had to be made in the economy; otherwise it would self-destruct. Such modifications have taken the form of what Boulding calls "grants"—tariffs, subsidies, franchises, licenses, for example. Only recently has the significance of these "grants" for the economy been recognized.

True, economists have known since at least Adam Smith's time that the market could not regulate all human relationships. Adam Smith himself wrote a book on the moral sentiments as well as one on the wealth of nations, and the so-called Scottish school of philosophy, especially moral philosophy, worked as hard on morals and justice and ethics as the political economists did on exchange. But only within the last few years have economists come to see both systems as part of a single whole. Boulding (1973) has been the outstanding representative of this movement. He and his associates have developed the concept of a "grants economy," a system of one-way transfers to complement the concept of the exchange economy. It has interesting implications for women.

Boulding defines the grants economy as that "segment of the total economy which deals with one-way transfers of exchangeables." They supplement the exchange economy by diverting resources from areas to which the market would not direct them and channeling them into areas that strengthen the community, such, for example, as education and research, even when the market would not endorse them. Boulding estimates that about 13 percent of the gross national product today falls into the grants economy.

The grants economy, in its turn, includes two subsystems, one an

---

transactions the exact obligations of both parties are simultaneously agreed upon; a given product is sold for a certain price. . . . Social exchange . . . entails supplying benefits that create diffuse future obligations. The nature of the return is invariably not stipulated in advance, cannot be bargained about, and must be left to the discretion of the one who makes it" (1968:454). He also excludes from any concept of social exchange any interaction based on force, on conformity with internalized norms (duty), or on uncontrollable impulse. The concept refers only to "voluntary social actions that are contingent on rewarding reactions from others and that cease when these expected reactions are not forthcoming." The relationships in the female network or in women's world do not conform to this model of exchange any more than to the economic.

"economy of love" which leads toward sociology, and one an "economy of threat" which leads toward political science. Both perform an integrative function or, perhaps better, both are part of an integrative system. Since women have had a relatively small part to play in the threat economy—they may be participating more in the future—it is their part in the "economy of love" aspect of the integrative system that is most relevant here.

Grants to Men and Grants to Women

If one does not have a market mechanism to guide decisions and policies for directing the use of resources, what is there? Boulding proposes "social integration and maintenance of a viable socio-economic system." This should be the "explicit norm in the preference function of the policy maker." Boulding claims ignorance on the part of economics with respect to the way the grants economy does actually operate. This appears a bit naive.

Grants have been distributed to men on the basis of power and competition. The New England mill cannot succeed in competition with the mill in India. The market or exchange economy should therefore let it disappear. Not, however, the grants economy. It is, after all, *our* country's mill. It is *our* workers whose standard of living must be protected. It is *our* socioeconomic system we have to maintain. We must, therefore, give the mill a "grant" in the form of tariff protection. This is, no doubt, an integrative gesture, as are a great many other grants that protect competitors from one another. Other grants, in addition to tariffs, have similarly been found essential: subsidies of one kind or another, licenses, franchises, quotas or import restrictions, concessionary loans, trading stipulations, tax benefits, and a host of other forms of one-way transfers. Whether they have served integrative functions, or not, these grants have been useful to specific groups of men. Women have had little benefit from the grants economy.

The development of the exchange economy and its complement, the grants economy, has had untoward effects on women. In preindustrial society, before it became organized on a monetary basis, there was a division of labor between the sexes as well as a differentiation of functions, and women were not at a severe disadvantage in the market. But as our economy moved from a stage in which the family was a major productive unit toward a stage in which it was primarily a distributive unit (Sawhill, Ross, and MacIntosh, 1973), the father's contribution in the form of wages or salary became, in the Boulding schema, a "grant," that is, a one-way transfer rather than a sharing in the division of labor. Women and children became recipients of grants.

When there was no husband and father to make such "grants" the community had to do so. There was little love in the one kind of grant that has touched women directly, the dole, as there is little love today in its current counterpart, "welfare." In women's world, women had given "charity" or love. They had engaged in "friendly visiting" among the poor; rich people had even engaged in "philanthropy" or acts expressing the love of mankind. But what the local parish gave in the form of the dole was a resented grant, even a punitive one. It has always been anathema to the principles of the economy.

We have long since noted the anomaly of granting subsidies to big farmers for not cultivating their land while granting grudging, penny-pinching "welfare" to the displaced workers. For the most part grants have been used to strengthen the already rich and powerful. Far from profiting from the grants economy, women have bestowed enormous subsidies on the economy, not in the form of monetary grants, but in the form of the unpaid services both in the home and in the community. Little by little, however, these services are acquiring monetary value, and are becoming part of the exchange economy. And as they do, the "grant" nature of their contribution becomes visible.

Monetization of the Integry

The principles of exchange have been invading the integry; it is becoming a part of the cash-nexus world. Increasingly we hear of plans for monetizing the work women have traditionally done on the basis of love or of duty, both in the home for what Caroline Shaw Bell (1972) calls "Consumer maintenance" and in the community for volunteer services. The world run on principles of love or duty and the exchange world held together by a cash nexus, once segregated from one another, have been converging. Boulding points out some of the policy problems this trend raises:

> A very interesting question in the area of social policy issues is the nature of the adjustment when there is danger that the voluntary labor supply will be inadequate to perform a necessary function. Should one move toward increasing the supply of voluntary labor for services . . . or should one go into the market and begin paying for the service, in which case there may be a change in the quality of the service itself? A church faces the same problem when it goes from a lay ministry to a professional ministry, as does charitable organization, professional society or club, when it moves toward professional management. Paid labor may be more efficient in the technical sense, but something is lost in the integrative system as we move from voluntary labor, which tends

to create integrative relationships, to paid labor, where the integrative relationship is almost inevitably lost. (Boulding, 1969:4)

Little by little the principles of the exchange world have been winning. This outcome may have been inevitable. The direct, personal, unmediated help that women traditionally supplied becomes more and more difficult in a market economy. Some other form of mutual aid is called for to perform the old functions. It may take the form of grants of one form or another.

I insert here parenthetically that I regret the fact that the love or duty world has been, in effect, co-opted. I would have preferred to see the love or duty world leaven the exchange world. I would have preferred to see policy makers seek ways to preserve the principles embodied in the integry. But public policy is heavy handed; public resources are limited; money is the policy maker's major tool.

Generalized Drawing Rights

In asking what new institutional forms might develop, what functions they might fulfill, and what their benefits will be, I would like to refer to the reply that its proponent, Gösta Rehn,[8] calls "generalized drawing rights" (1973:4), which would make available to women in monetary form the help no longer available to them in the form of unpaid mutual aid as a matter of course. The benefits would include income maintenance during years taken out of the working lives of women for motherhood. Services would not be performed directly for them, as in the past, but the wherewithal to buy them would be made available. It is part of the burgeoning movement toward more flexibility in the scheduling of our total working lives.

Thinking about "flexitime" has been extended to flexibility beyond hours, days, weeks, months, even years. It now aims to make possible the allocation of time to work, leisure, schooling, and retirement over a whole lifetime. In the following statement of the system I have added childbearing and child rearing as also legitimate allocation of a woman's time, a form of extended maternal leave with pay.

> Governments and industrial organizations should make it a policy goal to provide the individual with the greatest possible degree of freedom to determine the allocation of his [or her] own time among different uses. An endeavour should be made to achieve this freedom through well planned and prepared policy programmes rather than by reluctantly and belatedly yielding to the social pressures exerted in the

8. Dr. Rehn is OECD Director of Manpower and Social Affairs.

direction of greater flexibility. The individual should be free to switch between periods of income-earning work, education or training, [childbearing and child care], and leisure (including retirement) according to his [or her] own interests and wishes. . . . Decisions concerning retirement, vacations, [childbearing and child care], weekly hours, years of schooling and access to adult training and education are taken piecemeal. Instead they should be seen as an inter-related set of economic and social choices as to the utilization of growing resources, which should be taken into account in improving the quality of life. . . .

An integrated insurance system for transferring income between different periods of life (under appropriate risk-sharing) should be created in order to make the desired flexibility and freedom of choice a practical reality. The many separate schemes for maintenance of income during periods of voluntary and involuntary non-work which already exist are becoming chaotic, bureaucratic, costly, inequitable, yet at the same time insufficient. Often they tend to reduce rather than increase the individual's freedom by acting as "golden hand-cuffs." . . . Freedom of choice and flexibility in shaping one's own life presuppose an increased degree of self-determination in the use of the income transfer and maintenance systems. This freedom should apply both to timing and to interchangeability—a right within limits to sacrifice benefits of one kind during one period in order to get more of another kind during another period.

This could best be achieved by combining into one single, unified system of individualised accounting all those fees, taxes [unemployment, Social Security], study loan payments and other compulsory savings which are already used to provide the individual with liquid income during periods of non-work. Part of those future increases of hourly earning which could be regarded as compensation for shortened working time (as is customary in connection with reductions in weekly hours) would also have to be directed into this unified system. Each person would be given a right to draw on his [or her] account for purposes of his [or her] own choosing in a way that would be similar in a technical sense to the right to borrow on that part of one's private life insurance which is not needed to cover the risk-sharing involved. (Rehn, 1973:4)

This "flexitime" system could also provide for more part-time work in behalf of

those who . . . prefer shorter than average hours . . . legal obstacles to the use of non-standard working hours should be eliminated. In some countries existing social insurance legislation makes part-time work unnecessarily expensive. In others, hours-of-work rules limit variations in working hours to a very narrow range, and laws protecting working women sometimes tend to be detrimental to those they should protect. All such obstacles ought to be reconsidered so as to facilitate the introduction of "work à la carte," "flexitime" and other variable and unorthodox patterns for the allocation of working time over the day, the week, the year [and a lifetime]. (Ibid.)

Since I am neither an actuary nor an economist, I hope no one will raise technical questions about the implementation of this system of "generalized drawing rights." All I know is that although predictions cannot be made woman by woman, projections can be made for women as a population with respect to both motherhood and labor-force participation.

I see a serendipitous secondary benefit of such a system in the possibility that women would come to see their lives as a whole, as men have had to do, and plan for the pattern that is going to characterize their lives.

It is hard for me to find an answer to the question, What might this system cause us to lose? But if we ask if we can expect resistance to the development of these forms, I think the answer would have to be yes, perhaps. Antinatalists might argue that anything making it easier for women to integrate their roles as mothers and as workers might encourage natality, that the woman who was assured of income during the time she took out for childbearing and child care would prefer that use of her time to working. In reply I can only say that the check here would be the limits imposed by "appropriate risk sharing," written into the system, for all benefits have to meet at least minimum actuarial standards; and although they might be lenient in the case of mothers, they could not be expected to be without reasonable limits.

It would be reassuring, however impractical, if women could themselves support such a system of generalized drawing rights. It could then be conceptualized as simply a modernized form of the traditional "women's world" form of mutual aid. Women would be serving one another's needs in the traditional spirit but by means of new techniques imposed on them by the cash-nexus world. They would contribute from their earnings to the common pool and have the right to call on it for help for childbearing and child care. It would still be part of "women's world."

That, of course, is an impossible dream, clearly out of the question. Women have been too disadvantaged in the economy to bear by themselves the costs of any such mutual aid plan operating in a cash nexus. And, in any event, it might well be asked why women alone should pay the costs of motherhood. But even if male workers also contributed, supplementation would be called for.

It does not seem to me unreasonable for a generalized drawing rights system to call for support in the form of grants. In a certain sense every insurance system is based on individual "grants." There is a one-way transfer from all the members of the system to the particular individual who finally calls on it. The American Social Security system has included a very sizable "grant" by many working women who contribute for years only to find that their retirement benefits as their husbands' survivors are about as great as their own benefits as contributors. Their contribution to the system has been, in effect, a "grant." What, then, is the difference between "welfare" and "generalized drawing rights"? The same difference as that between Old Age Assistance and Social Security retirement benefits. Although the theory of the generalized drawing rights system is based on a shift toward individual debits, it could also be combined with a negative income tax for the reduction of income differences.

And while we are at it, I would like special insurance provisions made also to take care of the special hazards women are vulnerable to such as rape, abortion, unexpected pregnancies, abandonment, desertion, and physical violence in the home. Perhaps Lloyds of London might undertake such policies on a market basis, but certainly not with premiums within the range of the women who need them most. If women knew that there was a support system upon which they could depend, it would be far less true than now that most women are just one heartbeat away from the welfare rolls. It would relieve many from the frightened dependence on the economic support of a single male. Just knowing that there was a strong system available would give them an enormous morale lift. Sisterhood is admirable; we should not denigrate it. But, in addition, financial support would also help overcome the feeling of isolated, lonely, personal helplessness that overwhelms so many women.

Reprise

I would not like the specific "new societal form"—generalized drawing rights—I have presented here as an illustration to deflect attention from the basic underlying theme of this paper. That theme, in briefest form, is simply this: as more and more women become, as Figure 13.1 suggests they do, both mothers and labor-force participants, societal forms must be developed, analogous to the old female support systems, to make possible a suitable way to integrate their two roles.

In a recent highly acclaimed work, John Rawls (1971) answers a question that has become no easier since it was first asked by a perplexed judge some 2000 years ago—"What is justice?" Rawls answers with the statement that, in effect, it is fairness. As applied to women we might say that it is only fair that anything in the biology of women that imposes a disadvantage on her should be compensated for. To the extent that childbearing and child care constitute handicaps, it is fair that compensatory forms be made available for those who wish them. Such are among the new societal forms that are now in process of evolving.

References

Battle-Sister, Ann. 1971. Conjectures on the female culture system. *Journal of Marriage and the Family* 23 (August):411–420.

Bell, Caroline Shaw. 1972. Social security: Society's last discrimination. *Business and Society Review* No. 3 (Autumn):45-47.

Bernard, Jessie. 1971a. Changing life styles: One role, two roles, shared roles. *Issues in Industrial Society* 2:21–28

_____ . 1971b. *Women and the public interest: An essay on policy and protest.* Chicago: Aldine.

_____ . 1972. *The future of marriage.* New York: World, Bantam, 1973.

_____ . 1974. *The future of motherhood.* New York: Dial.

Blau, Peter M. 1968. Social exchange, in *International encyclopedia of the social sciences.* vol. 7. New York: Macmillan.

Boulding, Kenneth E. 1969. The grants economy. *Michigan Academician* 1 (Winter): 3-11.

_____ . 1973. *The economy of love and fear: A preface to grants economics.* Belmont, Calif.: Wadsworth.

Garfinkle, Stewart. 1969. Work in the lives of women. Paper prepared for the International Union for the Scientific Study of Population, London.

Holmstrom, Lynda Lyttle. 1972. *The two-career family.* Cambridge, Mass.: Schenkman.

LeMasters, E. E. 1957. *Modern courtship and marriage.* New York: Macmillan.

President's manpower report. 1974. Washington, D.C.: U.S. Government Printing Office.

Rapoport, Rhona, and Rapoport, Robert. 1971. *Dual-career families.* Gretna, La.: Pelican.

Rawls, John. 1971. *Theory of justice.* Cambridge: Harvard University Press.

Rehn, Gösta. 1973. For greater flexibility in working life. *OECD Observer* (February):3ff.

Sawhill, Isabel; Ross, Heather L.; and MacIntosh, Anita. 1973. *The family in transition.* Washington, D.C.: Urban Institute.

Smith-Rosenberg, Carroll. 1972. Molly and Helena, Edith and Mary: Some reflections on female sexuality in nineteenth century America. Unpublished paper.

INDEX

Sapirstein, Milton
  dependency, 36, 39
Sarohill, Isabel
  family, 235-36, 244, 246, 251-53
Saul
  turning point, 86
Seifer, Nancy
  working-class women, 191-92
Sex difference, 14n
  brain size, 11n
  in childhood, 36-37
  denial of, 14
  emphasis of, 14n
  and Freud, 9n, 11n
  and glands, 13n
  intra, 21-22, 31-32, 146-47, 171
  male values, 10-11
  and psychosomatic illness, 15
  and relation to roles, 15, 45-46
  research on 5, 7, 7n, 9
    female backlash in, 13-16
    male bias in, 11n, 13, 23
    objectives of, 7-10, 23
    superiority of men in, 10-13
  as sociological phenomenon, 7, 14-15, 66
  and technology, 27
  values placed on, 24
Sex roles
  atttitudes and age, 176n
  characteristics of, 12, 44-45, 76
  and children, 8, 16-17, 21, 47-48
  in children's books, 37, 41n
  and class, 2, 51, 62-63, 186-87, 189-90
  and culture, 15, 15n, 16n, 43-44, 225
  defined, 46
  development of, 46-49
  differentiation, 46-47, 223, 227
    and gender identity, 48, 49
  and ethnicity, 191-92
  integration of, 242
  and interdependence, 67
  models, 48
  political implications of, 175
  power in, 11n-12n
  and relation to sex differences, 15
  research, 242-48
  restructuring of, 2, 9, 77, 85-86, 181
  reversals, 15n
  socialization and, 16-18, 72, 73, 76, 105
  specialization, 44-45, 217-24, 224n, 233,
    237, 246-47, 255 See also, Androgyny

and television, 191
transcendence, 44-49, 66-67
transcenders, 49-66
values related to, 5
  see also, Men; Sex differences; Women
Sexes
  equality of, 8
  order of, 15n-16n
  polarity of, 22, 22n, 48, 55
  stereotyping of, 20-23
Sexism
  and racism, 200
    and employment, 204-6, 207, 212
    institutional nature of, 202-4
  defined, 202
  measures of, 204
Sexual intercourse
  initiation to, 86-89, 100
  premarital, 80-81
    see also, Virginity
Shostak, Arthur
  blue collar men, 231, 234
  working-class women, 191, 196
Shulman, Alix Kates
  fathers as providers, 230-31, 231n
Smith, Adam, 11, 270
Social class
  and marriage, 196-97
  research, 162
  and women's liberation movement,
    183-86, 186, 188-89, 189-90
  and working women, 163
Social roles and institutions, 19
Social Security Act, 148, 232, 276
Sorensen, Robert C.
  premarital sex, 80, 88n
Spiegel, John
  turning points, 75
Status quo, challenged, 19-20
Steinem, Gloria
  power and women, 26
Stereotyping of sexes, 20-23
  research and, 23
Stoller, Robert, J.
  gender identity, 64

Tchambuli
  and sex roles, 15
Tennyson, Alfred Lord
  mothers, 137